THE QUEST FOR UNITY:
ORTHODOX AND CATHOLICS IN DIALOGUE

THE QUEST FOR UNITY:
ORTHODOX AND CATHOLICS IN
DIALOGUE

*Documents of the Joint International Commission and
Official Dialogues in the United States
1965 - 1995*

Edited by
JOHN BORELLI AND JOHN H. ERICKSON

ST VLADIMIR'S SEMINARY PRESS
CRESTWOOD, NY 10707
and
UNITED STATES CATHOLIC CONFERENCE
WASHINGTON, DC 20017
1996

Library of Congress Cataloging-in-Publication Data

The quest for unity: Orthodox and Catholics in dialogue: documents of the Joint International
    Commission and Official Dialogues in the United States, 1965-1995/edited by John Borelli
    and John H. Erickson.
        p.   cm.
    Includes bibliographical references (p.)
    ISBN 0-88141-113-2
        1. Orthodox Eastern Church—Relations—Catholic Church.   2. Catholic Church—
    Relations—Orthodox Eastern Church.   3. Orthodox Eastern Church—Doctrines.
    4. Catholic Church—Doctrines.   5. Christian union conversations—History—20th century—
    Sources.   6. Christian union—United States—History—20th century—Sources.
    I. Borelli, John.   II. Erickson, John H.
    BX324.3.Q47   1996
    280'.042—dc20   96-23082
                                                                                              CIP

THE QUEST FOR UNITY: ORTHODOX AND CATHOLICS IN DIALOGUE

ISBN 0-88141-113-2

The National Conference of Catholic Bishops' Committee for Ecumenical and Interreligious Affairs
recommended this jointly prepared publication of the agreed statements of the official international and
U.S. Orthodox-Catholic Dialogues and approved it in its 1994 plans and programs. The oldest of these
dialogues is the U.S. Orthodox-Catholic Theological Consultation which first met in 1965 under the
joint sponsorship of the Standing Conference of Canonical Orthodox Bishops in America and the
National Conference of Catholic Bishops. Archbishop Rembert G. Weakland of Milwaukee and Bishop
Maximos of Pittsburgh, who currently co-chair this consultation, have written forewords for this volume.
The text has been reviewed by Archbishop Oscar Lipscomb, Chairman of the NCCB Committee for
Ecumenical and Interreligious Affairs, and it is authorized for publication by the undersigned.

Monsignor Dennis M. Schnurr
General Secretary, NCCB/USCC

PRINTED IN THE UNITED STATES OF AMERICA

CONTENTS

Section 2
The Mystery of the Church and Christian Unity

Section 3
The Sacrament of Order in the Life of the Church

Section 4
New Challenges to Orthodox-Catholic Dialogue: Recent Changes in Eastern Europe and the Present Search for Full Communion

Section 5
Pastoral Care for Orthodox-Catholic Marriages

❖   ❖   ❖   ❖

Editors' Note

Fall 1995 marks the thirtieth anniversary and the fiftieth meeting of the U.S. Orthodox-Catholic Theological Consultation. The present collection of agreed statements seeks to make the work of the consultation accessible to a wide audience, beyond the usual circle of specialists. Also included in the collection are the agreed statements of two other bodies whose work has been especially important for the U.S. Consultation: the Joint International Commission for Theological Dialogue between the Catholic Church and the Orthodox Church, which held its first plenary session in 1980, and the U.S. Joint Committee of Orthodox and Catholic Bishops, established in 1981.

From its inception this was a joint project intended to present the history and current state of dialogue between our churches in an even-handed and dispassionate way. There was a distribution of tasks: Dr. Borelli (Catholic) was chiefly responsible for arrangement of the documents, the bibliography of documentation, and the introductions to sections 1 and 5. Prof. Erickson (Orthodox) was chiefly responsible for the general introduction and the introductions to sections 2, 3 and 4. Yet both editors carefully reviewed the entire text for accuracy and objectivity. Their hope is that the reader will not be able to say immediately, "this was written by a Catholic," or "this was written by an Orthodox."

Many hierarchs, scholars, pastors and faithful of both churches have contributed in diverse ways to Orthodox-Catholic dialogue and to the realization of this project. The editors would like to express their thanks, first of all, to colleagues past and present on the Consultation, whose tireless and sometimes thankless labors have brought our churches closer to the day when we will share one chalice; to Archbishop Rembert G. Weakland and Bishop Maximos (Aghiorgousis), current co-chairmen of the Consultation, whose personal commitment to the cause of Orthodox-Catholic unity has been a never-failing source of encouragement and joy; and especially to Fr. Michael Fahey, executive co-secretary of the Consultation from 1979-1995. His study of the history of the Consultation which appears in this volume is but one example of his many scholarly contributions to the Consultation's ongoing work. A special word of thanks also goes to Mr. Theodore Bazil of St. Vladimir's Seminary Press and Mr. Richard W. Daw of the United States Catholic Conference's Publishing and Promotion Services for having confidence in the editors and their project; to Ms. Thérèse Bermpohl of the Secretariat for Ecumenical and Interreligious Affairs, who accomplished the essential task of ordering the documents, entering them into a computer file, and preparing the near-perfect collection that forms the heart of this book; and to Miss Amy Odum of St. Vladimir's Seminary Press, whose technical expertise brought the book swiftly through the process of publication.

John Borelli
Secretariat for Ecumenical and Interreligious Affairs
National Conference of Catholic Bishops

John H. Erickson
St. Vladimir's Orthodox Theological Seminary

FOREWORD
Archbishop Rembert G. Weakland, O.S.B.

The embrace of Pope Paul VI and Patriarch Athenagoras I on the Mount of Olives at their first meeting on January 6, 1964, remains to this day a powerful image. That photo portrays the mutual affirmation of the quest for unity among both Roman Catholics and Orthodox. It heralded their common initiation of the dialogue of love to heal centuries of estrangement between the Eastern Church and the Western Church. In photographic stillness, we witnessed that outpouring of the spirit of unity coursing through the churches in those days and that so many of us were experiencing. For Catholics the scene occurred at the mid-point in the remarkable event that revitalized the Western Church for the modern world, the Second Vatican Council. For the Orthodox, the reconciliation of patriarch and pope was a sign of hope, a way of taking one more step out of isolation, and a witness to mutual support in the midst of the turmoil all churches feel in this twentieth century.

Events moved quickly for Rome and Constantinople in those days. Later in 1964, during the Council's third session, the Decrees on Ecumenism and on the Eastern Churches were adopted by overwhelming majorities. By December 1965, a joint commission for restoring relations between East and West had met and the mutual excommunications between the two sees were removed from the memory of the Church. In July of 1967, first Pope Paul VI visited the patriarchate of Constantinople. Then Athenagoras I, in turn, visited the Vatican in October of that same year. Correspondence and gestures of affection amassed until, ten years later, in 1978, the successor of Athenagoras, Patriarch Dimitrios I, assured the newly elected Pope John Paul II that he was one with him in desiring an international theological dialogue to begin meeting as soon as possible.

When that announcement by Patriarch Dimitrios I came in 1978, I had begun to attend the sessions of the United States Orthodox-Catholic Theological Consultation. In that year, the Consultation met twice, comprising its seventeenth and eighteenth sessions. It is a happy thought to realize that we are celebrating the fiftieth session of that group in 1995.

1

Foreword

We in North America have played a significant role in this major ecumenical drama of Orthodox-Roman Catholic relations in our time. Archbishop Iakovos, Primate of the Greek Orthodox Archdiocese of North and South America, served as a bridge-builder for the first official contacts between Rome and Constantinople. Then, after initial contacts in New York and Massachusetts under his direction and that of the newly established National Conference of Catholic Bishops, the Theological Consultation held its first meeting in early September 1965. We must remember that this occurred before the start of the final session of the Second Vatican Council. The Consultation's eighteen agreed statements that would follow in the next thirty years constitute an outstanding record of scholarly cooperation to the goals of mutual understanding and removal of obstacles to full communion. This theological dialogue, which usually met semiannually, gave rise to a second official dialogue, an annual meeting of Orthodox and Roman Catholic Bishops. This dialogue was the initiative of Archbishop Iakovos and took as its aim the pastoral considerations of the search for unity. The ecumenical journey of these Orthodox and Roman Catholic bishops from the United States to Rome and Constantinople in 1995 marked their fourteenth meeting. Both of our dialogues have continued to meet, deliberate, and pray together, even through these latter days when events and developments in Eastern Europe have strained relations and given rise to unpleasant accusations and grave demands on one another. The trust and good-will established over the years has made these dialogues most beneficial and productive.

My personal association with both dialogues, for most of their history, has been a fulfilling aspect of my ecumenical ministry as a bishop. I know first hand how much intense work both of scholarship and discussion has been put into each of the United States statements collected in this volume. Their publication with the work of the Joint International Commission will, it is hoped, draw Catholics and Orthodox especially in the United States closer together. It can be a tool to acknowledge and learn from the methods used in this mutual record of dialogue, a way to study jointly the agreements and reflections contained herein, and a stimulus to envision together the restoration of unity so much hoped for and prayed for.

FOREWORD
Bishop Maximos of Pittsburgh

The memory of the first theological meeting of the Orthodox-Roman Catholic Consultation in the United States—the previous two were organizational—is still very vivid in my mind. It took place at the John Power Center in Worcester, MA, hosted by Bishop Bernard Flanagan. I remember the first papers by Frs. John Romanides (who was not present) and Charles Von Euw on "Theological Diversity and Unity," John Meyendorff and Myles Bourke on "Intercommunion," and Leonidas Contos and Edward Malone on "Common Witness in Theological Education." I remember the words of Archbishop Iakovos: "There is no such thing as 'intercommunion.' There will either be communion or nothing!" I remember the kind hospitality of Bishop Flanagan and of the Kotsidas-Tonnas family, with their tasty "table-talk pies." This memorable meeting set the tone for meaningful talks for the next thirty years.

The spirit which has prevailed in the dialogue all these years has been one of mutual respect and love, kindness and understanding, together with honesty and commitment to truth. Our commitment has been not only to seeking and "speaking the truth in love" but also to sharing in the lives and experiences of our churches. Common prayer and participation as far as possible in the prayer life of the other church has also been part of our lives together in dialogue. And now, it is time to stop and reminisce about what has happened over these thirty years of theological dialogue in the United States, fifteen years of dialogue as pastors and bishops, and fifteen years of international dialogue. We are happy to see the results gathered in this volume.

We have produced a variety of agreed statements, beginning—significantly enough—with one on the holy eucharist. We have tried to give direction regarding common pastoral issues, beginning with inter-church marriages. We have responded to the work of the Joint International Commission for the dialogue between our two sister churches, the "two lungs" of the one Church of Christ. These two have to synchronize anew their breathing, so that the Church of Christ may begin breathing properly again. How

3

much more will it take for this to happen? It depends upon the kind of work that people like us do, as we listen to the guidance of God's Holy Spirit. It depends upon the work of our leaders, and it depends upon the prayers of God's holy people. As Patriarch Bartholomew of Constantinople recently said, "the Spirit talks to our churches today," as in the past. Let us hope that all of us will hear His voice and respond to His promptings.

INTRODUCTION
From Estrangement to Dialogue

Unlike most Christian divisions, that between the Orthodox Churches of the East and the Roman Catholic Church in the West cannot be dated with precision nor can its immediate causes be specified easily. To be sure, the year 1054 once figured prominently in presentations of East-West ecclesiastical relations. For example, according to the eighteenth-century historian Edward Gibbon, the mutual excommunications of Patriarch Michael Cerularius of Constantinople and the papal legate Humbert of Silva Candida in that year marked "the consummation of the schism." Most scholars these days would be less categorical. Schisms prompted by jurisdictional rivalry and by diverse theological and disciplinary issues divided the churches of East and West many times before 1054. As for the schism of 1054 itself, few if any at the time viewed it as absolute or irreversible. Most Christians in East and West were unaware of any change in relations between the churches. Much more significant, in the view of many scholars, was the shock of the Fourth Crusade in 1204, when knights from the West sacked Constantinople and established a Latin Kingdom on the ruins of the Byzantine Empire. But in fact it may be misleading to identify "the consummation of the schism" with any single event or date. It would be more accurate to speak of a progressive alienation of the churches, which, although this would be experienced and expressed in various ways, eventually led each side to regard the other as estranged from right belief and practice, as being outside the fullness of the mystery of the Church

Christianity was born and grew up within the Roman Empire, then a far-flung political and economic entity comprising many different nationalities and cultures. While Jesus and his immediate followers in Palestine spoke Aramaic, the Gospel message spread through the Roman world chiefly in Greek, the common language of the age. By the third century, other languages also begin to be used by Christian communities—Syriac in parts of the East, for example, and Latin in the West. Just as the Gospel message had been "translated" into the language and forms of thought comprehensible to the Greek world, so now other distinctive expressions of Christianity begin to emerge. This demonstrated the universality of the Gospel message, but it could also cause problems in mutual under-standing. More than one of the theological controversies of antiquity was exacerbated by difficulties in translating the concepts of one language into another.

It has become commonplace to contrast the Greek mind, inclined toward philosophy and intellectual speculation, and the Latin mind, with its genius for law and administration. While there is a measure of truth in this generalization, it would be a mistake to exaggerate the importance of linguistic and cultural differences, as though these in themselves could account for the eventual estrangement of the churches. Consider, for example, the Emperor Justinian (483-565). A native-speaker of Latin, the great codifier of Roman Law, he also was the builder of Hagia Sophia in Constantinople, the very symbol of Orthodox Christianity, and he molded subsequent Byzantine conceptions of church-state relations as did no other. Like many in both East and West, Justinian was devoted to the notion of a Christian *oikoumenê,* one Christian commonwealth, in which linguistic and cultural differences could be transcended.

Transcended—but not obliterated, for certainly such differences re-mained. In the realm of doctrine this is evident most notably in Eastern and Western approaches to the mystery of the Holy Trinity. How can God be both three and one? The eastern approach, as epitomized in the work of the Cappadocian Fathers of the fourth century, begins with the three divine persons and only then moves to consideration of their common essence: God is one because the Father is the single Source and Cause (*archê*) from whom the Son is eternally begotten and the Spirit eternally proceeds. By contrast, the western approach, as set forth especially by St. Augustine, begins with the divine essence and only then considers the relationship of the three persons. The Holy Spirit thus can be seen as the bond of love uniting the Father and His only-begotten Son in one single Godhead. These differences of approach coexisted for many centuries in the Church, and in certain respects they may be regarded as complemen-tary; but as subsequent history indicates, when pursued in isolation, oblivious to each other's fundamental concerns and intuitions, these differences of approach could become divisive.

As we look at East and West in Christian antiquity, we may also detect certain differences in their conceptions of church order. Consider the wording of canon 3 of the First Council of Constantinople (381, reckoned by both Catholics and Orthodox as the second ecumenical council, though it was exclusively eastern in its composition): "The bishop of Constantinople," the new co-capital of the Roman Empire, "shall have the primacy of honor after the bishop of Rome, because Constantinople is New Rome." The same line of thinking can be seen in canon 28 of the Council of Chalcedon (451, the fourth ecumenical council), which was approved in the absence of the Roman legates: Just as "Old Rome" was honored because it was the imperial capital, so now Constantinople, the "New Rome," is to be honored—and given a greatly expanded patriarchal jurisdiction surpassing that of the other ancient eastern patriarchates and rivaling that of Old Rome. According to the eastern conception revealed in these canons, differences in rank arise not from any essential inequality of the churches but rather from conciliar decision based upon the secular importance of their cities. The Church of Rome, on the other hand, insisted that its primacy was *iure divino*, based not on secular importance or even conciliar decision but rather on Christ's promise to Peter: "Thou art Peter, and on this rock I will build my Church" (Matt. 16:18). Here again, the differing approaches of East and West were not necessarily mutually exclusive. Despite recurrent tensions relating to church order, the churches remained in communion for centuries save when dogmatic issues were at stake. But neither were these approaches neatly complementary. Issues relating to church order, above all to papal primacy, would in time prove church-dividing.

Notwithstanding their differences in antiquity, both the Greek East and Latin West shared Emperor Justinian's ideal of one Christian commonwealth. More concretely, they simply took for granted the existence of one Christian Roman Empire. But with the barbarian invasions of the West in the fifth and sixth centuries and the rise of Islam in the seventh, the existence of this empire was threatened. For a time these shared vicissitudes seemed to draw Old Rome and the New closer together. With the loss of the Near East to the Muslim Arabs, Constantinople was no longer tempted to compromise with theologically dissident elements there and instead emphasized its solidarity with Rome and the West. At the same time, the Popes looked to the imperial authority in Constantinople for protection against barbarian depredations, and a flood of refugees fleeing the Islamic tide made Rome more "eastern" than ever before. To be sure, cultural differences were beginning to cause friction, as is evident from some of the canons of the Byzantine Synod in Trullo (691-92), which criticized certain Latin practices. On the whole, however, relations remained correct and even cordial. In 710 Pope Constantine I even visited Constantinople, where he was received with every honor. Unfortunately there would not be another event of this sort until Pope Paul VI's historic visit to Patriarch Athenagoras of Constantinople in 1967.

The eighth century was to witness significant changes in relations between Rome and Constantinople. The Byzantine Empire was rent by controversy over an imperially initiated program of iconoclasm. In Rome Popes Gregory II and III refused to go along with this new heresy, and in retaliation Emperor Leo III transferred jurisdiction over Illyricum (the western half of the Balkan peninsula) and southern Italy from Rome to Constantinople, a move that was to complicate ecclesiastical relations long after the defeat of iconoclasm. The military situation in central Italy posed a more immediate problem for the papacy, however. Byzantine power there was on the wane, and incursions by the Lombards threatened Rome. A new protector was needed and found in the person of Pepin, King of the Franks, who invaded Italy to "restore" to the popes the "patrimony of St. Peter," *i.e.* the territories which they hitherto had governed on behalf of the emperor in Constantinople. This new papal-Frankish alliance received powerful symbolic confirmation in 800, when Pope Leo III crowned Pepin's son Charlemagne "Emperor of the Romans." The political unity which hitherto had facilitated amicable relations between the two Romes was effectively at an end.

The papacy was now in an independent but delicate position between Byzantium and the Franks. Communion with Constantinople was restored with the condemnation of iconoclasm at the Second Council of Nicaea (787), the seventh and last ecumenical council which the churches would hold together, but this was challenged by Charlemagne's Frankish bishops who, misled by a faulty translation of the council's acts and eager to demonstrate their own theological acumen, castigated its teaching on images. Pope Hadrian I was left with the difficult task of soothing their ruffled feelings. Another point of discord focused on the wording of the creed. In its original form, preserved unaltered in the East, the "Nicene" or "Nicaeo-Constantinopolitan" creed spoke of "the Holy Spirit who proceeds from the Father." In Spain the phrase "and from the Son" (*filioque*) had been added in the sixth century to emphasize the full divinity of the Son against the Arian heresy. From Spain the phrase spread to what is now France and Germany, where Charlemagne's theologians accused the Greeks of heresy for *omitting* it from the creed! For the time being, at least, Rome tactfully but firmly rejected the interpolation, and Pope Leo III had the creed without *filioque* set up on silver plaques in St. Peter's.

In the ninth-century Photian Schism, many of these tensions and disagreements over theological, jurisdictional, ecclesiological and disciplinary issues inherited from earlier generations were raised to the level of open controversy. What, for example, was the proper role of the Roman Church and its bishop within the communion of the churches? In Constantinople, the incumbent patriarch, Ignatius, had been deposed (not, of course, without imperial pressure), and a new patriarch, Photius, had been elected. Pope Nicholas I of Rome claimed the right to review these proceedings. In Constantinople, however, this was regarded as an unjustified meddling in the internal affairs of a sister church. Speaking for the Byzantine Church, Patriarch Photius appealed to the ancient eastern concept of the pentarchy, the idea that the five patriarchates—Rome, Constantinople, Antioch, Alexandria and Jerusalem—are like unto the five senses in the body of Christ, whose well-being depends upon their communion, harmony, mutual support, coordination and consensus. According to this conception, Rome is indeed the first see, but neither Rome nor any other single see could claim full authority to the exclusion of the others.

This dispute over papal authority was complicated by the fact that both Constantinople and Rome claimed jurisdiction over what is present-day Bulgaria in ancient Illyricum. And while the czar of that emerging nation was being courted by those great ecclesiastical centers, his people witnessed a disedifying contest between Frankish missionaries from Germany, who were insisting on Western disciplinary and liturgical practices such as clerical celibacy and the exclusive use of Latin in the mass, and missionaries from Byzantium, who followed the Eastern practice of permitting married men to be ordained priests and used the nearly-vernacular Slavonic in the liturgy. Even worse, in the eyes of Byzantium, was the fact that the Frankish missionaries in Bulgaria were reciting the creed with the interpolated *filioque*. This provoked a major reaction on the part of Patriarch Photius, who vigorously attacked both the interpolation and the less-than-subtle version of Augustine's trinitarian teaching which Charlemagne's theologians had developed to support it.

The result of this conflict—over authority, over disciplinary matters, over trinitarian doctrine—was schism. But in little more than a decade this schism was healed. A union council was held in Constantinople in 879—a council whose success has led both Catholic and Orthodox theologians in recent decades to hail it as an appropriate model for our own day. Patriarch Photius and Pope John VIII, successor to Nicholas I, made peace, and communion was restored between the Church of Constantinople and the Church of Rome. Given the many issues in dispute, how was this possible? At least two reasons may be suggested:

—First, *filioque* was not yet an issue between Rome and Constantinople. The interpolated creed was still confined to the Frankish realms. It was therefore easy for Pope John VIII to agree to the decisions of the union council of 879 rejecting the interpolation. At the same time, the theological issues which had come to be associated with the interpolation had not been fully discussed, much less resolved. The council of 879 was able to achieve the reunion of the churches but only by tacitly agreeing to ignore issues which later generations would again take up.

—Another and perhaps more important reason why reunion was possible in 879 is the fact that Rome and Constantinople still shared the same underlying ecclesiology, or at least they shared enough elements of it so that any differences could be ignored. Rome and the Eastern churches still shared the idea that the Church is essentially an ordered communion of local churches. On Rome's side this meant that Constantinople was recognized as a real sister church—as fully Church, one, holy, catholic and apostolic, and not just the branch office of a universal organization. For its part, Constantinople freely recognized Rome's priority. It was certainly the first among the churches of the pentarchy. Like the sense of sight in the human body, Rome had the oversight of the whole body of Christ. But practically speaking, how was this oversight to be exercised in maintaining the communion of the churches? What limits if any were there to the exercise of papal authority? At the union council of 879 this ecclesiological issue, like the theological issue of the procession of the Holy Spirit, was not fully resolved.

In the tenth century Byzantine might and culture was nearing its apex, while the prestige of the papacy, now under the degrading domination of the Roman nobility, was at its nadir. A revival of imperial aspirations in Germany and increased German influence in Rome did little to improve matters. Early in the eleventh century the *filioque* was introduced in Rome, probably on the occasion of the coronation of German Emperor Henry II; and perhaps as a consequence, the names of the popes ceased to be commemorated in the diptychs in Constantinople, that is, the official list of hierarchs with whom the Patriarch of Constantinople was in communion. Yet on the whole apathy rather than hostility characterized relations between the churches. From the mid eleventh century this situation began to change. Byzantium's complacent sense of superiority was shaken by the advances of the hostile Normans in southern Italy and the Seljuk Turks in Asia Minor. Support from the papacy and other potential allies in the West became highly desirable. In the West, however, a powerful reforming movement, most often called the Gregorian Reform after its most illustrious proponent, Pope Gregory VII, was seeking to free the Church from lay domination and other abuses that had arisen in feudal society, and it was doing so by stressing the universal authority of the pope in a manner quite unfamiliar in the East.

Such is the broader context of the schism of 1054 and its aftermath. The irascible Cardinal Humbert had been sent to Constantinople to negotiate an alliance with the emperor against the Normans, but there he encountered the equally irascible Patriarch Michael Cerularius. The issues initially in dispute between them were disciplinary in nature, the most noteworthy being over whether the bread of the eucharist should be leavened or unleavened—an issue which few if any Orthodox or Catholics today would regard as church-dividing. Quickly enough however, unresolved issues from the past were reintroduced. The issue of the *filioque* now divided Rome and Constantinople. In addition, the Gregorian conception of papal authority sharpened ecclesiological differences. In the West the older ecclesiology of *koinonia*, of the communion of sister churches, was giving way to an ecclesiology focused on a single church, the Roman, in such a way that "Roman Church" and "Universal Church" become virtually synonymous. Conformity with the Church of Rome, the see of Peter, comes to be regarded as a necessary aspect of belonging to the one Church of Christ. The concept of the pentarchy still favored in the East did not fit easily into this new perspective.

Unlike the Photian schism of the ninth century, the schism of 1054 was not quickly healed, but this was not for want of trying on both sides. Negotiations began almost at once. Though differences had grown sharper, dimming prospects for reunion, these were diplomatically ignored in order to facilitate an alliance against the Turks. The ensuing crusades brought closer contact between Latins and Greeks but did little to resolve their religious differences. The Greeks were shocked by the crusaders' rapaciousness and resented the establishment of a Latin hierarchy in the crusaders' principalities in the East. The Latins in turn blamed Greek treachery and ecclesiastical insubordination for the crusades' failures. Hostility culminated in 1204 with the Fourth Crusade and its sack of Constantinople. Despite the passage of centuries, Eastern Christians still feel the pain of that tragic attempt to impose the union of the churches by force.

After 1204 the sense of mutual interiority—of common participation in the mystery of the Church—which had persisted even after the schism of 1054 gives way to a sense of mutual exteriority: The Orthodox Church and Catholic Church are on their way to becoming mutually exclusive, each viewing the other as somehow "outside" that one Church confessed in the creed. Yet efforts at reunion continued. Among the Easterners the idea of the pentarchy was not dead, notwithstanding ecclesiological developments in the Latin West. Needed, in the opinion of many churchmen, among them the most conservative, was a new union council like that of 879, a true ecumenical council in which all the patriarchates would be represented and the outstanding theological issues would be discussed and resolved. At first the Latins were not enthusiastic. Needed, in their opinion, was due submission of the Easterners to papal authority, not debate in a common council. This was to be their approach at the time of the

Council of Lyon in 1274, where the only dogmatic decisions were reached before the tiny Greek delegation arrived; all that remained was for the Byzantine emperor to make his personal submission. It is little wonder that the union negotiated there proved ephemeral, however much it might have served the emperor's political interests. But new developments in the West in the later Middle Ages, above all the rise of conciliarism, in time made the Latins more receptive to the idea of a union council.

At the resulting Council of Florence (1438-39), the East was incomparably better represented than at Lyon 160 years earlier, and many of the outstanding issues between East and West were debated at length. By this point, however, the two sides no longer shared a "universe of discourse." The Greeks were uncomfortable with the scholastic theology which had developed in the West, and the Latins had little appreciation for the mystical theology of late Byzantium. Insights from both traditions which might have moved discussion of issues like the *filioque* to a deeper level, enriching both sides, were largely ignored. While all but one of the weary Greek delegates signed the council's decree of union, back in the East Florence was almost unanimously rejected as a betrayal of the true faith. While in many ways quite different from the Council of Lyon, Florence was no more successful than it in uniting the churches. In fact, these councils themselves may have served to deepen the estrangement of the churches, since the churches came to evaluate them in very different ways, Catholics regarding them as universally authoritative—indeed as ecumenical—and as offering an appropriate model and basis for any future union and the Orthodox rejecting them altogether. Fortunately in recent years churchmen on both sides have become more sensitive to the historical circumstances of these unsuccessful attempts at reunion, permitting a more nuanced evaluation of their ecclesiological significance. Indicative of this trend is the willingness of Pope Paul VI, on the nine-hundredth anniversary of Lyon in 1974, to refer to that council as "the sixth of the general synods held in the West" rather than as ecumenical.

The fall of Constantinople to the Turks in 1453 brought enormous changes not only to the internal life of the Orthodox Churches but also to their ways of relating to others. Within the Ottoman Empire, the *milet* system allowed the Church to survive as a distinct religious and cultural entity but severely limited possibilities for education and other intellectual pursuits. In distant Russia and other regions beyond Muslim domination, church life was not subject to the same restrictions, but for centuries spiritual energies there were directed more towards artistic expression—the "theology in colors" of the icon—than towards intellectual activity. For the most part, Eastern Christians were isolated from developments which were dramatically changing the Christian West—the Renaissance, the Protestant Reformation, the Enlightenment. To be sure, some points of contact remained. Bright young scholars from the East studied in the West. Merchants, diplomats and members of religious orders from the West made their presence felt in the East. But the manifest imbalance of resources both economic and intellectual made genuine dialogue virtually impossible. Given the growing dominance of Western culture, Eastern Christians quite understandably tended to adopt its vocabulary and categories of thought, even though this often obscured many of the deeper and more distinctive insights of their own Eastern tradition.

Changes within the West in this period also had important consequences for Orthodox-Catholic relations. Religious and economic rivalries pitted the Protestant and the Catholic powers against each other not only in Western Europe but also in the East, where they tried to manipulate the Orthodox in diverse ways. In addition, in response to the challenge of the Protestant Reformation, Catholic theologians from the Council of Trent onward cultivated what has been described as "soteriological and ecclesiological exclusivism," that is, the idea that no salvation is possible outside the visible institutional structures of the (Roman) Catholic Church. An earlier sacramental approach to ecclesiology, which even as late as Florence could envision reunion above all as the restoration of communion between sister churches, gives way to a predominantly institutional ecclesiology aimed at the "conversion" of individual "schismatics" to the Roman Church, "the Head, the Mother and the Teacher of all the churches," and their "submission" to the Roman Pontiff, its visible head. Under these circumstances, it is understandable why the Orthodox were inclined to view Western ecclesiastical activities in the East with suspicion. All too often the educational and charitable enterprises of the Western missionaries were agencies for proselytization. Worse yet, in the eyes of Orthodox Church leaders, was the formation of the Eastern

Catholic Churches (or Uniate Churches, as the Orthodox more often have called them), that is, groups of Eastern Christians who, while keeping their own liturgical rites and customs, submitted to Roman authority and accepted Roman doctrine. While generalizations about the origins and nature of these very diverse churches require considerable qualification, few scholars today would deny that "extra-ecclesial interests" (for example, Polish, Austrian, French pressure or influence) played a role, just as "extra-ecclesial interests" at other times would play a role in their restriction or suppression. At the same time, as recent studies of the first of these unions, that of Brest in 1595-96, suggest, those Easterners who initiated the union were by no means insincere opportunists. Like Easterners at the time of Florence, they envisioned union as a restoration of communion between sister churches. By this time in Rome, however, the new spirit of soteriological and ecclesiological exclusivism prevailed, and the union was understood rather as a legal act of submission. At any event, neither Brest nor subsequent partial unions succeeded in achieving a wider reunion of the Orthodox and the Catholic Churches. If anything, they served to sharpen their division, as each came to regard itself as the exclusive bearer of salvation. Symptomatic on the Catholic side is a 1729 order of the Propaganda Fide forbidding any *communio in sacris* with the "dissident orientals." Symptomatic on the Orthodox side is the 1756 decision of the Patriarchate of Constantinople that henceforth Catholic converts to Orthodoxy were to be rebaptized.

During the nineteenth century, two papal documents about the Christian East, from Pius IX in 1848 and Leo XIII in 1894, appealed for reunion, but in them reunion was clearly conceived as a return to the see of Rome. The Orthodox responded by taxing Rome for its doctrinal "innovations," above all its conception of papal primacy, and by urging it to return to the faith and practice of the undivided Church of the first millennium. This was not an atmosphere conducive to fruitful dialogue. Yet by the closing decades of our own twentieth century, relations between Catholics and Orthodox have improved to the point that leaders on both sides can speak of communion between the churches as being almost complete. Many factors have contributed to this remarkable change. For example, a growing historical consciousness has allowed both Catholics and Orthodox to view their own histories as well as the history of their

15

estrangement in a new light. But certainly especially important among these factors has been the modern ecumenical movement. Faced by common challenges in a rapidly changing world, Christians from many different traditions increasingly became aware of the scandal of disunity and of the need for reconciliation and cooperation. One of the earliest testimonies to this movement for Christian unity is the 1920 encyclical letter of the Ecumenical Patriarchate of Constantinople "to all the churches of Christ, wherever they may be," which has rightly been hailed as the charter of modern Orthodox ecumenism. During the interwar years the Orthodox pursued both bilateral and multilateral ecumenical contacts, and in 1948 they played an important role in the establishment of the World Council of Churches. Unfortunately the Communist Revolution of 1918 curtailed participation of the Russian Orthodox Church in such ecumenical activities. For decades the very survival of this martyred church was threatened. Following World War II, overt persecution subsided and institutional church life could be reestablished, but during the years of the cold war the Russian Church and now also the other Orthodox churches of Eastern Europe remained aloof from the ecumenical movement. This situation changed dramatically in 1961, however, when these churches became members of the World Council of Churches and began to cultivate closer contacts with other Christian groups.

The official attitude of the Catholic Church towards the ecumenical movement was at first negative, then cautious. When John XXIII was elected pope in 1958, few anticipated the major reorientation in policy and attitude which he would initiate, above all through the Second Vatican Council (1962-65) which he convoked. The council marked a significant shift not only in Catholic thinking on ecumenism but also in basic ecclesiology, as the strongly institutional model of the Church set forth at Trent and Vatican I gave way to a more sacramental understanding of the Church as communion—an understanding inspired among other things by a rediscovery of the ecclesiology of the early Church. The vision of the Church and of Christian unity set forth in the council's documents, above all in the Decree on Ecumenism (*Unitatis Redintegratio*), the Decree on the Eastern Churches (*Orientalium Ecclesiarum*) and the Dogmatic Constitution on the Church (*Lumen Gentium*), created a new climate for dialogue especially with the Orthodox.

16

In view of the new spirit of openness, the second of the Pan-Orthodox "Rhodes Conferences" (1963) accepted the principle of "a dialogue on equal footing" with the Catholic Church. The third Rhodes Conference (1964) reiterated its support for dialogue but added that "a dialogue of charity" would be needed first in order to create appropriate conditions for official theological dialogue. Accordingly, each autocephalous Orthodox Church was authorized to initiate contacts aimed at restoring good will between Orthodox and Catholics. Such contacts included a series of theological conversations between the Russian Orthodox Church and the Roman Catholic Secretariat for Promoting Christian Unity, beginning in 1967. But the most noteworthy events by far in this "dialogue of charity" involved Rome and Constantinople. These included the historic meeting and embrace of Pope Paul VI and Patriarch Athenagoras I of Constantinople in Jerusalem (1964), the mutual lifting of the anathemas of 1054 (1965) and exchanges of visits to Rome and Constantinople by pope and patriarch (1967).

In December 1975, in the course of celebrations marking the tenth anniversary of the mutual lifting of anathemas, patriarchal envoy Metropolitan Meliton of Chalcedon announced the establishment of an inter-Orthodox commission responsible for preparing for official theological dialogue with the Catholic Church. A comparable commission was established on the Catholic side, and in 1976 these two commissions began their work. In 1978 a Joint Coordinating Group from these commissions completed a document detailing objectives and methodology for the dialogue for submission to church authorities on both sides (pp. 47-52 below). The document sets forth the purpose of the dialogue in simple but eloquent terms:

> The purpose of the dialogue between the Roman Catholic Church and the Orthodox Church is the re-establishment of full communion between these two churches. This communion, based on unity of faith according to the common experience and tradition of the early Church, will find its expression in the common celebration of the eucharist. (Joint Preparatory Plan I)

As for methodology, it was agreed that the dialogue should begin "with the elements that unite the Orthodox and Roman Catholic Churches" (Joint Preparatory Plan II), with what Orthodox and Catholics have in common rather than with what divides them. Specifically, the dialogue should begin with the sacraments, particularly as they relate to ecclesiology.

Yet another year passed before Pope John Paul II and Patriarch Demetrios I of Constantinople officially announced the beginning of the dialogue. The new Joint International Commission for Theological Dialogue between the Catholic and Orthodox Churches was to be comprised of experts appointed by both sides in equal number. On the Orthodox side these would include two representatives, typically a hierarch and a theologian, from each of the fourteen universally recognized autocephalous and autonomous Orthodox Churches. On the Catholic side these would be appointed by the Secretariat (now Pontifical Council) for Christian Unity. The first plenary session of the new commission, held on Patmos and Rhodes, May 29-June 4, 1980, was devoted to organizational matters. The plan for dialogue set forth in the 1978 document was approved. Cardinal Johannes Willebrands, head of the Secretariat for Christian Unity, and the Patriarchate of Constantinople's Archbishop Stylianos of Australia were chosen as co-presidents. (In 1989 Cardinal Willebrands would be succeeded by Cardinal Edward Idriss Cassidy.) In addition, three sub-commissions were established. These would be responsible for preparing study papers to serve as the basis for draft documents for discussion in plenary session. It was anticipated that plenary sessions would be held every two years and that the sub-commissions would meet during the alternate years.

The Joint International Commission's second plenary session, held in Munich, June 30-July 6, 1982, succeeded in completing the Commission's first agreed statement, "The Mystery of the Church and of the Eucharist in the Light of the Mystery of the Holy Trinity" (pp. 53-64 below). The third plenary session, held on Crete, May 30-June 8, 1984, considered a draft document on "Faith, Sacraments, and the Unity of the Church," but because of time constraints and certain reservations on the part of the Orthodox concerning the order of Christian initiation in the Roman Catholic Church, the text could not be finalized at that time. It was to be taken up again at the next plenary session in Bari, May 29-June 7, 1986. That gathering, however, was boycotted by several Orthodox Churches because of alleged Catholic proselytism and support for schismatic elements in Macedonia, so final revision and approval of "Faith, Sacraments, and the Unity of the Church" was deferred to a second gathering in Bari, June 9-16, 1987 (pp. 93-104 below). At its fifth plenary session, held at the New Valamo monastery in Finland, June 19-17, 1988, the Joint International Commission was able to adopt its third agreed statement, "The Sacrament of Order in the Sacramental Structure of the Church, with Particular Reference to the Importance of Apostolic Succession for the Sanctification and Unity of the People of God" (pp. 131-142). By that time, however, new tensions relating to the reemergence of the Eastern Catholic Churches in Eastern Europe prompted the commission to establish a special sub-commission to study the question of "uniatism." The next plenary session, scheduled for Munich/Freising in 1990, was to take up "Ecclesiological and Canonical Consequences of the Sacramental Structure of the Church: Conciliarity and Authority in the Church." In the interval, however, the situation had become more urgent. By the time that the special sub-commission met in Vienna in January 1990, the Berlin Wall had fallen and ecclesiastical relations in Eastern Europe were deteriorating rapidly. As newspaper headlines announced the death of communism, the inside pages told of recrudescent ethnic and religious strife, suggesting the death also of ecumenism as Orthodox and Catholic churchmen and theologians had known it during the "dialogue of charity."

When the sixth plenary session of the Joint International Commission gathered in Munich/Freising in June 1990, at the insistence of the Orthodox membership it set aside the draft document on "Ecclesiological and Canonical Consequences of the Sacramental Structure of the Church." Interrupting the normal progression for the dialogue as set forth in the Joint Preparatory Plan, the Commission agreed to turn its attention to the subject of "uniatism" and released a brief communiqué announcing this decision and sketching its initial reaction to the subject (see the introduction to Section 4, below pp. 159-166). The document concluded by noting that "the study of this question will be carried forward." In accordance with its standard operating procedure, the Joint International Commission entrusted preparation of a draft text to three joint sub-commissions and then to its joint coordinating committee. Contrary to standard operating procedure, however, the draft text completed by the coordinating committee working at Arricia (near Rome) in June 1991 was published later that month by the Orthodox side. This Arricia text would eventually be taken up at the Joint International Commission's seventh plenary session, where it formed the basis for the Commission's fourth and most recent agreed statement, "Uniatism, Method of Union of the Past, and the Present Search for Full Communion" (pp. 175-183). The plenary session originally had been scheduled to meet at Balamand, Lebanon in June 1992, but civil strife there forced postponement to June 17-23, 1993. Even then, for a wide range of reasons, six of fourteen Orthodox Churches did not send representatives. Since its appearance, the Balamand Statement has generated considerably more discussion, much of it quite passionate, than the Joint International Commission's first three agreed statements. All this suggests that the issue of "uniatism" remains a neuralgic point in Orthodox-Catholic relations. While leaders on both sides have vowed that the dialogue will go forward, it is evident that much remains to be done if the estrangement of centuries is to be overcome.

The work of the Joint International Commission represents Orthodox-Catholic theological dialogue at the highest church level, but this is not the only level at which such dialogue has been taking place. Discussion groups and formal dialogues exist on national and local levels both in Europe and in the United States. In France, for example, a sixteen-member Catholic-Orthodox Joint Commission has met regularly since 1985. Its work has included an important statement on "The Roman Primacy within the Communion of the Churches" (1991; English translation in the periodical *One in Christ* vol. 29 [1993], pp. 156-64) and a reaction (highly favorable) to the Joint International Commission's Balamand Statement (1993; English translation in *Eastern Churches Journal* vol. 1 [1994], pp. 57-62).

Especially noteworthy has been the work of the U.S. Orthodox-Roman Catholic Theological Consultation, which has met regularly since 1965 under the joint auspices of the United States Catholic Bishops (since 1966 the National Conference of Catholic Bishops, NCCB) and the Standing Conference of Canonical Orthodox Bishops in America (SCOBA). The first Orthodox co-chairman of the Consultation—and for many years its animating spirit—was Archbishop Iakovos, primate of the Greek Orthodox Archdiocese of North and South America and President of SCOBA. In 1984 he was succeeded as co-chairman by Metropolitan Silas of New Jersey (Greek Orthodox Archdiocese), and in 1987 by Bishop Maximos (Aghiorgoussis) of Pittsburgh (Greek Orthodox Archdiocese), the current co-chairman. The first Roman Catholic co-chairman was Bishop Bernard Flanagan of Worcester, Massachusetts. His successors have been Cardinal William Baum of Washington (1973-80), Archbishop Rembert G. Weakland of Milwaukee (1980-84), Bishop Arthur O'Neill of Rockford, Illinois (1984-94), and—for a second time—Archbishop Weakland, the current co-chairman. The remainder of the membership—averaging a dozen on each side—includes theologians, canonists, Scripture scholars, historians and liturgiologists. Catholic members are appointed by the NCCB through the Bishops' Committee for Ecumenical and Interreligious Affairs; Orthodox members are appointed by the hierarchs of SCOBA in such a way as to reflect the multijurisdictional character of that body. Executive co-secretaries, currently Fr. Michael Fahey (Roman Catholic) and Fr. Thomas FitzGerald (Orthodox) and staff support from the NCCB and SCOBA facilitate the on-going work of the Consultation.

The U.S. Consultation was established within a year of the Second Vatican Council's Decree on Ecumenism and the third of the Pan-Orthodox Rhodes Conferences, which officially authorized such dialogues for Catholics and Orthodox respectively. The excitement of those early years of ecumenical contact can be seen in the comments of one participant who, with some hyperbole, observed that this was the first time Orthodox and Catholic theologians had met face to face officially since the conclusion of the Council of Florence in 1439. It is not surprising that such contact should come first in the United States, a land of immigrants, far from the traditional homelands of both Catholicism and Orthodoxy. Despite an obvious disparity in numbers (there are approximately sixty million Catholics in the United States compared to perhaps four million Orthodox), Catholics and Orthodox meet and share the challenges of this pluralistic society on an equal footing. As Archbishop Iakovos reflected in an early meeting of the Consultation, "Here we can conduct the dialogue free of the national pressures which would first have to be overcome in overwhelmingly Catholic countries like Spain or Italy or in a predominantly Orthodox country like Greece."

At the same time, the American situation presents certain unique challenges especially for effective implementation of the results of dialogue. In its homelands, Orthodoxy, true to its basic understanding of ecclesiology, has maintained a territorial principle of church order: In each place all the faithful regardless of ethnic or racial or socio-economic particularities are brought together as one body of Christ, as one catholic church, with a single church structure. In America as in other regions of the so-called "diaspora," by contrast, for various historical reasons Orthodox Christians are divided into a number of territorially overlapping jurisdictions which reflect, in diverse ways, the particularities of a multitude of immigrant groups. Desire for greater structural coherence and cooperation in matters of common concern led to the formation SCOBA in 1960, but while SCOBA has facilitated coordination in such areas as ecumenical dialogue, it has not succeeded in bringing full structural unity to Orthodoxy in America. Of the present constellation of jurisdictions, the largest, the Greek Orthodox Archdiocese of North and South America, as well as several smaller groups is under the jurisdiction of the Ecumenical Patriarchate of Constantinople. Another, the Orthodox Church in America (OCA), traces its history to the eighteenth-century Russian mission in Alaska; after many decades of estrangement in the wake of the Communist Revolution, it entered into negotiations with the Russian Orthodox Church and in 1970 received autocephalous (lit. "self-headed") status, making it the only completely self-governing Orthodox church in North America. This autocephaly, however, has been hotly contested by the Patriarchate of Constantinople and is not recognized by many of the other autocephalous Orthodox Churches, thus further complicating inter-Orthodox relations in the United States. Still other jurisdictions—the Antiochian Orthodox Christian Archdiocese, the three Serbian dioceses, the Romanian Orthodox Missionary Episcopate, the Bulgarian diocese—are subject to other Old World patriarchates. While SCOBA serves as a useful umbrella organization for these various jurisdictions, it remains a consultative body. It has no juridical authority comparable to that which the NCCB has in certain areas. If the canonical implications of a major ecumenical issue need to be addressed, the NCCB can raise the matter with the appropriate Vatican offices. For SCOBA, major issues often must be referred to the various Old World patriarchates. But these churches themselves do not have a common centralized structure comparable to that of the Roman Catholic Church. They act together on the basis of consensus, and as the history of the Joint International Commission also indicates, consensus is not always easy to achieve.

This "structural imparity" reflects at least in part certain basic differences between Orthodox and Catholic ecclesiology. Such issues are a matter of concern especially for the Orthodox, who are working to address them on a Pan-Orthodox basis on the international level (see especially section 2 below), but they also have important implications for the future of Orthodox-Catholic relations. The creation of the U.S. Joint Committee of Orthodox and Catholic Bishops in 1981 represents an important attempt to deal with practical difficulties related to this "imparity." The membership of the Committee, at present eight bishops on each side plus SCOBA and NCCB staff, is intended to be representative of the Catholic and the Orthodox episcopate in the United States. On the Orthodox side it includes one or more bishops from most of the jurisdictions represented in SCOBA. On the Catholic side it includes both Eastern and Latin Catholic bishops, many of whom come from parts of the country where Orthodox Christians are numerous. The Roman Catholic co-chairman is Archbishop Rembert G. Weakland of Milwaukee; the Orthodox co-chairman is Metropolitan Silas of New Jersey (Greek Orthodox Archdiocese). At their annual meetings, the bishops explore pastoral implications of the work of the U.S. Theological Consultation and other areas of mutual concern, and in their agreed statements they seek to give practical expression to the work of the theologians. By holding liturgical services and other public events in the course of their meetings they seek to bring the work of Orthodox-Catholic dialogue to a wider audience. A joint visit to Rome and Constantinople in late November 1995 gave them a unique opportunity to express their concerns and views in those historic centers of the two churches.

Joint commissions and consultations, theological papers, agreed statements, personal contacts, pilgrimages—all these have been instruments in the present quest for Orthodox-Catholic unity. Given centuries of estrangement, the quest may be long and difficult. When siblings have drifted apart and have not seen each other for many years, they may have difficulty recognizing each other at first. If they have not been on speaking terms, they may for a time only stammer; their awkward gestures at reconciliation may even be misunderstood. But with the churches just as with such siblings, no real reunion will be possible without dialogue. This must be a dialogue of truth, for no enduring relationship can be based on a lie, but it must also continue to be a dialogue of charity, a dialogue of love.

THE ORTHODOX-CATHOLIC CONSULTATION IN THE UNITED STATES

Michael A. Fahey, S.J.

The Orthodox-Catholic Consultation in the United States came into being in 1965. Although there had been some informal and unpublicized meetings between Orthodox and Catholic theologians in the 1950s at the Russian Center, Fordham University, New York City, and in Boston, the more immediate occasion for closer contact came from a meeting on January 29, 1965, between the third and fourth sessions of the Second Vatican Council, in New York City, attended by Catholics: Monsignor William Baum, Frs. John Long, Thomas Stransky, Paul Mailleux, Donald Campion and several others, together with Orthodox representatives: Frs. John Meyendorff, Alexander Schmemann, and Paul Schneirla. The meeting sketched various topics that might be explored in the future. Msgr. Baum and Fr. Long met with Archbishop Iakovos on February 2, 1965, at the Greek Orthodox Archdiocese in New York City, to discuss possible forms of cooperation.

Catholics had been moved by the Second Vatican Council's Decree on Ecumenism, *Unitatis Redintegratio,* which was promulgated on November 21, 1964. The Orthodox took inspiration from the second Pan-Orthodox Rhodes Conference (1963) when Ecumenical Patriarch Athenagoras and his fellow bishops accepted the principle of "a dialogue on equal footing with the Catholic Church." The third Rhodes Conference reiterated support for "a dialogue of charity" needed to create appropriate conditions for official theological dialogue. Each local Orthodox Church was authorized starting in 1964 to initiate contacts aimed at restoring good will between Orthodox and Catholics.

On March 5, 1965, Fr. Paul Schneirla, General Secretary of the Standing Conference of the Canonical Orthodox Bishops in America (SCOBA), wrote to Cardinal Lawrence Shehan, chairman of the Bishops' Commission for Ecumenical Affairs. Schneirla noted that SCOBA, at its most recent general meeting, had resolved to propose "a continuing theological dialogue between representatives of the Orthodox Church in the United States and theologians of the Roman Catholic Church." His letter stated that "It is the hope of the [Orthodox] bishops that such a program would increase mutual understanding between the two bodies and contribute further to the cause of Christian reunion." Schneirla concluded: "...I take great pleasure in informing Your Eminence of this brotherly proposal, offered in the spirit of Christian love and with the intention of working for the dissolution of any barriers that may remain between the Christian communions." Although Fr. Schneirla was writing on behalf of SCOBA, it is easy to recognize in his choice of words the wise inspiration of Archbishop Iakovos.

Several days later, on March 10, 1965, the U.S. Catholic Bishops' Commission for Ecumenical Affairs met for the first time under the chairmanship of Cardinal Shehan of Baltimore. In response to the SCOBA invitation they set up a subcommission to foster dialogue between the Orthodox and Catholics in the U.S.A. Bernard J. Flanagan, Bishop of Worcester, MA, was asked to assume the chairmanship of this subcommission. He lost no time. Already on March 15 he wrote to the man who would be his principal adviser in these matters, Fr. Charles K. Von Euw, Professor of Patristics at St. John's Seminary, Brighton, MA, to enlist help to set up a committee of Catholic theologians and to plan the first of what eventually became fifty meetings. By May, Bishop Flanagan had chosen ten Catholic members (not all of whom attended each and every early meeting): Rev. Charles K. Von Euw, Rev. Paul Mailleux, S.J. (John XXIII Center, Fordham University), Monsignor Myles M. Bourke (Professor of New Testament at St. Joseph's Seminary, Yonkers), Rt. Rev. Francis Dvornik (Byzantine Research Institute at Dumbarton Oaks, Washington, D.C.), Rev. Maurice B. Schepers, O.P. (Washington), Rev. George Maloney, S.J. (John XXIII Center, Fordham), Very Rev. John Jadaa, B.S. (St. Basil's Seminary, Methuen, MA), Rev. John T. Feeney (Auburndale, MA), Rev. Edward F. Malone, M.M. (Maryknoll Seminary, Maryknoll, NY), and Mr. (later Dr.) Thomas E. Bird (Princeton). Also present was the staff member of the Bishops' Conference, Msgr. William W. Baum. By July, the place and date had been set for the first meeting: St. Spyridon's Orthodox Church, Worcester, on September 9, 1965.

The Orthodox members appointed to the dialogue about this time were, in addition to the co-presider Archbishop Iakovos, Frs. Paul Schneirla, George Bacopulos, Panteleimon Rhodopoulos, John Romanides and George Tsoumas of the Greek Orthodox Archdiocese; Frs. John Meyendorff and Alexander Schmemann and Professor Serge Verhovskoy of the Russian Metropolia; Professor Veselin Kesich of the Serbian diocese; Fr. Seraphim Surrency of the Russian Exarchate; and Fr. Florian Galdau of the Romanian Episcopate.

The first meeting on September 9, 1965, was short and not very substantive. Some of the Orthodox delegates, Fr. Romanides in particular, objected strongly to the presence among the Catholic delegation of so-called "Uniate" members: Fr. John Jadaa, B.S., a Melkite priest from St. Basil's Seminary, Methuen, MA, and presumably three other priests who also celebrated the Divine Liturgy according to the Byzantine rite: Frs. Mailleux, Maloney, and Malone. There was little if any formal exchange of views. Writing about this to Bishop Flanagan several weeks later, on September 21, 1965, Archbishop Iakovos stated: "We greatly regret the complication that arose in Worcester over the presence of the Uniate members of your Committee and we wish to assure you that we intended them no offense." He went on to say that he himself was simply being sensitive especially to the Ukrainian and Carpatho-Russian groups who felt that U.S. Uniates were practising proselytism. Archbishop Iakovos continued: "We would therefore suggest to Your Excellency that for the present, at least, until the situation becomes more clarified and stable, that the Uniate members of your delegation be limited to an occasional consultant role serving in the capacity of Eastern Rite experts. We hope that the American Bishops' Commission for Ecumenical Affairs will understand the reason for this and will agree thereto."

The second meeting took place a year later on September 29, 1966, this time at the headquarters of the Greek Orthodox Archdiocese in Manhattan. The Catholics were represented by the same group, except that Fr. Mailleux was now replaced with the new director of the John XXIII Center, Fr. Feodor Wilcock. This time we have detailed minutes of that meeting (eleven pages composed jointly by Fr. Von Euw and Fr. Schneirla). We are able to verify who in fact attended. The Catholics were: Bishop Bernard Flanagan, Msgr. William Baum, Dr. Thomas Bird, Msgr.

Myles Bourke, Fr. John Feeney, Fr. John Jadaa, Fr. Edward Malone, Fr. George Maloney, Fr. Charles Von Euw, and Fr. Feodor Wilcock. The Orthodox in attendance were: Archbishop Iakovos, Fr. George Bacopulos, Fr. Leonidas Contos, Fr. John Meyendorff, Fr. Iakovos Pililis, Fr. John Romanides, Fr. (William) Paul Schneirla, Fr. Alexander Schmemann, Fr. Robert Stephanopoulos, Fr. Eusebius Stephanou, and Fr. John Zanetos.

During the second meeting, Archbishop Iakovos reported that Patriarch Athenagoras had extended his blessing to those at the meeting and requested that an agenda be submitted to him and to the Holy Synod. Bishop Flanagan replied that the Catholic Church was committed to this work which had begun "somewhat haltingly and falteringly." He went on to say, as the minutes note: "Although there will be frustration, we undertake this effort in the knowledge of Christ's own prayer that we may be one." This in fact was a truly prophetic utterance.

During the session, the influence of Fr. Alexander Schmemann was especially notable. In dramatic tones, he urged the members to define the committee's tone, scope, and basis of discussion. In his view, it should address two levels: (1) renewal of theological discussion broken off at the Council of Florence in 1438, and (2) meeting problems seen in pastoral and jurisdictional terms inasmuch as the delegates live in the pluralistic American society. There must be a deep theological discussion of those practical matters which constantly irritate us, said Schmemann. At the end of this one-day meeting it was decided to meet again in May of the following year in Worcester, and to focus on three topics: (a) "Theological Diversity and Unity" (Fr. John Romanides and Fr. Charles Von Euw); (b) "Intercommunion" (Msgr. Myles Bourke and Fr. John Meyendorff); (c) "Common Witness in Theological Education" (Fr. Leonidas Contos and Fr. Edward Malone).

The third meeting took place as scheduled May 5-6, 1967, at the Fr. John Power Center of the Roman Catholic Diocese of Worcester (Pleasant and Chestnut St., one block from City Hall and St. Paul's Cathedral). This was the first overnight meeting, and also the first to have formal papers written in advance for discussion. Experience would eventually teach the members that their initial agendas were far too ambitious for short meetings. On the first topic, "Theological Diversity and Unity," Frs. Romanides and Von Euw were asked to rework the topic for next meeting. The second topic regarding common witness in theological education was only lightly touched upon. Most of the discussion focused on inter-communion and centered around a five-page report prepared by Msgr. Bourke and Fr. Meyendorff. The Orthodox were concerned that the Second Vatican Council seemed to have given *carte blanche* to intercommunion; they wanted to distance themselves from what they perceived to be the lax Catholic position. It was argued that intercommunion should not be posed on the basis of unity in faith with regard to the eucharist, but of total unity of the communicant with the bishop-celebrant of the eucharist.

Not only could one note the lively interest in the theological discussions, but a new note of realism also emerged. Clearly, future agendas had to be less ambitious, less grandiose. But no one imagined that the next meeting would not take place until nineteen months later in December 1968, at the Maryknoll Seminary in New York. Why this long hiatus? Several meetings were either cancelled or postponed. A partial reason for these delays may have been tensions in the wider North American Ortho-dox community concerning the canonical status of what was then the "Russian Orthodox Greek Catholic Church of America" or the "Metro-polia," as it was more commonly known.

The fourth meeting took place December 6-7, 1968, at Maryknoll, NY. Since Fr. Romanides had since moved to Saloniki, Prof. Kesich, the Orthodox secretary of the dialogue, wrote to Fr. Contos on November 9, 1968, asking that a substitute be appointed. Fr. Contos responded on November 13 that Fr. Maximos Aghiorgoussis had been chosen to replace Romanides. For the meeting Fr. Edward Kilmartin (who was appointed to the dialogue on March 25, 1968) had prepared a study on intercom-munion called "Sharing in Common Worship: Catholic and Orthodox." This would ultimately become an early draft of what came to be a consensus statement on the eucharist by the next meeting.

Another year went by before meeting number five would take place, at Worcester, December 12-13, 1969. The period between those Decembers of 1968 and 1969 was most turbulent for a number of reasons. The original plan was to have a March 5, 1969, meeting at Holy Cross, Brookline. In February, however, the Orthodox asked to postpone the meeting and a new date was proposed, May 7, 1969, again at Brookline's

Holy Cross Greek Orthodox School of Theology. On April 22, 1969, Flanagan announced that Fr. Schneirla had just informed him that "the Theological Consultation scheduled between our Ecumenical Commission and the Roman Catholics for Wednesday, May 7, must be postponed because of the assignment of several theologians to an emergency project." It was asked that some time in the autumn be considered. Bishop Flanagan was concerned that the future of the dialogue was in jeopardy, and he met with Archbishop Iakovos in June 1969. In July 1969 Msgr. Frederick McManus was asked to join the Catholic team.

A great loss occurred during the summer of 1969 when the Catholic executive secretary, Fr. Charles von Euw, died suddenly of a heart attack. From August to November 1969, Bishop Flanagan was confined to St. Vincent's Hospital, Worcester, where he underwent corrective surgery and therapy on his right hip. Amazingly, during this whole time, he carried on a lively correspondence with members of the Consultation, especially its new co-secretary, Fr. Edward Kilmartin.

Finally, the fifth meeting took place on December 12-13, 1969, again at St. Spyridon's Orthodox Church Hall, Worcester, MA. The agenda included discussion of Orthodox and Catholic views of the eucharist and membership in the Church (papers produced by Kilmartin and Aghiorgoussis). The session was notable especially for producing the first of eighteen consensus statements: "An Agreed Statement on the Holy Eucharist."

The momentum created by the fifth meeting poured over into the sixth meeting held only five months later, May 19-20, 1970, in New York City. Four topics were on the agenda but only the issue of marriage between Orthodox and Catholics was addressed. Rather unwisely one could say in retrospect, the Consultation formulated in some haste a second consensus statement: "On Mixed Marriages." It turned out that two meetings later on November 4, 1971, in Barlin Acres near Worcester, MA, a revised version of the text was required. This became the definitive "second U.S. statement."

The statement on marriage raised interest in the study of marriage liturgies in both East and West as well as the similarities and differences in the theological exposition of the sacrament. At the seventh meeting (December 4-5, 1970) at the Greek Orthodox School of Theology in Brookline, MA, four papers were planned on marriage. A new pattern was slowly beginning to take shape. Papers on the theme(s) were prepared in advance and, at least theoretically, distributed beforehand for study and comment. After the meeting, Msgr. Bernard Law of the BCEIA asked the Catholic members to reflect on the successes and problems of the dialogue so far. In the archives we have one of these assessments (both forthright and pessimistic) by the late Fr. Michael Blecker, O.S.B., a medieval scholar, who astutely argued that "As the larger communion with considerable responsibility of the schism, I think we [Catholics] should go out of our way in sustaining whatever conversations the Orthodox wish to have with us."

It would be another full year before the dialogue group met for its eighth meeting, this time at Barlin Acres, November 3-4, 1971, to reflect on ethical considerations of marriage introduced by two visiting scholars: Fr. Stanley Harakas (Holy Cross Greek Orthodox School of Theology, Brookline) and Fr. Roger Couture, O.M.I. (Weston Jesuit School of Theology). It was at this meeting, as we have noted, that a revision of the earlier agreed statement on mixed marriage was formulated. At the meeting there was an attempt to produce a common statement on the sanctity of Christian marriage, a text based mostly on a draft prepared by Fr. Kilmartin. Approval would be slow and complicated; the text, much reworked and refined, did not obtain joint approval until the meeting held seven years later on December 7-8, 1978. When the meeting at Barlin Acres concluded, no one could have guessed that there would be a full two-year hiatus before the next meeting. As it turned out, this would be the last meeting co-presided over by Bishop Bernard Flanagan. Despite his retirement from the Consultation, he would maintain great interest in its progress during the years to come.

The two-year gap posed a serious problem. Much of the earlier momentum was beginning to wane. The reasons for delays are doubtlessly complex. Study of the archives in Washington, at the Greek Orthodox Archdiocese and elsewhere will be needed to understand all the reasons for these delays. The meeting did eventually take place in New York City for one day, December 6, 1973.

To review the work done to date, Fr. John Hotchkin read at that meeting some "Historical Notes" about the dialogue. The meeting again looked at a draft on the sanctity of marriage. It was suggested that more work needed to be done on it and that two separate statements might be formulated, one on ethical considerations, especially abortion, and a second on the theology of marriage. This is what in fact later happened; two agreed statements were published "On Respect for Life" (May 24, 1974) and "On the Sanctity of Marriage" (December 8, 1978).

This ninth meeting of December 6, 1973, was a veritable turning-point. Never again would the Consultation know so many cancellations or lengthy time gaps. The Consultation had now entered a creative stage in terms of theological and historical research. Meetings were now held regularly, and many scholarly background papers were produced. Agreed statements appeared on "The Church" (December 10, 1974), "Pastoral Office" (May 19, 1976); and "The Principle of 'Economy'" (also May 19, 1976). The group returned to the topic of Christian marriage, focusing on the "Spiritual Formation of Children of Marriages between Orthodox and Roman Catholics" (October 11, 1980). It also responded to the major ecumenical document of the Faith and Order Commission of the World Council of Churches on *Baptism, Eucharist and Ministry* (October 27, 1984).

Additional stimulus to the U.S. Consultation came from the news that progress had been made by a Pan-Orthodox decision to convoke a Great and Holy Council of the Church. A council was announced (date to be determined) to explore six agenda items: the sources of revelation; revisions concerning fasting; participation of the laity in church life and liturgy; impediments to marriage; the church calendar; and the principle of "economy" (*oikonomia*), meaning the Church's ability to depart, especially in regard to the sacraments, from strict application of the canons, somewhat analogous to the Western concept of *dispensatio*. Work on the agenda topics was divided up among the different Orthodox jurisdictions. The fact that the U.S. Orthodox-Catholic Consultation spent two years studying the preliminary report on *oikonomia* and then published a consensus statement on the concept shows how the proposed Great and Holy Council and the U.S. Consultation were interacting. At its 16th meeting on September 29, 1977, the U. S. Consultation published an agreed statement entitled "Reaction to the Agenda of the Great and Holy Council of the Orthodox Church."

Of all the agenda items listed for that Great Council, Christian unity was the most important for dealings with the Catholics. Orthodoxy's commitment to official dialogue with the Church of Rome was dramatically announced on December 14, 1975, when Metropolitan Meliton, personal representative of the Ecumenical Patriarch Demetrios I, announced to Pope Paul VI in the Sistine Chapel the Pan-Orthodox decision to establish a special inter-Orthodox theological commission, the purpose of which was to prepare, for the Orthodox side, for formal theological dialogue with Roman Catholics. Pope Paul greeted the news with the stunning gesture of falling to his knees and kissing the feet of Metropolitan Meliton, who conveyed the good news, thereby evoking St. Paul's words citing Isaiah in Rom. 10:15: "How beautiful are the feet of those who preach the good news!" That gesture of reconciliation and joy may well be seen as the most moving experience of Pope Paul's pontificate.

The work of the International Commission has been already described. These international meetings and the publication of their consensus statements influenced the work of the U.S. Consultation. Not only did the Americans react to the International Commission's agreed statements such as the documents of Munich (tenth U.S. statement, May 25, 1983); Bari (13th U.S. statement, June 2, 1988); Valamo (14th U.S. statement, October 28, 1989); and Balamand (18th U.S. statement, October 15, 1994), but they also suggested to the International Commission before publication of their documents what they perceived to be useful emphases or issues to highlight: "Apostolicity as God's Gift in the Life of the Church" (12th U.S. statement, November 1, 1986); "Conciliarity and Primacy in the Church" (15th U.S. statement, October 28, 1989); "On Current Tensions between Our Churches in Eastern Europe" (16th U.S. statement, October 20, 1990); and "Tensions in Eastern Europe Related to 'Uniatism'" (17th U.S. Statement, May 28, 1992). The U.S. Consultation saw itself in partnership with the International Commission. Suggestions by the U.S. Consultation were sometimes cited during plenary discussions of the International Commission, and the U.S. Consultation received on several occasions appreciative recognition by Cardinal Cassidy and Archbishop Stylianos, the two co-presiders.

Another important role of the U.S. Consultation was its encouragement and help in establishing a Joint Committee of Orthodox and Roman Catholic Bishops in 1981. This idea, first proposed by Fr. Nicon

Patrinacos, has led to a series of thirteen meetings held to date and which in late 1995 will meet at the Vatican and the Phanar.

The meetings of the U.S. Orthodox-Catholic Consultation since its inception have been co-presided over by hierarchs of the two churches. For the Orthodox, Archbishop Iakovos served as co-presider from 1965 to 1984, Bishop Silas of New Jersey from 1984 to 1986, and Bishop Maximos of Pittsburgh from 1987 to the present date (1995); for the Catholics, Bishop Bernard J. Flanagan of Worcester, MA, from 1965 to 1971; Archbishop (later Cardinal) William W. Baum of Washington from 1973 to 1979, Archbishop Rembert Weakland, O.S.B., of Milwaukee, from 1979 to 1983 and from 1994 to the present (1995), and finally Bishop Arthur O'Neill of Rockford, IL, from 1984 to 1993. There have been a few occasions when a hierarch has been absent. In the case of the Catholics, there have occasionally been several substitutes: Cardinal Shehan co-presided for the 14th meeting, Bishop Ernest Unterkoefler, for the 21st, and Eparch Michael Dudick for the 44th.

Despite the gradual changeover in the membership among the theological consultants for the Consultation, there has been a remarkable continuity of purpose and mission over the thirty years. Some who forged agreed statements and were devoted to the dialogue have entered eternal life, among whom could be mentioned Alexander Schmemann, John Meyendorff, Nicon Patrinacos; Lawrence Shehan, Paul Mailleux, Charles Von Euw, Michael Blecker, and Edward Kilmartin. The friendships that have developed from the meetings and genuine mutual respect for one another that is ever present are two additional gifts of the Consultation. Although there has never been intercommunion between the two groups, each meeting has devoted time for liturgical prayer and devotions. As the Consultation approaches the new millennium there is fervent hope that prayers for the unity of the sister churches will be realized.

Section 1

The Holy Eucharist: Sanctification of the Faithful and Sign of Unity

INTRODUCTION TO SECTION ONE

The twentieth century could be described as the century of the Church. Throughout these past ten decades, Christians through various means have sought to restore unity among themselves and to renew the life of the Church within their own communions. Hand in hand with a revitalization of the idea of the Church as a communion of persons has been a rediscovery of the fundamental place of the eucharist in church life. In this context, therefore, not only the renewal of the liturgy with the Constitution on the Sacred Liturgy (1963) but also the presentation of the eucharist as both sign of the Church's unity and source of spiritual nourishment were significant ecumenical endowments of the Second Vatican Council.

The latter theme, as it applies to relations between Eastern Christians in communion with the Church of Rome and separated Eastern Christians, was articulated in the Decree on the Eastern Churches (*Orientalium Ecclesiarum*, 1964, ¶¶26-29). There, in a discussion of *communicatio in sacris* (mutual sharing in sacred things), the "less rigorous course" of offering the means of salvation to all as a witness to charity among Christians is presented as the basis for a "more relaxed regulation," under certain circumstances and with a few factors considered, for sharing the sacraments of reconciliation, eucharist, and anointing of the sick with separated Eastern Christians. Furthermore, Catholics were told by their bishops that they could present themselves for these sacraments to ministers in whose church there are valid sacraments, provided necessity or spiritual benefit recommended it and access to a Catholic priest was not possible.

These same principles, as well as some further elucidation of the status of separated Eastern Christians, are conspicuous in the Decree on Ecumenism (*Unitatis Redintegratio*), promulgated by the council on the same date as the Decree on the Eastern Churches. The following paragraph on the Eastern Churches separated from the Catholic Church would be often repeated and later expanded by Catholics in subsequent decades:

> These Churches, although separated from us, yet possess true sacraments, above all—by apostolic succession—the priesthood and the Eucharist, whereby they are still joined to us in closest intimacy. Therefore some *communicatio in sacris*,

given suitable circumstances and the approval of Church authority, is not merely possible but is encouraged. (¶15)

In addition, both conciliar texts call for watchfulness on the part of local bishops and consultation with the bishops of separated churches.

Response by the Orthodox Churches was almost immediate. The decrees were issued in late November 1964. On January 22, 1965, SCOBA issued a statement "On the Discipline of Holy Communion," which welcomed the new expressions of yearning for fellowship and unity but asserted unequivocally that reception of Holy Communion is the end of unity, not a means to that end. Therefore, the Orthodox bishops stated, decisions on sacramental sharing "reached by Christian bodies outside the Orthodox Church have no significance or validity for the Orthodox Church or her members." The council documents, the response of SCOBA, and a general public clamor for more explanation of these differences in church policy, as well as the general optimism that the ecumenical movement was getting underway for the Catholic Church, were a large measure of the context when the first meeting of the U.S. Orthodox-Catholic Theological Consultation took place on September 9, 1965. That meeting, occurring a few months before the close of the Second Vatican Council, was largely devoted to organizational matters. The next, one year later on September 29, 1966, was the first meeting for which minutes were kept on file. As they indicate, discussion centered on the topic of the new Catholic policy on eucharistic sharing and on the diverse pastoral difficulties that can ensue when ecumenically sensitive gestures are made without ecumenical consultation.

The following year, the atmosphere became somewhat more tense when Patriarch Athenagoras I of Constantinople issued an encyclical, dated April 24, 1967, which made it clear that "the use of Roman Catholic, Protestant or other churches for the celebration of the Divine Liturgy, where no Greek Orthodox Church exists, is a matter of necessity and does not at all mean that our Orthodox faithful may receive the Grace of the Sacraments from a non-Orthodox priest, since no decision of this kind was ever taken and since intercommunion between the Orthodox and other Churches does not as yet exist." Then, just three weeks later, the first part of the Catholic Church's Directory Concerning Ecumenical Matters appeared (May 14). The Directory specified that the norms set out in the Decree on the Eastern Churches equally apply to the faithful of any rite in the Catholic Church. It further stated that "it is particularly opportune that the Catholic authority, whether the local one, the synod or the episcopal conference, does not extend permission for sharing in the reception or administration of the sacraments ...except after satisfactory consultations with the competent authorities (at least local ones) of the separated Oriental Churches." (¶42)

Without benefit of a forewarning either of the Ecumenical Patriarch's encyclical or Pope Paul VI's approval of the Ecumenical Directory, the third meeting of the U.S. Theological Consultation was scheduled for May 5-6, 1967. It convened to hear about the encyclical but could not anticipate the policies announced by Pope Paul VI ten days later. A paper on intercommunion, jointly prepared by an Orthodox and a Catholic participant, led to candid discussion which noted that public concern over the practice often failed to take into consideration important theological principles.

It is little surprise, then, that the first agreed statement of the U.S. Theological Consultation —and the first document to appear in this collection—is "An Agreed Statement on the Holy Eucharist," which appeared in 1969 following the fifth meeting of the consultation. No doubt from the record, there was unstoppable good will and charity, such that when the leadership suggested that Orthodox and Catholic representatives separately prepare lists of theses on the Holy Eucharist, the members of the dialogue were able to convert the two lists into a brief but profound set of six theses in one meeting. The agreed text covered but a page. Nevertheless it was a sign of ecumenical progress for Orthodox and Catholics alike. While acknowledging that serious differences exist which prevent communicating in one another's churches, the members of the Consultation could still affirm their "remarkable and fundamental agreement" on the eucharist.

It is also no surprise that thirteen years later the Joint International Commission should devote its first agreed statement to "The Mystery of the Church and of the Eucharist in the Light of the Mystery of the Holy Trinity" (Munich 1992). Compared to the short U.S. document, the international text is massive in size and spacious in scope. In it the eucharist, so central in the lived experience of both Orthodox and Catholics, becomes the point of departure for exploration of ecclesiology and other aspects of the faith. By thus beginning with what unites rather than what divides Catholics and Orthodox, the Joint International Commission was following the principles established in its own initial Plan for the dialogue. What is remarkable about the Munich Statement is not just that the Joint Commission was able to reach such a high level of agreement concerning the eucharist but that, building upon this agreement, it was able to reach such a high level of agreement on so many other areas concerning which the churches hitherto had appeared to disagree.

Reflecting the work of the Joint Commission's three subcommissions, the Munich Statement is divided into three main sections. The first addresses the question of how the Church and the eucharist are to be understood in relation to Christ and the Holy Spirit. What is the relationship between the Church's sacramental life, as epitomized in the eucharist, and christology, pneumatology and trinitarian theology? The statement begins by affirming that what God has done in Christ is given to us "through material and created realities" (¶I.1), above all in the eucharist. But this is accomplished "in the Holy Spirit...which proceeds eternally from the Father and manifests himself through the Son." "Christ, who is the sacrament *par excellence*, given by the Father for the world, continues to give himself for the many in the Spirit." (¶I.3) Striking here and throughout the Munich Statement is the emphasis placed on the role of the Holy Spirit, who, "by making present what Christ did once for all..., accomplishes it in all of us" (¶I.5). Much of the terminology used to describe this reality—"divinization" (*theôsis*), "divine energies," "*epiclêsis*"—will be more familiar to Orthodox than to Catholics, but this should not be interpreted as the "victory" of one side over the other. Rather, it suggests the high level of agreement which exists between the churches, notwithstanding historically conditioned differences in their ways of articulating the truths of the Christian faith. This means that it may now be possible to resolve a number of issues that have divided the churches in the past, such as the question of the procession of the Holy Spirit (*filioque*). The Munich Statement is able to state:

> Without wishing to resolve yet the difficulties which have arisen between the East and the West concerning the relationship between the Son and the Spirit, we can already say together that this Spirit, which proceeds from the Father as the sole source in the Trinity and which has become the Spirit of our sonship

since he is also the Spirit of the Son, is communicated to us particularly in the Eucharist by the Son upon whom he reposes in time and in eternity (¶I.6).

In this dense but rich passage and in others like it, distinct echoes of St. Gregory Palamas and other late Byzantine theologians can be discerned. Such sensitivity to the insights of the Eastern tradition is just one of many reasons why the Munich Statement can be considered a milestone in Orthodox-Catholic relations.

The second section of the Munich Statement examines the relationship between the eucharist celebrated around the bishop in the local church and the mystery of one God in the communion of three persons. The Church cannot be understood simply in sociological categories. It is above all a sacramental reality which "finds its model, its origin and its purpose in the mystery of God, one in three Persons" (¶II.1). At the same time, the Church is not an abstraction. Rather, it is a "local" reality, "placed" in the midst of the world to be the prototype of renewed human community. It is a *koinonia* which most fully realizes itself in the eucharistic assembly of the local church gathered around the bishop or the priest in communion with him as one body. The main lines of the "eucharistic ecclesiology" expressed here will be familiar to many Orthodox and Catholics. By calling attention to the sacramental nature of the Church and also to the sacramental nature of the bishop's ministry in the Church, the Munich Statement challenges both Orthodox and Catholics to go beyond the familiar old institutional and juridical models.

The third section of the statement turns to the relationship between the eucharistic celebration of the local church and the communion of all the local churches as the one body of Christ. Here again, the statement reflects the insights of modern "eucharistic ecclesiology" in its insistence on the ontological identity of the local churches as the one body of Christ. This identity

> comes from the fact that all by eating the same bread and sharing in the same cup become the same unique body of Christ into which they have been integrated by the same baptism. If there are many celebrations, there is nevertheless only one mystery celebrated in which all participate.... In the same way, the local church which celebrates the Eucharist gathered around its bishop is not a section of the body of Christ. The multiplicity of local *synaxes* [gatherings] does not divide the Church, but rather shows sacramentally its unity. (¶III.1)

From this understanding of the Church as a communion of local churches flows its understanding of the relationship of the churches' bishops in their common responsibility for oversight *(episkopê)* in the Church. "Because the one and only Church is made present in his local church, each bishop cannot separate the care for his own church from that of the universal Church" (¶III.4). In terms reminiscent of the Second Vatican Council's *Lumen Gentium,* the text goes on to state:

> The *episkopê* for the universal Church is seen to be entrusted by the Spirit to the totality of local bishops in communion with one another. This communion is expressed traditionally through conciliar practice. We shall have to examine further the way it is conceived and realized in the perspective of what we have just explained. (¶III.4)

With the Munich Statement theologians of the two churches were able to reach a remarkable level of agreement on many of the most basic issues in ecclesiology, but as the last sentence suggests, some major differences have yet to be addressed, most notably the place of the Bishop of Rome in the communion of churches.

The U. S. Theological Consultation issued a response to the Munich Statement in less than a year (1983), demonstrating its joy in receiving the work of the Joint International Commission and its eagerness to incorporate its achievements and contribute to the ongoing dialogue. A pattern of theological response developed: Each of the subsequent international agreed statements would be received and become the object of common theological reflection on the part of the members of the U.S. Consultation. The Consultation hailed the Munich text as "an important achievement" which "moves us farther away from our history of mutual estrangement and allows the churches to speak with one voice on matters at the heart of the Christian faith" (¶2). The Consultation offered practical and procedural comments about the text's intended audience, language, and other technical points. It also noted important points of theological concern and underscored certain ambiguities, for example, the referents for the term "sister churches" (¶7). Clearly the U.S. Theological Consultation was raising questions that the International Commission would need to answer in the future.

The interconnectedness of ecumenical activity today is particularly evident in the response of the U.S. Theological Consultation to the Lima document, *Baptism, Eucharist and Ministry*, of the Faith and Order Commission of the World Council of Churches. The Lima document appeared early in 1982, as the culmination of a long process in which representatives from numerous churches worldwide reached major agreement on these three fundamental areas of faith. The response of the U.S. Orthodox and Catholic scholars was produced at the Consultation's 29th meeting in 1984. (The Lima document is not reprinted in this volume but can easily be found elsewhere: *Baptism, Eucharist and Ministry,* Faith and Order Papers No. 111, Geneva, World Council of Churches, 1982; also published in *Growth in Agreement*, Ecumenical Documents II, edited by Harding Meyer and Lukas Vischer, New York, Paulist Press, 1984, pp. 465-95.) The Lima document, the Munich Statement, and the U.S. responses to both all appeared within a period of two years (1982-84). The articulation of faith in the eucharist between Orthodox and Catholics and the convergence of faith in the eucharist among all the participant churches in the Faith and Order movement are truly remarkable achievements of the ecumenical movement and great causes of hope for the restoration of unity among Christians. The churches not only have been brought closer together through ecumenical activity but also have experienced liturgical renewal.

Responding to the Lima document gave the Theological Consultation's members further opportunity to reflect on the considerable agreement on baptism, eucharist and ministry that they already shared. Although they saw the need for a number of clarifications in the baptism section, they agreed that "in the Lima Statement we can recognize to a considerable degree the faith of the Church in regard to baptism." In view of this agreement, they recommended "that our two churches explore the possibility of a formal recognition of each other's baptism as a sacrament of our unity in the body of Christ." The members of the Consultation found the section on the eucharist rich but succinct, and they called attention to the need for further discussion particularly of the eucharist's ecclesiological significance. In the ministry section, however, they found more serious disagreements. They appreciated the presentation of the threefold ordained ministry and its location in the apostolic tradition of the Church. Lacking, in their judgment, was a developed sense of the sacramentality of the ordained ministry and also of its non-repeatability. They also asked how the presence of the episcopal office will be adequately recognized if the churches hope to come together and noted that considerable agreement must be in place on matters of apostolic faith and practice before mutual recognition of ministries could ever be achieved.

AN AGREED STATEMENT ON THE HOLY EUCHARIST

U.S. Theological Consultation, 1969

We, the members of the Orthodox-Catholic Consultation, have met and discussed our understanding of the holy eucharist. After a dialogue, based on separately prepared papers, we affirm our remarkable and fundamental agreement on the following:

1. The holy eucharist is the memorial of the history of salvation, especially the life, death, resurrection, and glorification of Jesus Christ.

2. In this eucharistic meal, according to the promise of Christ, the Father sends the Spirit to consecrate the elements to be the body and blood of Jesus Christ and to sanctify the faithful.

3. The eucharistic sacrifice involves the active presence of Christ, the High Priest, acting through the Christian community, drawing it into his saving worship. Through celebration of the eucharist the redemptive blessings are bestowed on the living and the dead for whom intercession is made.

4. Through the eating of the eucharistic body and drinking of the eucharistic blood, the faithful, who through baptism became adopted sons of the Father, are nourished as the one body of Christ, and are built up as temples of the Holy Spirit.

5. In the eucharistic celebration we not only commend ourselves and each other and all our lives unto Christ, but at the same time accept the mandate of service of the Gospel of Jesus Christ to mediate salvation to the world.

6. Through the eucharist the believer is transformed into the glory of the Lord and in this the transfiguration of the whole cosmos is anticipated. Therefore the faithful have the mission to witness to this transforming activity of the Spirit.

Recognizing the importance of this consensus, we are aware that serious differences exist in our understanding of the Church, eucharistic discipline, and pastoral practice which now prevent us from communicating in one another's churches. Our task should consist in exploring further how these differences are related to the agreement stated above and how they can be resolved.

Worcester, MA
December 13, 1969
Fifth Meeting

PLAN TO SET UNDERWAY THE THEOLOGICAL DIALOGUE BETWEEN THE ROMAN CATHOLIC CHURCH AND THE ORTHODOX CHURCH

Joint International Commission, 1980

I. Purpose of the Dialogue

The purpose of the dialogue between the Roman Catholic Church and the Orthodox Church is the re-establishment of full communion between these two churches. This communion, based on unity of faith according to the common experience and tradition of the early Church, will find its expression in the common celebration of the holy eucharist.

II. Method of the Dialogue

Since this is the purpose of the dialogue between the Orthodox and Roman Catholic Churches, the best method for approaching and discussing the various problems involved should include the following points:

1. The dialogue should begin with the elements which unite the Orthodox and Roman Catholic Churches. This in no way means that it is desirable, or even possible, to avoid the problems which still divide the two churches. It only means that the dialogue should begin in a positive spirit and that this spirit should prevail when treating the problems which have accumulated during a separation lasting many centuries.

2. In examining the theological problems which exist between the Orthodox and Roman Catholic Churches, consideration must also be given to more recent developments both of a theological and of an ecclesial nature in relations between the two churches. The history of the past certainly should not be ignored, and perhaps it can even help the positive progress of the dialogue (for example, study of the Council of 879-880). Nonetheless, historical developments of the past must also be seen in the light both of further theological developments and of recent ecclesial practice in the Roman Catholic and Orthodox Churches.

In light of these, the points of difference between our churches can also be considered in a new way. Thus one can hope that it will be possible to overcome progressively and successively the concrete obstacles which stand in the way of the renewal of common life between our churches.

3. During discussion of existing problems, a distinction must be made between differences which are compatible with eucharistic communion and those which are incompatible and require that a solution and common agreement be found.

There are a large number of developments which are due to special historical conditions which have prevailed unilaterally either in the East or in the West. These developments do not constitute elements which necessarily are acceptable or unacceptable to the two sides. At the same time, without serious examination they cannot be considered as indifferent as far as eucharistic communion is concerned. It is therefore necessary, in each particular case, to search out criteria by which particular differences in both the Roman Catholic Church and the Orthodox Church may be judged.

4. We judge it useful that, in the dialogue, serious consideration be given to, and profit taken from, the work accomplished on various occasions by mixed study groups composed of Roman Catholic and Orthodox theologians.

5. The dialogue of love should continually accompany the theological dialogue in order to facilitate resolution of difficulties and to strengthen the deepening of fraternal relations between the two churches both on the local and on more general levels. For this, it would be profitable that some disagreeable situations be reconsidered, as, for example, the question of "uniatism," of proselytism, *etc.* In general, the theological dialogue can be fruitful only in an atmosphere of love, of humility and of prayer.

III. Themes of the First Stage of the Dialogue

1. As for the themes which should be the object of the dialogue during its first stage, we judge that the study of the sacraments of the Church is propitious for an examination, in depth and in a positive way, of the problems of the dialogue. Sacramental experience and theology express themselves the one through the other. For this reason, the study of the

sacraments of the Church presents itself as a very positive and natural theme. From the study of problems relating to the sacraments, one will normally come to an examination of ecclesiological as well as other aspects of the faith, without moving away from the lived character which is fundamental for theology.

2. While examining the theme of the sacraments within the framework of the dialogue, the Commission for Dialogue should free itself, as much as possible, from the problematic created by the theology of the schools of earlier days. In the formulation of the entire problematic concerning the theme of the sacraments, it is practically obligatory to study and give serious consideration to all the recent theological efforts in both Roman Catholic and Orthodox theology, so that these efforts may be connected to the tradition of the early Church.

3. The principal purpose of studying the theme of the sacraments is not to examine every aspect of this very wide theme, but primarily those aspects which touch upon the unity of the Church. Consequently the principal problems which should be proposed for discussion are related to ecclesiology in its broad theological sense. More particularly, these problems are related to the way in which the presence or absence of unity between Roman Catholics and Orthodox has an influence on communion in the sacraments and in the Christian life in general of the faithful of the two churches, and vice versa.

4. If one tries to reconnect the problematic regarding the sacraments to the tradition of the early Church, one will see that, in principle and in essence, it is not necessary to speak of several sacraments but rather of one sacrament, the "sacrament of Christ," which is expressed and realized by the Holy Spirit as the sacrament of the Church. The sacraments should not be conceived of principally as autonomous actions or as individualistic means for transmitting divine grace, but as the expression and realization of the unique sacrament of the Church.

5. This unique sacrament of the Church is expressed and realized in history above all in the holy eucharist. It is not by chance that all the particular sacraments were connected in the early Church, even in their liturgical dimensions, with the eucharist. The eucharist, then, should not be considered as one sacrament among others, but as the sacrament *par excellence* of the Church. Consequently, it should be the basis for every

examination of the theme of the sacraments within the framework of the dialogue.

6. On this basis, and with the sacrament of the holy eucharist as its point of departure, the Commission for Dialogue will be asked to examine the following fundamental problems:

(a) What is the relationship between the other "sacraments of initiation," that is, baptism and chrismation/confirmation, and the holy eucharist? In the West, these three sacraments have been separated from each other on the liturgical level in the baptism of children. In the East, these three sacraments have remained united. What importance does this question have for one's conception of the unity of the Church and even for the spiritual life of the faithful? Another question related to this one is the "recognition" of these sacraments between the churches. Up to what point is it possible to say that one recognizes the baptism of a church without participating in the eucharist of that church? How can we have unity with respect to only one or two of these sacraments of initiation?

(b) What is the relationship of the sacraments—always conceived of as connected with the holy eucharist—with the structure and government of the Church (or the canonical unity of the Church)? Here it is necessary to examine the following question: Can there exist in the Church an "administration" or a structure or a "canonical jurisdiction" which does not flow immediately and necessarily from the sacramental life of the Church, more particularly in the case of ordination and of the eucharist? It is evident that a host of problems concerning the relationship between sacraments and canonical jurisdiction present themselves at this point and are directly connected with the unity of the Church.

(c) Given that the Church is built up and is realized in time and space by means of the eucharist of the local community gathered around one sole bishop, what does this fact mean for the communion of all the local churches and their witness in the world?

(d) In what sense is right faith (orthodoxy) related to the sacraments of the Church? Is it a presupposition for communion in the sacraments—and, if so, in what sense or to what extent?—or is it rather the result and expression of such a communion? Or can both these things be true? This subject is essential above all in view of sacramental unity and, in particular, of eucharistic unity.

7. During the examination of these questions, we consider it indispensable that the entire discussion of the theme of the sacraments be continually presented in light of the following fundamental questions:

(a) How should the entire structure and the realization of the sacramental life of the Church be understood in relation to Christ and in relation to the Holy Spirit? What relationship exists between the sacraments and christology, pneumatology and triadology? Should there be placed in this perspective questions concerning, for example, the *epiclêsis* of the Holy Spirit, or the visible elements of the sacraments or again the connection between the celebrant and the community in relation to Christ and in relation to the Holy Spirit?

(b) Also connected to this should be the problem of the meaning of eschatology in the understanding of the sacraments. It is true that in the West an historical approach to the sacraments has more or less prevailed, while in the East the understanding of the mysteries has been rather "iconological" and "metahistorical." Are there problems arising out of this fact that might be essential for the unity of the Church?

(c) Finally, the anthropological question, which has different accentuations in the East and in the West, should not be neglected in studying the sacraments. For example, the question could be raised as to what is the new reality (the "new creation") which the sacramental life creates. In what does the new creation consist? Consideration must be given to the fact that for theology and tradition the sacraments, in the light of the holy eucharist, contain dimensions wider than the psychological and individual levels and reach out even unto the transformation of the social milieu as well as of the natural and cosmic milieu of mankind. How is this transformation conceived of, and what consequences can such a consideration have for the life of the faithful in the Church?

IV. List of Proposed Themes

1. The sacrament of Christ expressing itself and realizing itself, through the Holy Spirit, as the sacrament of the Church (section III.4 above). How should one understand the sacramental nature of the

Church in relation to Christ and in relation to the Holy Spirit? What is the connection between the sacraments and christology, pneumatology and triadology? (section III.7.a above)

2. The eucharist as sacrament *par excellence* of the Church (section III.5 above).

3. The sacraments of initiation, their interrelationship and the unity of the Church (section III.6.a above).

4. Relationship between the sacraments and the canonical structure of the Church (section III.6.b-c above).

5. Faith and communion in the sacraments (section III.6.d).

6. The sacraments in their relationship to history and to eschatology (section III.7.b).

7. The sacraments and the renewal of mankind and of the world (section III.7.c).

8. Ritual and canonical differences in the celebration of the sacraments.

V. Recommendations

The two preparatory commissions submit this report to their respective church authorities and unanimously recommend:

—that the commissions which should enter into dialogue be set up as soon as possible;

—that the proposed plan be the basis for the work of these commissions for the first stage of the dialogue;

—that each commission be composed of an equal number of members on each side.

Adopted Patmos/Rhodes
June 1, 1980
First Plenary Meeting

THE MYSTERY OF THE CHURCH AND OF THE EUCHARIST IN THE LIGHT OF THE MYSTERY OF THE HOLY TRINITY

Joint International Commission, 1982

Faithful to the mandate received at Rhodes, this report touches upon the mystery of the Church in only one of its aspects. This aspect, however, is particularly important in the sacramental perspective of our churches, that is, the mystery of the Church and of the eucharist in the light of the mystery of the Holy Trinity. As a matter of fact the request was made to start with what we have in common and, by developing it, to touch upon from inside and progressively all the points on which we are not in agreement.

In composing this document, we intend to show that in doing so we express together a faith which is the continuation of that of the apostles.

This document makes the first step in the effort to fulfill the program of the preparatory commission, approved at the first meeting of the Commission for Dialogue.

Since there is question of a first step, touching upon the mystery of the Church under only one of its aspects, many points are not yet treated here. They will be treated in succeeding steps as has been foreseen in the program mentioned above.

I

1. Christ, Son of God incarnate, dead and risen, is the only one who has conquered sin and death. To speak, therefore, of the sacramental nature of the mystery of Christ is to bring to mind the possibility given to man, and through him, to the whole cosmos, to experience the "new creation," the kingdom of God here and now through material and created realities. This is the mode (*tropos*) in which the unique person and the unique event of Christ exists and operates in history starting from Pentecost and reaching to the Parousia. However, the eternal life which God has given to the world in the event of Christ, his eternal Son, is

contained in "earthen vessels." It is still only given as a foretaste, as a pledge.

2. At the Last Supper, Christ stated that he "gave" his body to the disciples for the life of "the many," in the eucharist. In it this gift is made by God to the world, but in sacramental form. From that moment the eucharist exists as the sacrament of Christ himself. It becomes the foretaste of eternal life, the "medicine of immortality," the sign of the kingdom to come. The sacrament of the Christ event thus becomes identical with the sacrament of the holy eucharist, the sacrament which incorporates us fully into Christ.

3. The incarnation of the Son of God, his death and resurrection were realized from the beginning, according to the Father's will, in the Holy Spirit. This Spirit, which proceeds eternally from the Father and manifests himself through the Son, prepared the Christ event and realized it fully in the resurrection. Christ, who is the sacrament *par excellence*, given by the Father for the world, continues to give himself for the many in the Spirit, who alone gives life (Jn. 6). The sacrament of Christ is also a reality which can only exist in the Spirit.

4. The Church and the Eucharist:

(a) Although the evangelists in the account of the Supper are silent about the action of the Spirit, he was nonetheless united closer than ever to the incarnate Son for carrying out the Father's work. He is not yet given, received as a person by the disciples (Jn. 7:39). But when Jesus is glorified, then the Spirit himself also pours himself out and manifests himself. The Lord Jesus enters into the glory of the Father and, at the same time, by the pouring out of the Spirit, into his sacramental *tropos* in this world. Pentecost, the completion of the paschal mystery, inaugurates simultaneously the last times. The eucharist and the Church, body of the crucified and risen Christ, become the place of the energies of the Holy Spirit.

(b) Believers are baptized in the Spirit in the name of the Holy Trinity to form one body (cf. 1 Cor. 12:13). When the Church celebrates the eucharist, it realizes "what it is," the body of Christ (1 Cor. 10:17). By baptism and chrismation (confirmation) the members of Christ are "anointed" by the Spirit, grafted into Christ. But by the eucharist, the paschal event opens itself out into Church. The Church becomes that which it is called to be by baptism and chrismation. By the communion in the body and blood of Christ, the faithful grow in that mystical divinization which makes them dwell in the Son and the Father, through the Spirit.

(c) Thus, on the one hand, the Church celebrates the eucharist as expression here and now of the heavenly liturgy; but on the other hand, the eucharist builds up the Church in the sense that through it the Spirit of the risen Christ fashions the Church into the body of Christ. That is why the eucharist is truly the sacrament of the Church, at once as sacrament of the total gift the Lord makes of himself to his own and as manifestation and growth of the body of Christ, the Church. The pilgrim Church celebrates the eucharist on earth until her Lord comes to restore royalty to God the Father so that God may be "all in all." It thus anticipates the judgment of the world and its final transfiguration.

5. The mission of the Spirit remains joined to that of the Son. The celebration of the eucharist reveals the divine energies manifested by the Spirit at work in the body of Christ.

(a) The Spirit prepares the coming of Christ by announcing it through the prophets, by directing the history of the chosen people towards him, by causing him to be conceived by the Virgin Mary, by opening up hearts to his word.

(b) The Spirit manifests Christ in his work as Savior, the Gospel which is he himself. The eucharistic celebration is the *anamnêsis* (the memorial): Truly but sacramentally, the *ephapax* (the "once and for all") is and becomes present. The celebration of the eucharist is *par excellence* the *kairos* (proper time) of the mystery.

(c) The Spirit transforms the sacred gifts into the body and blood of Christ (*metabolê*) in order to bring about the growth of the body which is the Church. In this sense, the entire celebration is an *epiclêsis*, which becomes more explicit at certain moments. The church is continually in a state of *epiclêsis*.

(d) The Spirit puts into communion with the body of Christ those who share the same bread and the same cup. Starting from there, the

55

Church manifests what it is, the sacrament of the trinitarian *koinonia*, the "dwelling of God with men" (cf. Rev. 21:4).

The Spirit, by making present what Christ did once for all—the event of the mystery—accomplishes it in all of us. The relation to the mystery, more evident in the eucharist, is found in the other sacraments, all acts of the Spirit. That is why the eucharist is the center of sacramental life.

6. Taken as a whole, the eucharistic celebration makes present the trinitarian mystery of the Church. In it one passes from hearing the word, culminating in the proclamation of the Gospel—the apostolic announcing of the Word made flesh—to the thanksgiving offered to the Father and to the memorial of the sacrifice and to communion in it thanks to the prayer of *epiclêsis* uttered in faith. For the *epiclêsis* is not merely an invocation for the sacramental transforming of the bread and cup. It is also a prayer for the full effect of the communion of all in the mystery revealed by the Son.

In this way, the presence of the Spirit itself is extended, by the sharing in the sacrament of the Word made flesh, to all the body of the Church. Without wishing to resolve yet the difficulties which have arisen between the East and the West concerning the relationship between the Son and the Spirit, we can already say together that this Spirit, which proceeds from the Father (Jn. 15:26) as the sole source in the Trinity and which has become the Spirit of our sonship (Rom. 8:15) since he is also the Spirit of the Son (Gal. 4:6), is communicated to us, particularly in the eucharist, by this Son upon whom he reposes in time and in eternity (Jn. 1:32).

That is why the eucharistic mystery is accomplished in the prayer which joins together the words by which the Word made flesh instituted the sacrament and the *epiclêsis* in which the Church, moved by faith, entreats the Father, through the Son, to send the Spirit so that in the unique offering of the incarnate Son, everything may be consummated in unity. Through the eucharist, believers unite themselves to Christ, who offers himself to the Father with them, and they receive the possibility of offering themselves in a spirit of sacrifice to each other, as Christ himself offers himself to the Father for the many, thus giving himself to men.

This consummation in unity, brought about by the one inseparable operation of the Son and the Spirit, acting in reference to the Father in his design, is the Church in its fullness.

II

1. If one looks at the New Testament, one will notice first of all that the Church describes a "local" reality. The Church exists in history as local church. For a region one speaks more often of churches, in the plural. It is always a question of the Church of God, but in a given place.

Now the Church existing in a place is not formed, in a radical sense, by the persons who come together to establish it. There is a "Jerusalem from on high" which "comes down from God," a communion which is at the foundation of the community itself. The Church comes into being by a free gift, that of the new creation.

However, it is clear that the Church "which is in" a given place manifests itself when it is "assembled." This assembly itself, whose elements and requirements are indicated by the New Testament, is fully such when it is the eucharistic synaxis. When the local church celebrates the eucharist, the event which took place "once and for all" is made present and manifested. In the local church, then, there is neither male nor female, slave nor free, Jew nor Greek. A new unity is communicated which overcomes divisions and restores communion in the one body of Christ. This unity transcends psychological, racial, socio-political or cultural unity. It is the "communion of the Holy Spirit" gathering together the scattered children of God. The newness of baptism and of chrismation then bears its fruit. And by the power of the body and blood of the Lord, filled with the Holy Spirit, there is healed that sin which does not cease to assault Christians by raising obstacles to the dynamism of the "life for God in Christ Jesus" received in baptism. This applies also to the sin of division, all of whose forms contradict God's design.

One of the chief texts to remember is 1 Cor. 10:15-17: one sole bread, one sole cup, one sole body of Christ in the plurality of members. This mystery of the unity in love of many persons constitutes the real newness of the trinitarian *koinonia* communicated to men in the Church through the eucharist. Such is the purpose of Christ's saving work, which is spread abroad in the last times after Pentecost.

This is why the Church finds its model, its origin and its purpose in the mystery of God, one in three persons. Further still, the eucharist thus understood in the light of the trinitarian mystery is the criterion for the functioning of the life of the Church as a whole. The institutional elements should be nothing but a visible reflection of the reality of the mystery.

2. The unfolding of the eucharistic celebration of the local church shows how the *koinonia* takes shape in the church celebrating the eucharist. In the eucharist, celebrated by the local church gathered about the bishop or the priest in communion with him, the following aspects stand out, interconnected among themselves even if this or that moment of the celebration emphasizes one or another.

The *koinonia* is eschatological. It is the newness which comes in the last times. That is why everything in the eucharist as in the life of the Church begins with conversion and reconciliation. The eucharist presupposes repentance (*metanoia*) and confession (*exomologêsis*), which find in other circumstances their own sacramental expression. But the eucharist forgives and also heals sins, since it is the sacrament of the divinizing love of the Father, by the Son, in the Holy Spirit.

But this *koinonia* is also kerygmatic. This is evident in the synaxis not only because the celebration "announces" the event of the mystery but also because it actually realizes it today in the Spirit. This implies the proclamation of the word to the assembly and the response of faith given by all. Thus the communion of the assembly is brought about in the kerygma, and hence unity in faith. Orthodoxy (correct faith) is inherent in the eucharistic *koinonia*. This orthodoxy is expressed most clearly through the proclamation of the symbol of faith which is a summary of the apostolic tradition of which the bishop is the witness in virtue of his succession. Thus the eucharist is inseparably sacrament and word since in it the incarnate Word sanctifies in the Spirit. That is why the entire liturgy, and not only the reading of Holy Scriptures, constitutes a proclamation of the Word under the form of doxology and prayer. On the other hand, the Word proclaimed is the Word made flesh and become sacramental.

Koinonia is at once ministerial and pneumatological. That is why the eucharist is its manifestation *par excellence*. The entire assembly, each one according to his rank is *leitourgos* of the *koinonia*. While being a gift of the trinitarian God, *koinonia* is also the response of men. In the faith which comes from the Spirit and the Word, these put into practice the vocation and the mission received in baptism: to become living members, in one's proper rank, of the body of Christ.

3. The ministry of the bishop is not merely a tactical or pragmatic function (because a president is necessary) but an organic function. The bishop receives the gift of episcopal grace (1 Tim. 4:14) in the sacrament of consecration effected by bishops who themselves have received this gift, thanks to the existence of an uninterrupted series of episcopal ordinations, beginning from the holy apostles. By the sacrament of ordination, the Spirit of the Lord "confers" on the bishop, not juridically as if it were a pure transmission of power, but sacramentally, the authority of servant which the Son received from the Father and which he received in a human way by his acceptance of his passion.

The function of the bishop is closely bound to the eucharistic assembly over which he presides. The eucharistic unity of the local church implies communion between him who presides and the people to whom he delivers the word of salvation and the eucharistic gifts. Further, the minister is also the one who "receives" from his church, which is faithful to tradition, the word he transmits. And the great intercession which he sends up to the Father is simply that of his entire church praying with him. The bishop cannot be separated from his church any more than the church can be separated from its bishop.

The bishop stands at the heart of the local church as minister of the Spirit to discern the charisms and take care that they are exercised in harmony, for the good of all, in faithfulness to the apostolic tradition. He puts himself at the service of the initiatives of the Spirit so that nothing may prevent them from contributing to building up *koinonia*. He is minister of unity, servant of Christ the Lord, whose mission is to "gather into unity the children of God." And because the Church is built up by the eucharist, it is he, invested with the grace of priestly ministry, who presides at the latter.

But this presidency must be properly understood. The bishop presides at the offering which is that of his entire community. By consecrating the gifts so that they become the body and blood the community offers, he celebrates not only for it, nor only with it and in it, but through it. He appears then as minister of Christ fashioning the unity of his body and so creating communion through his body. The union of the community with him is first of all of the order of *mysterion* and not primordially of the juridical order. It is that union expressed in the eucharist which is prolonged and given practical expression in the "pastoral" relations of teaching, government and life. The ecclesial community is thus called to be the outline of a human community renewed.

4. There is profound communion between the bishop and the community in which the Spirit gives him responsibility for the Church of God. The ancient tradition expressed it happily in the image of marriage. But that communion lies within the communion of the apostolic community. In the ancient tradition (as the *Apostolic Tradition* of Hippolytus proves) the bishop elected by the people—who guarantee his apostolic faith, in conformity with what the local church confesses—receives the ministerial grace of Christ by the Spirit in the prayer of the assembly and by the laying on of hands (*cheirotonia*) of the neighboring bishops, witnesses of the faith of their own churches. His charism, coming directly from the Spirit of God, is given him in the apostolicity of his church (linked to the faith of the apostolic community) and in that of the other churches represented by their bishops. Through this his ministry is inserted into the catholicity of the Church of God.

Apostolic succession, therefore, means something more than a mere transmission of powers. It is succession in a church which witnesses to the apostolic faith, in communion with the other churches which witness to the same apostolic faith. The "see" (*cathedra*) plays an essential role in inserting the bishop into the heart of ecclesial apostolicity. On the other hand, once ordained, the bishop becomes in his church the guarantor of apostolicity and the one who represents it within the communion of churches, its link with the other churches. That is why in his church every eucharist can only be celebrated in truth if presided over by him or by a presbyter in communion with him. Mention of him in the anaphora is essential.

Through the ministry of presbyters, charged with presiding over the life and the eucharistic celebration of the communities entrusted to them, those communities grow in communion with all the communities for which the bishop has primary responsibility. In the present situation, the diocese itself is a *communion* of eucharistic communities. One of the essential functions of presbyters is to link these to the eucharist of the bishop and to nourish them with the apostolic faith of which the bishop is the witness and guarantor. They should also take care that Christians, nourished by the body and blood of him who gave his life for his brethren, should be authentic witnesses of fraternal love in the reciprocal sacrifice nourished by the sacrifice of Christ. For, according to the word of the apostle, "if someone sees his brother in need and closes his heart against him, how does God's love abide in him?" The eucharist determines the Christian manner of living the paschal mystery of Christ and the gift of Pentecost. Thanks to it there is a profound transformation of human existence always confronted by temptation and suffering.

III

1. The body of Christ is unique. There exists then only one Church of God. The identity of one eucharistic assembly with another comes from the fact that all, with the same faith, celebrate the same memorial, that all by eating the same bread and sharing in the same cup become the same unique body of Christ into which they have been integrated by the same baptism. If there are many celebrations, there is nevertheless only one mystery celebrated, in which all participate. Moreover, when the believer communicates in the Lord's body and blood, he does not receive a part of Christ but the whole Christ.

In the same way, the local church which celebrates the eucharist gathered around its bishop is not a section of the body of Christ. The multiplicity of local synaxes does not divide the Church but rather shows sacramentally its unity. Like the community of the apostles gathered around Christ, each eucharistic assembly is truly the holy Church of God, the body of Christ, in communion with the first community of the disciples and with all who throughout the world celebrate and have celebrated the memorial of the Lord. It is also in communion with the assembly of the saints in heaven, which each celebration brings to mind.

2. Far from excluding diversity or plurality, the *koinonia* supposes it and heals the wounds of division, transcending the latter in unity.

Since Christ is one for the many, so in the Church which is his body, the one and the many, the universal and local, are necessarily simultane-

61

ous. Still more radically, because the one and only God is the communion of three persons, the one and only Church is a communion of many communities and the local church a communion of persons. The one and unique Church finds her identity in the *koinonia* of the churches. Unity and multiplicity appear so linked that one could not exist without the other. It is this relationship constitutive of the Church that institutions make visible and, so to speak, "historicize."

3. Since the universal Church manifests itself in the synaxis of the local church, two conditions must be fulfilled above all if the local church which celebrates the eucharist is to be truly within the ecclesial communion.

(a) First, the identity of the mystery of the Church lived by the local church with the mystery of the Church lived by the primitive church—catholicity in time—is fundamental. The Church is apostolic because it is founded on and continually sustained by the mystery of salvation revealed in Jesus Christ, transmitted in the Spirit by those who were his witnesses, the apostles. Its members will be judged by Christ and the apostles (cf. Lk. 22:30).

(b) Today, mutual recognition between this local church and the other churches is also of capital importance. Each should recognize in the others, through local particularities, the identity of the mystery of the Church. It is a question of mutual recognition of catholicity as communion in the wholeness of the mystery. This recognition is achieved first of all at the regional level. Communion in the same patriarchate or in some other form of regional unity is first of all a manifestation of the life of the Spirit in the same culture or in the same historical conditions. It equally implies unity of witness and calls for the exercise of fraternal correction in humility. This communion within the same region should extend itself further in the communion between sister churches.

This mutual recognition, however, is true only under the conditions expressed in the anaphora of St. John Chrysostom and the first Antiochene anaphoras. The first condition is communion in the same kerygma, and so in the same faith. Already there in baptism, this requirement is made explicit in the eucharistic celebration. But it also requires the will for communion in love (*agapê*) and in service (*diakonia*), not only in words but in deeds.

Permanence through history and mutual recognition are particularly brought into focus in the eucharistic synaxis by the mention of the saints in the canon and of the heads of the churches in the diptychs. Thus it is understood why these latter are signs of catholic unity in eucharistic communion, responsible, each on its own level, for maintaining that communion in the universal harmony of the churches and their common fidelity to the apostolic tradition.

4. We find then among these churches those bonds of communion which the New Testament indicated: *communion* in faith, hope and love, *communion* in the sacraments, *communion* in the diversity of charisms, *communion* in the reconciliation, *communion* in the ministry. The agent of this communion is the Spirit of the risen Lord. Through him the Church universal, catholic, integrates diversity or plurality, making it one of its own essential elements. This catholicity represents the fulfillment of the prayer of chapter 17 of the Gospel according to John taken up in the eucharistic *epicleses*.

Attachment to the apostolic communion binds all the bishops together, linking the *episkopê* of the local churches to the college of the apostles. They too form a college rooted by the Spirit in the "once for all" of the apostolic group, the unique witness to the faith. This means not only that they should be united among themselves by faith, charity, mission, reconciliation but that they have in common the same responsibility and the same service to the Church. Because the one and only Church is made present in his local church, each bishop cannot separate the care for his own church from that of the universal Church. When, by the sacrament of ordination, he receives the charism of the Spirit for the *episkopê* of one local church, his own, by that very fact he receives the charism of the Spirit for the *episkopê* of the entire Church. In the people of God, he exercises it in communion with all the bishops who are here and now in charge of churches and in communion with the living tradition which the bishops of the past have handed on. The presence of bishops from neighboring sees at his episcopal ordination "sacramentalizes" and makes present this communion. It produces a thorough fusion between his solicitude for the local community and his care for the Church spread throughout the world. The *episkopê* for the universal Church is seen to be entrusted, by the Spirit, to the totality of local

63

bishops in communion with one another. This communion is expressed traditionally through conciliar practice. We shall have to examine further the way it is conceived and realized, in the perspective of what we have just explained.

Munich
July 6, 1982
Second Plenary Meeting

A RESPONSE TO THE JOINT INTERNATIONAL COMMISSION FOR THEOLOGICAL DIALOGUE BETWEEN THE ORTHODOX CHURCH AND THE ROMAN CATHOLIC CHURCH REGARDING THE MUNICH DOCUMENT: "THE MYSTERY OF THE CHURCH AND OF THE EUCHARIST IN THE LIGHT OF THE MYSTERY OF THE HOLY TRINITY"

U.S. Theological Consultation, 1983

1. The Munich common statement of the Joint International Commission for Theological Dialogue between the Orthodox Church and the Roman Catholic Church regarding "The Mystery of the Church and of the Eucharist in the Light of the Mystery of the Holy Trinity," dated July 6, 1982, is a landmark in the recent history of Orthodox-Roman Catholic relations. The text is a creative statement about the high degree of agreement that already exists between the two churches. The Commission deserves commendation for its achievement. What follows is a response to the text on the part of the Orthodox-Roman Catholic Consultation in the United States established by the Standing Conference of Canonical Orthodox Bishops in America (SCOBA) and the National Conference of Catholic Bishops (NCCB) which was reached unanimously at its 26th meeting, May 23-25, 1983, in New York.

2. That a joint statement was published by the Commission is in itself an important achievement. The text moves us farther away from our history of mutual estrangement and allows the churches to speak with one voice on matters at the heart of the Christian faith. The decision to publish the text promptly for wider reaction was welcome. We hope that this procedure will be continued in the future.

3. The text requires careful reading, and to some its language may seem unfamiliar, despite many biblical and liturgical allusions. A clear attempt is made not to impose specific terminologies of either Roman Catholic or Orthodox theology. Rather, the text appropriately uses new formulations as needed in order to hand on the faith to men and women of our time.

For example, use of the word "event" (*événement, to gegonos*) found in I, 1, bis; I, 2; I, 3; I, 4b; I, 5d, para. 2; II, 1, para. 3; II, 2, para. 3, is helpful in stressing the work of the Trinity. However, this word, as well as others such as "sacrament," "mystery," "word," and "energies," are open to various interpretations and thus call for further elucidations.

4. We have several suggestions which, if followed, might facilitate discussion and assessment of this and future documents.

(a) It is not always clear to whom the document is addressed. If addressed to the Church at large, then much in the text is inaccessible.

(b) Criticism of omissions or overemphases could often be forestalled if the document were situated within the context of the long-range agenda of the Commission. The publication of an annotated text of this agenda would be appreciated.

(c) Publication of commentaries or background papers by the Commission would be helpful in explicating the document and would make it more accessible to non-specialists.

(d) In formulating texts, a more systematic and consistent numbering of paragraphs would be desirable.

(e) The document itself recognizes that this is but "the first step in the effort to fulfill the program." It is to be hoped therefore that this text will be reformulated in the light of critical responses and the developments of other sections of the dialogue. This process has proved extremely useful in other international dialogues.

5. Our Consultation took note of several specific doctrinal themes raised in the document. In discussing the synaxis, or eucharistic celebration (especially in I, 5, b, c and I, 6), the text states clearly that the eucharistic celebration is the *anamnêsis* of the work of Christ as Savior made manifest by the Spirit, but also that the Spirit transforms the sacred gifts into the body of Christ in order to effect the growth of the body of Christ which is the Church. Particularly welcome are the assertions that "the entire [eucharistic] celebration is an *epiclêsis*, which becomes more explicit at certain moments" and that "the Church is continually in a state of *epiclêsis*" (I, 5, c).

6. The formulation of the relationship between the Son and the Spirit (I, 6, para. 2), though it does not address the *filioque* question directly,

does state that "the Spirit which proceeds from the Father (Jn. 15:26) as the sole source in the Trinity ... is communicated to us particularly in the eucharist by this Son upon whom he reposes in time and eternity." The text thus gives a solid basis for further statements about the Spirit in the treatment of the mission of the Spirit. Indeed the entire section which discusses the relation of the Spirit's activity to the historical mission of Christ and to the mystery of the risen Christ (I, 4 to I, 6) is well formulated.

7. Collegiality and the synodal nature of the Church are affirmed by the references to "communion in the same patriarchate" or "in some other form of regional unity" or "communion between sister churches" (III, 3, b), as well as to a bishop's "solicitude for the local community" and "his care for the Church spread throughout the world" (III, 4, para. 2). However, the appeal to the term "sister churches" is unclear. Does it refer to patriarchates or jurisdictions in full communion or to the special relationship between the Orthodox Church and the Roman Catholic Church?

8. The expression the "*episkopê* of the entire Church" (III, 4, para. 2) needs further exploration in the context of the separated Christian churches. The way in which the document focuses on the "local church" through eucharistic ecclesiology does not readily correspond to the actual situation of bishops and their churches today. Although this model offers some useful insights, the character, numerical size, and geographical extent of most local churches makes application problematic.

9. Regarding the office of *episkopos* and other institutions, such as ordination and sacramental practices, the text does not pay sufficient attention to historical development, creating an impression of oversimplification. For example, the appeal to the "uninterrupted series of episcopal ordinations, beginning from the holy apostles" (II, 3), or the "college of the apostles" (III, 4, para. 2) needs refinement. Other statements about apostolicity and apostolic faith are better developed, as in II, 4, para. 2. Further, the use of New Testament texts lacks rigor and does not coincide with the requirements of responsible historico-critical scholarship.

10. The text should have discussed the diversity of ministries within the one body (cf. II, 1, para. 4); likewise, some reference to the priesthood proper to all the faithful would have been in order. The relation between

the bishop's ministerial priesthood and that of all the faithful is not adequately explored. The relation of the bishop and the presbyter is not sufficiently addressed. We hope that significant aspects of these major problems will be addressed in future documents.

11. The sections of the document regarding kerygmatic aspects of *koinonia* and its relationship to the "unity in faith" (II, 2, para. 3) and "communion in the same kerygma, and so in the same faith" (III, 3, b, para. 2) need clarification. It is not always apparent that the text sufficiently distinguishes between faith (or credal) affirmations and theological explanations about faith that need not require unanimity.

12. The document is open to criticism for not sufficiently recognizing the social dimensions of Church and eucharist. It seems to prescind from concrete social problems. When mention is made of social issues, this seems to be an afterthought (*e.g.*, II, 4, para. 3). When the text mentions the transformative aspects of Church and eucharist, this is usually in the context of individual repentance, conversion, self-sacrifice (cf. I, 6, para. 3; II, 1, para. 3; II, 2, para. 2). It neglects the Christian's vocation to contribute to the transformation of society (I, 1).

13. The sections which discuss the eucharist should situate it more clearly in the context of Christian initiation and the total sacramental life of the Church. It is encouraging therefore that the International Commission has taken as its next task the study of the sacraments of baptism, chrismation and the eucharist and the unity of the Church.

Jamaica, NY
May 25, 1983
26th Meeting

AN AGREED STATEMENT ON THE LIMA DOCUMENT: *BAPTISM, EUCHARIST AND MINISTRY*

U.S. Theological Consultation, 1984

The Eastern Orthodox-Roman Catholic Consultation in the United States, during its 28th and 29th meetings (1983-84), studied the *Baptism, Eucharist and Ministry* document of the Faith and Order Commission of the World Council of Churches.

We welcome the *Baptism, Eucharist and Ministry* document, and we take this opportunity to comment on its separate sections. In what follows we call attention to those elements which we particularly appreciate and affirm as representative of the faith of the Church and note those which we judge to require further clarification.

I. Baptism

The presentation of the theological meaning of baptism as renewal of life in Christ, participation in Christ's death and resurrection, cleansing from sin, the gift of the Spirit, incorporation into the body of Christ, and a sign of the kingdom, sets forth essential elements of faith in regard to this sacrament. Chief among these are the affirmation that Christian baptism is in water and the Spirit, in the name of the Trinity, and that baptism is an unrepeatable act. We particularly appreciate the way in which the document relates the sacrament of baptism so intimately to faith and views baptism as the foundation of a life-long process of growth in Christ. In this and in its treatment of the practice of baptism, the document offers an approach to the resolution of historical controversies over baptism, especially those about infant and adult baptism. In regard to both practices, the document gives due significance to the faith and life of the Church. Because faith is so central to baptism, we agree with the document's admonition to the churches to exercise discernment in their baptismal practice, particularly but not exclusively in the baptism of infants. At the same time we are mindful that baptism is a divine gift received and celebrated in the context of the community of faith. For this

69

reason, we also agree that the celebration of baptism should include, as far as possible, the local community of faith.

The issue of the unity of the sacraments of initiation is treated in a sensitive way. We affirm with the Lima Statement that baptism, in its full meaning, signifies and effects both "participation in Christ's death and resurrection" and "the receiving of the Spirit." We further recognize that each of our churches expresses this unity in its rites, though there are significant differences in practice. For the Orthodox, the conferring of baptism, chrismation, and eucharist takes place in a single liturgical celebration, whether for adults or infants. For Roman Catholics, reception of eucharist and confirmation are delayed in the case of infant baptism. These practices are based on different pastoral and theological concerns. However we affirm with the document that catechesis and nurture in the Christian life are necessary in all cases.

Within this agreement on the essentials of baptism, we also recognize the need for further clarification of a number of points.

First, the action and role of the Holy Spirit in the structure of the rite of Christian initiation should be as strongly developed in the section on baptism as it is in the section on eucharist.

Second, the role of the faith of the Church in baptism is not clearly enough explained. In our view it is not sufficient to treat this matter merely in the section on baptismal practice.

Third, the way in which the unity of the sacraments of initiation is expressed in practice has doctrinal implications which need further consideration and which suggest the need for revision of practice. For the Orthodox, the unity of the sacraments of initiation is maintained in both adult and infant baptism by the acts of chrismation and reception of the holy eucharist. For Roman Catholics, this unity is clearly expressed in the Rite of Christian Initiation of Adults, although it is not as obvious in the practice of infant baptism. The Consultation agrees that the practice of admitting or not admitting baptized infants to the eucharist needs further exploration.

Finally, we find the document's use of the terminology contrasting "believer's baptism" and "infant baptism" to be unfortunate. Despite the disclaimers in the Commentary (12), it suggests, against our convictions, that baptized infants are unbelievers or that faith is lacking in the case of infant baptism. In so doing the document misses an opportunity to move the discussion beyond the terms of historical debates.

Despite the need for such clarifications, the Consultation agrees that in the Lima Statement we can recognize to a considerable degree the faith of the Church in regard to baptism. Because of this agreement, we recommend that our two churches explore the possibility of a formal recognition of each other's baptism as a sacrament of our unity in the body of Christ, although we acknowledge that any such recognition is conditioned by other factors.

II. Eucharist

We welcome the recognition of the centrality of the eucharist in the life of the Church and the theological breadth of the document's presentation of the meaning of the eucharist. In its treatment of eucharist as thanksgiving, memorial, invocation, communion, and meal of the kingdom, *Baptism, Eucharist and Ministry* succeeds in conveying a sense of the full significance of the eucharistic celebration. Its accent on frequent celebration of the eucharist and participation in communion we also find in keeping with the faith of the Church. The strong emphasis on the trinitarian dynamics of the eucharist, especially the balanced presentation of the role of the Holy Spirit and the role of Christ, makes it possible to move beyond the terms of some historical controversies. The emphasis on the epicletic nature of the entire eucharistic celebration may help to overcome controversy about the moment of consecration. Similarly, the affirmation of Christ as High Priest and host who gathers the community and is present in the eucharistic gifts in a unique way may help to overcome excessive concentration on the eucharistic elements in isolation from the liturgical action of the community.

We also affirm the document's view of the eucharist as the sacrament of the unique and unrepeatable sacrifice of Christ in behalf of all. We likewise appreciate the way in which *Baptism, Eucharist and Ministry* expresses the social and ethical dimensions of eucharist by seeing in Christ's self-offering the source and model of Christians' self-offering as "living and holy sacrifices in their daily lives," as servants of reconciliation in the world. In addition we welcome the document's emphasis on the eucharist's role as uniting the whole world to the offering of Christ, and as preparing for the sanctification and transformation of all creation. Eucharist is thus integrated into the whole of life and cannot be understood as an isolated liturgical event or simply as an expression of individual piety.

Because the presentation of the eucharist is remarkably rich yet succinct, there are inevitably some points that require further clarification or development.

First, we would welcome fuller discussion of the way in which eucharist manifests the nature of the Church as the body of Christ. Eucharist is related to the very being of the Church and cannot be seen simply as a strengthening of the grace of baptism.

Second, the relationship between Christ's sacrifice and his presence in the eucharist requires further clarification, particularly in regard to his offering of himself to the Father and his giving of himself to us as spiritual food.

Third, we note that *Baptism, Eucharist and Ministry* mentions the practice of reservation of the eucharist without presenting an adequate theological rationale for it. For the Roman Catholic and Orthodox churches, it is our faith that the bread and wine become and remain the body and blood of Christ that allows us to reserve the sacrament. We would therefore welcome further elaboration of this point.

Finally, concerning the possibility of eucharistic sharing, we do not find that growing consensus on eucharistic theology and practice is of itself sufficient for such sharing among our churches. The resolution of questions connected with ministry and the nature and faith of the Church are also important, as we note below.

Although we find such clarifications and further considerations necessary, we nevertheless are in agreement that the section on eucharist represents to a considerable degree the faith of the Church.

III. Ministry

By locating the ordained ministry in the context of the Church as the people of God, *Baptism, Eucharist and Ministry* appropriately relates ordained ministry to the ministry of all Christians, while also clearly distinguishing the two. We appreciate its affirmation of the diverse and complementary gifts for ministry of all the baptized. At the same time, we recognize the importance of its assertion that the ordained ministry, tracing its origins to apostolic times, is a permanent and constitutive element of the life of the Church. In this regard, we also commend especially the recognition that "a ministry of *episkopê* is necessary to express and safeguard the unity of the body."

We find helpful the treatment of the historical development of the three-fold ministry, and the delineation of the functions of bishop, presbyter, and deacon, to be adequately outlined and balanced.

Apostolic succession is rightly interpreted as involving the total life of the Church. The view that ordained ministry is an integral part of the apostolic tradition is especially useful in advancing ecumenical discussion. Ordained ministry is thus understood as one of the expressions of the Church's apostolicity. This understanding, in our judgment, is confirmed by the act of ordination within the believing community which signifies the bestowal of the gift of ministry through the laying on of hands of the bishop and the *epiclêsis* of the Holy Spirit.

We commend the treatment of the authority of the ordained ministry as an authority of service exercised through love. We affirm with the document that ordained ministry derives from Jesus Christ and is to be exercised in a manner that is personal, collegial, and communal. Thus interdependence and reciprocity between the faithful and their ordained ministers is rightly emphasized.

We welcome the document's invitation to all the churches to reexamine their understanding and practice of ordained ministry. Some churches are challenged by the possibility of recognizing the ministry of *episkopê* in those churches which have not maintained the historical pattern of the three-fold ministry. Other churches are challenged by the possibility of recognizing the value of the historical pattern and incorporating it into their structure. These challenges may offer a fruitful way toward ecumenical agreement on the ordained ministry.

Along with the areas of agreement indicated above, there is need for clarification on other matters treated in this section.

Baptism, Eucharist and Ministry attempts to integrate two approaches to ministry: one—personal, the other—functional, by recognizing the charism of ministry as a gift of God in and for the Church. We appreciate this effort but do not find it entirely successful. For example, the non-repeat-ability of ordination is mentioned only in passing in the context of conditions for ordination; its theological rationale is not adequately developed.

In general, the document presents as possible, even laudable opinions, certain aspects of ordained ministry that we consider normative for the Church's life and structure. These normative aspects include the three-fold ministry; the historical succession of office holders in the episcopal ministry; the exclusive conferral of ordination by those entrusted with the *episkopê* of the community; and the presidency of the eucharist exclusively by an ordained minister.

Although *Baptism, Eucharist and Ministry* recognizes, at least to a degree, the sacramental nature of the ordained ministry, it does not adequately develop this important aspect of ministry. This is particularly evident in its failure to relate more closely ordained ministry to the eucharist, as the central sacrament and expression of the Church's reality. While we appreciate the description of ordained ministry as having a priestly character, we would require a treatment of the differences between the priesthood of all believers, the ministerial priesthood, and of their relation to the priesthood of Christ.

In addition to the document's emphasis on *episkopê* as necessary min-istry in the Church, we affirm that the episcopal office is a constitutive element of the structure of the Church. This office exercises primacy in teaching, leadership of worship, and government in the local church and has a responsibility for ordering the local church to the universal Church. It follows that complete reconciliation of the churches will depend on the presence in those churches of this episcopal office.

In its commendable attention to the communal context of ordained ministry, *Baptism, Eucharist and Ministry* only implies the prophetic dimension of ministry, that is to say, the God-given authority to chal-lenge, confront, and correct the community. In this context the historical role of binding and loosing could well have been developed.

Finally, we understand mutual recognition of ministries as part of a process of growth toward unity, marked by several steps. In our view, agreement on the understanding of ordained ministry and mutual recog-nition of ministries are important steps in this process but they are not of themselves sufficient for the restoration of full communion among the churches. Further doctrinal consensus is required. For example, because of traditional and theological reasons the question of ordination of women to the priesthood is of greater consequence and hence a greater obstacle to eucharistic sharing than the document suggests. A prerequisite for the restoration of eucharistic sharing is the satisfactory articulation of our apostolic faith.

Douglaston, NY
October 27, 1984
29th Meeting

Section 2

The Mystery of the Church and Christian Unity

INTRODUCTION TO SECTION TWO

Both Catholics and Orthodox lay claim to the same reality. Both believe that, notwithstanding human frailty and sin, the fullness of the apostolic tradition is faithfully and fully preserved in their respective churches. This affirmation inevitably leads both to ask how and to what extent can they recognize each other's ecclesial status and, underlying this, each other's sacramental life. The success or failure of the present quest for unity will depend in large measure on whether mutually satisfactory answers can be given to such questions.

So far, theological dialogue on the national and international levels has revealed a high measure of agreement concerning the nature of the Church. This is evident in the U.S. Consultation's 1974 "Agreed Statement on the Church." Though brief in comparison to the Joint International Commission's 1982 Munich Statement on "The Mystery of the Church," it shows many of the same characteristics. Eschewing the highly juridical and institutional models of some earlier periods, the statement calls attention to the reality of the Church as sacrament, as mystery, rooted in and reflecting the mystery of the Holy Trinity, "in which there is both distinction of persons and unity based on love, not subordination" (¶2). Like the Munich Statement, it calls special attention to the role of the Spirit, who in each place and each new historical context constitutes the Church as the body of Christ. Again like the Munich Statement, it shows the impact of modern "eucharistic ecclesiology" in its presentation of the local church and of the relationship of local churches one to another. The statement goes on to recognize the existence of "a real hierarchy of churches" notwithstanding their "fundamental equality" (¶6). But as it immediately points out, "the Catholic and Orthodox Churches explain differently the meaning of this hierarchy of churches," that is, they have a different understanding of the nature of primacy in the Church (¶7). On this issue the U.S. Consultation in 1974 could only state that "our two traditions are not easily harmonized" (¶8). It would return to the issue of primacy—perhaps the most important issue still separating Catholics and Orthodox—in its 1989 "Agreed Statement on Conciliarity and Primacy in the Church."

While Orthodox and Catholic theologians have made great progress towards agreement concerning the nature of the Church, they would also agree that primacy is not the only ecclesiological issue in need of resolution. Full *koinonia,* which is the express aim of current dialogue, implies mutual recognition of sacraments and mutual recognition precisely as churches. But such recognition has not been easy to achieve for at least two reasons:

—It is relatively easy to identify the Catholic "position" on the subject of sacramental and ecclesial recognition, especially since the Second Vatican Council. According to the council's Constitution on the Church, *Lumen Gentium,* the Church of Christ "subsists in the Catholic Church, which is governed by the successor of Peter and by the bishops in communion with him," but at the same time "many elements of sanctification and of truth can be found outside her visible structure" (¶8), albeit in varying measure, in other churches and ecclesial communities. To the extent that these elements are present, the one Church of Christ is effectively present in them, creating a "certain communion, albeit imperfect," with the Catholic Church. As for the Orthodox, "although these churches are separated from us, they possess true sacraments, above all—by apostolic succession—the priesthood and the eucharist, whereby they are still joined to us in a very close relationship" (Decree on Ecumenism, *Unitatis Redintegratio,* ¶15). The Orthodox, on the other hand, have not articulated their "position" on the ecclesial status of those outside the visible structures of the Orthodox Church in a comparably clear and authoritative manner. Individual Orthodox theologians and church figures have responded to many of the ecclesiological issues raised by the ecumenical movement, but in a wide variety of ways not easily harmonized.

—This imparity in the articulation of ecclesiology arises at least in part from the "structural imparity" of the Orthodox and the Catholic Churches. Notwithstanding the Second Vatican Council's recognition of the importance of subsidiarity, the Catholic Church remains relatively centralized. By contrast, the Orthodox Church is a communion of autocephalous churches, that is, fully self-governing churches which have the capacity to elect all their own bishops, including the head of the church (patriarch, archbishop, metropolitan), without obligatory reference to another church. While the Patriarch of Constantinople possesses a "primacy of honor," he is "first among equals." He may take the initiative in matters affecting the Orthodox Church as a whole, but major decisions depend upon the consensus of the autocephalous churches. In the twentieth century the Orthodox churches have recognized the need for greater unity among themselves, but diverse external pressures, ranging from ethnic tensions and nationalism to Communist oppression to the precarious position of the Ecumenical Patriarchate of Constantinople in modern Turkey, have hindered progress in this area. Already in 1923 a preparatory meeting began to prepare the agenda for a general council of the Orthodox Church, but serious efforts got underway only with the Pan-Orthodox "Rhodes Conferences" in the 1960s. In 1968 an Inter-Orthodox Preparatory Commission for the "Great and Holy Council" was established, but it was not until 1976 that the first Pan-Orthodox Preconciliar Conference was able to meet and finalize an agenda, and since then preparations for the council have proceeded very slowly indeed. While it may be hoped that an eventual Great and Holy Council will address the kinds of ecclesiological issues that at present hinder fruitful dialogue, it is difficult to predict when it actually will meet.

The U.S. Theological Consultation has followed Orthodox efforts to address these "imparities" with great interest, since they have an important bearing on the future of Orthodox-Catholic dialogue. This is especially evident in two joint efforts from the mid-seventies: "The Principle of Economy: A Joint Statement" (May 1976) and "Reaction of the Orthodox-Roman Catholic Dialogue to the Agenda of the Great and Holy Council of the Orthodox Church" (September 1977).

The subject of the former document, "economy" (*oikonomia*), had figured in the agenda originally announced for the Great and Holy Council by the Inter-Orthodox Preparatory Commission. As the joint statement indicates, the Greek word *oikonomia* has a wide and rich range of meanings. In relatively recent times, it has come to be used in connection with the sacraments and their relation to the Church. According to some presentations of this subject, "all non-Orthodox sacraments, from the point of view of strictness, are null and void," but "the Orthodox Church can, by economy, treat non-Orthodox sacraments as valid" (¶9b); thus in principle Catholic converts, for example, should be (re)baptized, and if "by economy" they have not been, this in no way implies recognition of their previous baptism, since this was administered outside the Orthodox Church. This approach, in the judgment of the Consultation, does not "do justice to the genuine whole tradition underlying the concept and practice of economy." The Consultation instead suggests that "a proper understanding of economy involves the exercise of spiritual discernment," and it expresses the hope "that our churches can come to discern in each other the same faith, that they can come to recognize each other as sister churches celebrating the same sacraments, and thus enter into full ecclesial communion" (¶10).

Six months after the issuance of the U.S. Consultation's statement on "economy," the first Pan-Orthodox Preconciliar Conference approved a revised agenda for the Great and Holy Council. Certain topics, among them "economy," were dropped, and others, relating especially to inter-Orthodox relations, were added. The resulting ten-point agenda included (1) fasting regulations, (2) marriage impediments, (3) calendar revision, (4) the Orthodox "diaspora," (5) the relationship of the Orthodox Church to other Christian churches and communities, (6) the diptychs, that is, the order of precedence of the Orthodox Churches, (7) autocephaly, (8) autonomy, (9) Orthodoxy and the ecumenical movement, and (10) peace and justice. In its Reaction to this agenda, the U.S. Consultation noted that its aims were primarily practical but that it also raised deeper theological issues. High among these, certainly, would be the Church's relation to the modern world and also "the ecclesial status of 'separated Christians' and 'separated churches'" (reaction to topic 5).

After the relative ease and speed with which the Joint International Commission was able to produce its well-received first agreed statement (Munich 1982), one might have expected work on its second agreed statement to go smoothly. This was not the case. The Commission was unable to reach agreement on a final text at its third plenary session (Crete 1984) or at the first meeting of its fourth plenary session (Bari 1986). It was able to issue "Faith, Sacraments and the Unity of the Church" only at a second meeting in Bari in 1987. In its final form, the agreed statement is divided into two unequal sections. The first and stronger is devoted to faith and communion in the sacraments. Faith, as the statement affirms, is inseparably the gift of God and the response of the human person, but "in its profound reality it is also an *ecclesial* event" (¶2). Sacramental *koinonia* is inseparable from the faith of the Church. As the Response of the U.S. Consultation puts it, "the Church is the locus for the flowering of faith," but at the same time "the Church's faith constitutes the norm and the criterion of the personal act of faith" (¶2). The first section of the Bari Statement then goes on to explore the relationship between the content of the faith and its articulation in the form of creeds. It affirms that "a certain diversity in its formulation does not compromise the *koinonia* between the local churches when each church can recognize, in the variety of formulations, the one authentic faith received from the apostles" (¶25), and it attempts to formulate criteria for such recognition. More problematic is the second section of the Bari Statement, which reviews a number of differences between East and West in the administration of the sacraments of Christian initiation. Its final paragraph (¶53), with its reference to the union council of 879, implies that a certain diversity in the practice of Christian initiation is not incompatible with mutual recognition and church unity. But with this reference, the Bari Statement ends abruptly. It stops short of making a specific judgment concerning the legitimacy of the present differences in practice. It stops well short of the mutual recognition of sacraments that some Catholics and Orthodox had been expecting on the basis of earlier statements by individual church leaders on both sides.

AN AGREED STATEMENT ON THE CHURCH

U.S. Theological Consultation, 1974

Issued by the Orthodox-Roman Catholic Bilateral Consultation in the U.S.A.

1. Christianity is distinguished by its faith in the Blessed Trinity. In the light of this revelation Christianity must interpret the world and every aspect of it. This revelation has obvious implications for the interpretation of the nature of the Church.

2. The Church is the communion of believers living in Jesus Christ and the Spirit with the Father. It has its origin and prototype in the Trinity in which there is both distinction of persons and unity based on love, not subordination.

3. Since the Church in history is constituted by the Spirit as the body of Christ, the continuity of the Church with its origin results from the active presence of the Spirit. This continuity is expressed in and by historical forms (such as Scripture and sacraments) which give visibility to the continuing presence of the Spirit but it does not result merely from a historical process.

4. Sharing in Christ and the Spirit, the local church is at once independent in its corporate existence: a church, and at the same time interdependent in relation to other churches.

The independent existence of the local church is expressed best in its eucharistic celebration. The sacramental celebration of the Lord's presence in the midst of his people through the working of the Spirit both proclaims the most profound realization of the Church and realizes what it proclaims in the measure that the community opens itself to the Spirit.

5. The independence of local eucharistic communities, in the disciplinary and constitutional spheres, was curtailed in the early church as soon as priests became leaders of the local churches. The dependence of local churches on the territorial bishop found its counterpart in the dependence of bishops on the "first" bishop (archbishop, metropolitan, patriarch) as territories were divided among bishops.

The interplay of independence and communality on the local, territorial, and patriarchal levels mirrors the Church's prototype: the Trinity, which the Church can only approach.

6. The fundamental equality of all local churches is based on their historical and pneumatological continuity with the Church of the apostles. However, a real hierarchy of churches was recognized in response to the demands of the mission of the Church. Still this did not and cannot exclude the fundamental equality of all churches.

7. The Catholic and Orthodox Churches explain differently the meaning of this hierarchy of churches.

The Catholic Church recognizes that the position of Peter in the college of the apostles finds visible expression in the Bishop of Rome who exercises those prerogatives defined by Vatican Council I within the whole Church of Christ in virtue of this primacy.

The Orthodox Church finds this teaching at variance with its understanding of primacy within the whole Church. It appears to destroy the tension between independence and collegiality. For interdependence, a basic condition for collegiality, appears to be removed as a consequence of the jurisdictional and teaching role attributed to the Patriarch of the West by Vatican Council I. The Orthodox believe that a necessary primacy in the Church depends on the consent of the Church and is at present exercised by the Patriarch of Constantinople.

8. Our two traditions are not easily harmonized. Yet we believe that the Spirit is ever active to show us the way by which we can live together as one and many. We have the hope that we will be open to his promptings wherever they may lead. "For only so will harmony reign, in order that God through the Lord in the Holy Spirit may be glorified, the Father and the Son and the Holy Spirit" (Apostolic Canons, canon 34).

New York, NY
December 10, 1974
11th Meeting

THE PRINCIPLE OF ECONOMY: A JOINT STATEMENT

U. S. Theological Consultation, 1976

1. Members of the Orthodox-Roman Catholic Bilateral Consultation in the United States, having met since 1965, have examined openly, in a spirit of Christian faith and fraternal charity, a wide spectrum of theological questions judged to be crucial for mutual understanding between our two churches.

2. One topic which has been discussed with particular interest, especially during 1975 and 1976, has been *oikonomia* or ecclesiastical "economy." Because of the possible relevance of economy to the question of mutual recognition of churches, this topic, which has been important for the Orthodox, has received increasing attention among Anglicans and Roman Catholics in recent years.

3. In its discussion of economy the Consultation considered an introductory report prepared in 1971 by the Inter-Orthodox Preparatory Commission for the forthcoming Great Council of the Orthodox Church. Some Orthodox and Roman Catholic members were dissatisfied with the interpretation it gave to certain texts and historical incidents but found it a useful beginning for further discussion.

4. Our investigation has shown:

(a) The wealth of meanings which economy has had over the centuries;

(b) Some weaknesses in recent presentations of economy;

(c) The significance of economy for our ongoing ecumenical discussion.

5. At the most basic level, the Greek word *oikonomia* means management, arrangement, or determination in the strictly literal sense. A few overtones add to this basic meaning. *Oikonomia* may imply accommodation, prudent adaptation of means to an end, diplomacy and strategy and even dissimulation and the "pious lie." But *oikonomia* can also have highly positive connotations. It suggests the idea of stewardship, of management on behalf of another, on behalf of a superior.

6. In the New Testament the word *oikonomia* occurs nine times: Luke 16:2, 3, 4; 1 Corinthians 9:17; Ephesians 1:10, 3:2; 3:9; Colossians 1:25,

and 1 Timothy 1:4. In the parable of the steward, Luke 16, the word refers generically to stewardship, house management. In other New Testament usages such as Ephesians 3:9, the word is used to refer to God's purpose or *prothesis,* the economy of the mystery hidden for ages in God who created all things.

Also in Ephesians 1:8-10 we read that God "has made known to us in all wisdom and insight the mystery of his will, according to his purpose which he set forth in Christ as a plan for the fullness of time (*oikonomian tou plêromatos tôn kairôn*) to unite all things in him, things in heaven and things on earth." This usage is closely related to the patristic idea that in and through his person the incarnate and risen Christ brings to fulfillment all of creation (*anakephalaiôsis*). The Pauline corpus of letters uses *oikonomia* to refer to Paul's own ministry or pastoral office to make the word of God fully known.

7. These New Testament usages of *oikonomia* are further expanded by the fathers' understanding as summarized by the Inter-Orthodox Preparatory Commission's report which states:

> Apart from the meaning which concerns us here, the term *oikonomia* also denotes the divine purpose or *prothesis* (Eph. 1:10, 3:9-11), the mode of existence of the one Godhead in Trinity through mutual indwelling (*perichoresis*), its broad action in the world through the Church, divine providence, the savior's incarnation, the whole redeeming work of our Lord Jesus Christ and all the operations through which human nature was made manifest in the Son, from the time of his incarnation to his ascension into heaven.

God is seen as arranging all for the purpose of man's salvation and eternal well-being; and man, fashioned in the image and likeness of God, is viewed as being called to imitate this divine activity.

8. The word *oikonomia* later acquired additional uses in ecclesiastical contexts, in particular:

(a) The administration of penance, the arranging or managing of a penitent's reconciliation to the Church;

(b) The reception of those turning to the Church from heresy or schism;

(c) The restoration of repentant clergy and the reception of heretical or schismatic clergy as ordained.

In all these areas, however, the understanding of economy as responsible stewardship, imitating the divine economy, is maintained, excluding arbitrariness or capriciousness.

9. Recent presentations of economy often have included the following elements:

(a) Economy understood as a departure from or suspension of strict application (*akribeia*) of the church's canons and disciplinary norms, in many respects analogous to the West's *dispensatio*.

(b) Economy applied not only to canon law and church discipline, but to the sacraments as well. In this context, it has been argued, for example, that all non-Orthodox sacraments, from the point of view of strictness, are null and void but that the Orthodox Church can, by economy, treat non-Orthodox sacraments as valid. These views imply that the application of economy to the sacraments may vary according to circumstances, including such pastoral considerations as the attitude of the non-Orthodox group toward Orthodoxy, the well-being of the Orthodox flock, and the ultimate salvation of the person or groups that contemplate entering Orthodoxy.

10. These recent interpretations do not, in the judgment of the Consultation, do justice to the genuine whole tradition underlying the concept and practice of economy. The Church of Christ is not a legalistic system whereby every prescription has identical importance, especially when ancient canons do not directly address contemporary issues. Nor can the application of economy make something invalid to be valid, or what is valid to be invalid. Because the risen Christ has entrusted to the Church a stewardship of prudence and freedom to listen to the promptings of the Holy Spirit about today's problems of church unity, a proper understanding of economy involves the exercise of spiritual discernment.

We hope and pray therefore that our churches can come to discern in each other the same faith, that they can come to recognize each other as sister churches celebrating the same sacraments, and thus enter into full ecclesial communion.

Washington, DC
May 19, 1976
14th Meeting

REACTION OF THE ORTHODOX-ROMAN CATHOLIC DIALOGUE TO THE AGENDA OF THE GREAT AND HOLY COUNCIL OF THE ORTHODOX CHURCH

U.S. Theological Consultation, 1977

Introduction

The agenda for the forthcoming Great and Holy Council of the Orthodox Church was formulated by the Pre-Synodal Pan-Orthodox Conference, in Chambésy, Geneva, November 21-28, 1976. At the recommendation of His Eminence Metropolitan Meliton, chairman of the Conference, and at the invitation of His Eminence Archbishop Iakovos, co-chairman of our Consultation, the Orthodox-Roman Catholic Consultation in the U.S.A. discussed this agenda during its meeting in Washington, D.C., September 28-29, 1977. The Consultation welcomed the agenda as an important step toward the future Great and Holy Council of the Orthodox Church. The following suggestions summarize various observations on the agenda by members of the Consultation. We hope that these suggestions may be of some value and of some service in the preparation of the study documents to be used as the basis of the Great Council's initial discussions.

The Agenda

Topics 1-3. The first three topics (fasting regulations, impediments to marriage, calendar) involve practical issues which deserve the attention of the Orthodox Churches. They are a fitting subject of a Great Council both because a common solution to these issues would enhance the daily life of the Orthodox Christians, and because they offer to the council the opportunity for reflection on religious issues in the context of today's world.

Topic 1. We understand that some changes in fasting practices are advisable in view of the changing conditions and rhythm of life in some geographical areas of the Orthodox Church. It is not altogether clear, because of insufficient study, what has been the result of the changes pertaining to fasting regulations within the Roman Catholic Church. This should provide the basis for the exercise of caution in the matter of proposed changes within the Orthodox Church. Disciplinary changes pertaining to fasting practices do not automatically bring about the hoped-for spiritual fruits without careful preaching and instruction about the reasons for these adaptations. Another question to be raised with regard to these changes is to what extent common practices are necessary to preserve the unity of the Church. Finally, discussion about fasting practices should, above all, seriously raise the question of the proper Christian attitudes toward the material world, modern consumerism, availability of foods, modern hedonism, ecology, religious discipline in contemporary society, and the like.

Topic 2. The issue regarding impediments to marriage, pertaining to both clergy and laity, as well as the possible issue of the eligibility of married clergy for the episcopate, requires discussion on the basis of an explicitly formulated theology of marriage, the presbyterate, and the episcopate. Other related themes to be dealt with are human sexuality in general, celibacy and monasticism.

Topic 3. With regard to the calendar question, the impact of Christian agreement on a common Easter date would be considerable both within and without the Christian world. The calendar question also offers an opportunity to address the question of the relationship of the Church to modern science. However, a caution may also be sounded: Unprepared changes in calendar matters could signal enormous pastoral problems.

Topic 4. It seems to us that the resolution of the *diaspora* problem might serve to better express the communion ecclesiology of the Orthodox Church. The question of the *diaspora* should be investigated against the background of the idea of the *catholicity* of the Church. An attempt in this regard has already been made at the Second World Conference of Orthodox Schools of Theology, Penteli, Athens, August 19-29, 1976.

Topic 5. On the question of the relationship of the Orthodox Church to other Christian churches and communities, special attention should be given to promoting closer relations with the Oriental Churches, the Roman Catholic Church, the Old Catholic Church, and the Anglican Communion. We see that this may involve a thorough study of the principles which have traditionally determined Orthodox views regarding the *ecclesial status* of "separated Christians" and "separated churches."

Topic 6. The question of the ranking of autocephalous churches raises the issue of the practical and theological significance of rank *per se* within the Orthodox Churches. Why, for instance, has the actual importance—past or present—of certain churches in fostering the life of the entire Church been the crucial factor in their gaining prominence in rank among their family of churches?

Topic 7. It seems to us that under the theme of autonomy and autocephaly some consideration should be given to the *limits of uniformity* compatible with the unity of the Church.

Topic 8. We feel that the consideration of the terms under which autonomy is granted to local churches might take in view the history of the Roman Catholic Church's practice of removing the status of "missionary church" from locally established churches. The history of the relationship between Rome and the Roman Catholic Church of North and South America, as well as Africa, may be useful in this matter. In this connection, the Anglican model of granting independence to missionary churches may also be instructive for the Orthodox Church.

Topic 9. We hold that the presence of the Orthodox Church in the World Council of Churches is a valuable witness of the apostolic and catholic tradition. We feel that Orthodox participation in the ecumenical movement as outlined by the Patriarchal Encyclical of 1920 is an indispensable factor in Christian efforts toward cooperation and unity between Christian churches and communities.

Topic 10. We believe that in proclaiming Christian ideals to the world the Church may explicitly call attention to what it has learned from its experience in the world concerning basic Christian ideals. Hence theological reflection is needed on the presence of the Holy Spirit in the world outside the Church and the values of the world in the eyes of the Church. Under this topic the following specific themes may be given special attention:

(a) Justice and human rights;

(b) Ethical consensus on many important issues such as sexuality, cohabitation without marriage, abortion, medical issues pertaining to the preservation of life, and the like; and

(c) Study of the roles and methods of effective preaching, Christian education, and liturgical celebration toward spiritual renewal, *i.e.*, the nature of the experience of the living God over against contemporary secularism and the modern experience of the "absence of God."

Conclusion

The agenda of the Great and Holy Council of the Orthodox Church has in view the status and unity of the Orthodox Church primarily in practical terms. However, these matters cannot be adequately discussed without raising deeper theological issues about the nature of discipline, unity, the Church, the Gospel, and life. The Great Council can settle the practical issues in order to strengthen the life of the Orthodox Church. It can also make a real contribution to the proclamation of the Gospel in today's world through the witness of an effective Orthodox consensus on important theological issues pertaining to the Church's presence in to-day's world.

Washington, D.C.
September 29, 1977
16th Meeting

FAITH, SACRAMENTS AND THE UNITY
OF THE CHURCH

Joint International Commission, 1987

Introduction

1. After our meeting in Munich in 1982 and in accord with the Plan adopted by our commission during its first meeting at Rhodes in 1980, this fourth session of the commission has undertaken to consider the question of the relation between faith and sacramental communion.

2. As was stated in the Plan of our dialogue, which was approved at Rhodes, unity in faith is a presupposition for unity in the sacraments and especially in the holy eucharist. But this commonly accepted principle raises some fundamental issues which require consideration. Does faith amount to adhering to formulas or is it also something else? Faith, which is a divine gift, should be understood as a commitment of the Christian, a commitment of mind, heart, and will. In its profound reality it is also an *ecclesial* event which is realized and accomplished in and through the communion of the Church in its liturgical and especially in its eucharistic expression. This ecclesial and liturgical character of the faith must be taken seriously into consideration.

3. Given this fundamental character of faith, it is necessary to affirm that faith must be taken as a preliminary condition, already complete in itself, which precedes sacramental communion; and also that it is increased by sacramental communion, which is the expression of the very life of the Church and the means of the spiritual growth of each of its members. This question has to be raised in order to avoid a deficient approach to the problem of faith as a condition for unity. It should not, however, serve to obscure the fact that faith *is* such a condition, and that there cannot be sacramental communion without communion in faith both in the broader sense and in the sense of dogmatic formulation.

4. In addition to the question of faith as a presupposition of sacramental communion and in close connection with it, following the Plan of the dialogue, we have also considered in our meetings the relation of what are

called sacraments of initiation—*i.e.,* baptism, confirmation or chrismation and eucharist—to each other and to the unity of the Church. At this point it is necessary to examine if our two churches are confronted simply with a difference in liturgical practice or also in doctrine, since liturgical practice and doctrine are linked to one another. Should we consider these three sacraments as belonging to one sacramental reality or as three autonomous sacramental acts? It should also be asked if, for the sacraments of initiation, a difference in liturgical practice between the two traditions raises a problem of doctrinal divergence which could be considered as a serious obstacle to unity.

I. Faith and Communion in the Sacraments

5. Faith is inseparably both the gift of God who reveals himself and the response of the human person who receives this gift. This is the synergy of the grace of God and human freedom. The locus of this communion is the Church. In the Church, revealed truth is transmitted according to the tradition of the apostles based on the Scriptures, by means of the ecumenical councils, liturgical life and the fathers of the Church, and is put into practice by the members of the body of Christ. The faith of the Church constitutes the norm and the criterion of the personal act of faith. Faith is not the product of an elaboration or of a logical necessity, but of the influence of the grace of the Holy Spirit. The apostle Paul received grace "in the obedience of faith" (Rom. 1:15). St. Basil says on this subject: "Faith precedes discourse about God; faith and not demonstration. Faith, which is above logical methods, leads to consent. Faith is born not of geometric necessities, but of the energies of the Spirit" (*In Ps.* 115:1).

6. Every sacrament presupposes and expresses the faith of the Church which celebrates it. Indeed, in a sacrament the Church does more than profess and express its faith: It makes present the mystery it is celebrating. The Holy Spirit reveals the Church as the body of Christ, which he constitutes and makes grow. Thus the Church nourishes and develops the communion of the faith of its members through the sacraments.

1. True faith is a divine gift and free response of the human person.

7. Faith is a gift of the Holy Spirit. Through faith, God grants salvation. Through it, humanity has access to the mystery of Christ, who

constitutes the Church and whom the Church communicates through the Holy Spirit, who dwells in it. The Church can only transmit what causes it to exist. Now, there is only one mystery of Christ and God's gift is unique, whole and irrevocable (Rom. 11:29). As for its content, faith embraces the totality of doctrine and church practice relating to salvation. Dogma, conduct and liturgical life overlap each other to form a single whole and together constitute the treasure of faith. Linking in a remarkable fashion the theoretical and practical character of faith, St. John Damascene says: "This [faith] is made perfect by all that Christ decreed, faith through works, respect for and practice of the commandments of the One who has renewed us. Indeed, the one who does not believe according to the tradition of the catholic Church or who by unseemly works is in communion with the devil is an infidel" (*De fide orthodoxa* IV, 10, 83).

8. Given by God, the faith announced by the Church is proclaimed, lived and transmitted in a local, visible church in communion with all the local churches spread over the world, that is, the catholic Church of all times and everywhere. The human person is integrated into the body of Christ by his or her *koinonia* (communion) with this visible church, which nourishes this faith by means of the sacramental life and the word of God, and in which the Holy Spirit works in the human person.

9. One can say that, in this way, the gift of faith exists in the single Church in its concrete historical situation, determined by the environment and the times, and therefore in each and all of the believers under the guidance of their pastors. In human language and in a variety of cultural and historical expressions, the human person must always remain faithful to this gift of faith. Certainly, one cannot claim that the expression of the true faith, transmitted and lived in the celebration of the sacraments, exhausts the totality of the richness of the mystery revealed in Jesus Christ. Nevertheless, within the limits of its formulation and of the persons who receive it, it gives access to the whole truth of the revealed faith, that is, to the fullness of salvation and life in the Holy Spirit.

10. According to the Letter to the Hebrews, this faith is "the substance of things to be hoped for, the vision of unseen realities" (11:1). It grants a share in divine goods. It is also understood in terms of an existential confidence in the power and love of God, in acceptance of the eschatological promises as fulfilled in the person of Jesus Christ. Yet, as this Letter to the

Hebrews further indicates, faith also requires an attitude toward the milieu of existence and the world. This attitude is marked by readiness to sacrifice one's own will and to offer one's life to God and to others as Christ did on the cross. Faith brings one into association with the witness of Christ and with "a cloud of witnesses" (12:1) which envelop the Church.

11. Faith therefore involves a conscious and free response from the human person and a continual change of heart and spirit. Consequently, faith is an interior change and a transformation, causing one to live in the grace of the Holy Spirit who renews the human person. It seeks a reorientation toward the realities of the future kingdom, which even now is beginning to transform the realities of this world.

12. Faith is a presupposition of baptism and the entire sacramental life which follows it. Indeed, one participates through baptism in the death and resurrection of Jesus Christ (Rom. 6). Thus begins a process which continues all through Christian existence.

2. The liturgical expression of the faith.

13. In the Church, the sacraments are the privileged place where the faith is lived, transmitted and professed. In the Byzantine liturgical tradition the first prayer for entrance into the catechumenate asks the Lord for the candidate: "Fill him/her with faith, hope and love for you that he/she may understand that you are the one true God, with your only Son our Lord Jesus Christ and your Holy Spirit." Similarly, the first question the Church puts to the candidate for baptism in the Latin liturgical tradition is: "What do you ask of the Church?" and the candidate answers: "Faith." — "What does faith give you?" —"Eternal life."

14. Our two churches express their conviction in this matter by the axiom: *Lex orandi lex credendi.* For them the liturgical tradition is an authentic interpreter of revelation and hence the criterion for the expression of the true faith. Indeed, it is in the liturgical expression of the faith of our churches that the witness of the fathers and of the ecumenical councils celebrated together continues to be for believers the sure guide of faith. Independently of diversity in theological expression, this witness, which itself renders explicit the kerygma of the Holy Scriptures, is made

present in the liturgical celebration. In its turn, the proclamation of the faith nourishes the liturgical prayer of the people of God.

3. The Holy Spirit and the sacraments.

15. The sacraments of the Church are "sacraments of faith" where God the Father hears the *epiclêsis* (invocation) in which the Church expresses its faith by this prayer for the coming of the Spirit. In them, the Father gives his Holy Spirit, who leads us into the fullness of salvation in Christ. Christ himself constitutes the Church as his body. The Holy Spirit edifies the Church. There is no gift in the Church which cannot be attributed to the Spirit (Basil the Great, PG 30, 289). The sacraments are both gift and grace of the Holy Spirit, in Jesus Christ in the Church. This is expressed very concisely in an Orthodox hymn of Pentecost: "The Holy Spirit is the author of every gift. He makes prophecies spring forth. He renders priests perfect. He teaches wisdom to the ignorant. He makes fishermen into theologians and consolidates the institution of the Church."

16. Every sacrament of the Church confers the grace of the Holy Spirit because it is inseparably a sign recalling what God has accomplished in the past, a sign manifesting what he is effecting in the believer and in the Church, and a sign announcing and anticipating the eschatological fulfillment. In the sacramental celebration the Church thus manifests, illustrates and confesses its faith in the unity of God's design.

17. It will be noted that all sacraments have an essential relationship to the eucharist. The eucharist is the proclamation of faith *par excellence* from which is derived and to which every confession is ordered. Indeed, it alone proclaims fully, in the presence of the Lord which the power of the Spirit brings about, the marvel of the divine work. For the Lord sacramentally makes his work pass into the Church's celebration. The sacraments of the Church transmit grace, expressing and strengthening faith in Jesus Christ, and are thus witnesses of faith.

4. The faith formulated and celebrated in the sacraments: the symbols of faith.

18. In the eucharistic assembly the Church celebrates the event of the mystery of salvation in the eucharistic prayer (*anaphora*) for the glory of God. The mystery it celebrates is the very one which it confesses, while receiving the saving gift.

19. Although the content and finality of this eucharistic celebration have remained the same in the local churches, they have however used varied formulas and different languages which, according to the genius of different cultures, bring into relief particular aspects and implications of the unique salvation event. At the heart of ecclesial life, in the eucharistic *synaxis* (assembly), our two traditions, eastern and western, thus experience a certain diversity in the formulation of the content of the faith being celebrated.

20. From earliest times there has been joined to the administration of baptism a formulation of faith by means of which the local church transmits to the catechumen the essential content of the doctrine of the apostles. This symbol of the faith enunciates in compact form the essentials of the apostolic tradition, articulated chiefly in the confession of faith in the Holy Trinity and in the Church. When all the local churches confess the true faith, they transmit, in the rite of baptism, this one faith in the Father, Son and Holy Spirit. Nevertheless, at different times and in different places, the formulation has been expressed differently as circumstances required, using terms and propositions which were not identical from one formulary to another. All, however, respected the content of faith. The Eastern Church in its baptismal rite uses the Niceo-Constantinopolitan Creed. Faithful to its own tradition, the Western Church conveys to the catechumen the text called "the Apostles' Creed." This diversity of formulas from one church to another does not in itself indicate any divergence about the content of the faith transmitted and lived.

5. *Conditions for communion of faith.*

21. The first condition for a true communion between the churches is that each church makes reference to the Niceo-Constantinopolitan Creed as the necessary norm of this communion of the one Church spread throughout the whole world and across the ages. In this sense the true faith is presupposed for a communion in the sacraments. Communion is possible only between those churches which have faith, priesthood and the sacraments in common. It is because of this reciprocal recognition that the faith handed down in each local church is one and the same (as are the priesthood and the sacraments as well), that they recognize each other as genuine churches of God and that each of the faithful is welcomed by the churches as a brother or sister in the faith. At the same time, however, faith is deepened and clarified by the ecclesial communion lived

in the sacraments in each community. This ecclesial designation of faith as the fruit of sacramental life is verified at various levels of church life.

22. In the first place, by the celebration of the sacraments, the assembly proclaims, transmits and assimilates its faith.

23. Furthermore, in the celebration of the sacraments each local church expresses its profound nature. It is in continuity with the Church of the apostles and in communion with all the churches which share one and the same faith and celebrate the same sacraments. In the sacramental celebration of a local church, the other local churches recognize the identity of their faith with that church's and by that fact are strengthened in their own life of faith. Thus the celebration of the sacraments confirms the communion of faith between the churches and expresses it. This is why a member of one local church, baptized in that church, can receive the sacraments in another local church. This communion in the sacraments expresses the identity and unicity of the true faith which the churches share.

24. In the eucharistic concelebration between representatives of different local churches, identity of faith is particularly manifested and reinforced by the sacramental act itself. This is why councils, in which bishops led by the Holy Spirit express the truth of the Church's faith, are always associated with the eucharistic celebration. By proclamation of the one mystery of Christ and sharing of the one sacramental communion, the bishops, the clergy and the whole Christian people united with them are able to witness to the faith of the Church.

6. True faith and communion in the sacraments.

25. Identity of faith, then, is an essential element of ecclesial communion in the celebration of the sacraments. However, a certain diversity in its formulation does not compromise the *koinonia* between the local churches when each church can recognize, in the variety of formulations, the one authentic faith received from the apostles.

26. During the centuries of the undivided Church, diversity in the theological expression of a doctrine did not endanger sacramental communion. After the schism occurred, East and West continued to develop, but they did this separately from each other. Thus it was no longer possible for them to take unanimous decisions that were valid for both of them.

27. The Church as "pillar and bulwark of truth" (1 Tim. 3:15) keeps the deposit of faith pure and unaltered while transmitting it faithfully to its members. When the authentic teaching or unity of the Church was threatened by heresy or schism, the Church, basing itself on the Bible, the living tradition and the decisions of preceding councils, declared the correct faith authentically and infallibly in an ecumenical council.

28. When it is established that these differences represent a rejection of earlier dogmas of the Church and are not simple differences of theological expression, then clearly one is faced with a true division about faith. It is no longer possible to have sacramental communion. For faith must be confessed in words which express the truth itself. However, the life of the Church may occasion new verbal expressions of "the faith once and for all delivered to the saints" (Jude 3) if new historical and cultural needs call for them, as long as there is explicit desire not to change the content of the doctrine itself. In such cases, the verbal expression can become normative for unanimity in the faith. This requires criteria for judgment which allow a distinction between legitimate developments, under the inspiration of the Holy Spirit, and other ones.

Thus:

29. The continuity of the tradition: The Church ought to give suitable answers to new problems, answers based on the Scriptures and in accord and essential continuity with the previous expressions of dogmas.

30. The doxological meaning of the faith: Every liturgical development in one local church should be able to be seen by the others as in conformity with the mystery of salvation as it has received that mystery and celebrates it.

31. The soteriological meaning of the faith: Every expression of the faith should envision the human being's final destiny, as a child of God by grace, in his or her deification (*theôsis*) through victory over death and in the transfiguration of creation.

32. If a formulation of the faith contradicts one or another of these criteria, it becomes an obstacle to communion. If, on the other hand, such a particular formulation of the faith contradicts none of these criteria, then this formulation can be considered as a legitimate expression of faith and does not make sacramental communion impossible.

33. This requires that the theology of *theologoumena* be seriously considered. It is also necessary to clarify what concrete development occurring in one part of Christianity can be considered by the other as a legitimate development. Furthermore, it should be recognized that often the meaning of terms has changed in the course of time. For this reason, an effort should be made to understand every formula according to the intention of its authors so as not to introduce into it foreign elements or eliminate elements which, in the mind of the authors, were obvious.

7. The unity of the church in faith and sacraments.

34. In the Church the function of ministers is above all to maintain, guarantee and promote the growth of communion in faith and sacraments. As ministers of the sacraments and doctors of the faith, the bishops, assisted by other ministers, proclaim the faith of the Church, explain its content and its demands for Christian life and defend it against wrong interpretations which would falsify or compromise the truth of the mystery of salvation.

35. Charitable works of ministers, or their taking positions on the problems of a given time or place, are inseparable from the two functions of the proclamation and teaching of the faith, on the one hand, and the celebration of worship and sacraments, on the other.

36. Thus, unity of faith within a local church and between local churches is guaranteed and judged by the bishop, who is witness to the tradition, in communion with his people. It is inseparable from unity of sacramental life. Communion in faith and communion in the sacraments are not two distinct realities. They are two aspects of a single reality which the Holy Spirit fosters, increases and safeguards among the faithful.

II. The Sacraments of Christian Initiation: Their Relation to the Unity of the Church

37. Christian initiation is a whole in which chrismation is the perfection of baptism, and the eucharist is the completion of the other two.

The unity of baptism, chrismation and the eucharist in a single sacramental reality does not deny, however, their specific character. Thus, baptism with water and the Spirit is participation in the death and resurrection of Christ and new birth by grace. Chrismation is the gift of the Spirit to the baptized as

101

a personal gift. Received under the proper conditions, the eucharist, through communion in the body and blood of the Lord, grants participation in the kingdom of God, including forgiveness of sins, communion in divine life itself and membership in the eschatological community.

38. The history of the baptismal rites in East and West, as well as the way in which our common fathers interpreted the doctrinal significance of the rites, shows clearly that the three sacraments of initiation form a unity. That unity is strongly affirmed by the Orthodox Church. For its part, the Catholic Church also preserves it. Thus, the new Roman Ritual of Initiation declares that "the three sacraments of Christian initiation are so closely united that they bring the faithful to full capability for carrying out, through the Spirit, the mission which, in the world, belongs to the entire assembly of the Christian people" (*Prenotanda Generalia*, 2).

39. The pattern of administration of the sacraments which developed very early in the Church reveals how the Church understood the various stages of initiation as accomplishing, theologically and liturgically, incorporation into Christ by entering into the Church and growing in him through communion in his body and his blood in this Church. All of this is effected by the same Holy Spirit who constitutes the believer as a member of the body of the Lord.

40. The early pattern included the following elements:

41. 1. For adults, a period of spiritual probation and instruction during which the catechumens were formed for their definitive incorporation into the Church;

42. 2. Baptism by the bishop assisted by his priests and deacons, or administered by priests assisted by deacons, preceded by a profession of faith and various intercessions and liturgical services;

43. 3. Confirmation or chrismation in the West by the bishop or in the East by the priest when the bishop was absent, by means of the imposition of hands or by anointing with holy chrism or by both;

44. 4. The celebration of the holy eucharist, during which the newly baptized and confirmed were admitted to the full participation in the body of Christ.

45. Those three sacraments were administered in the course of a single, complex liturgical celebration. There followed a period of further

catechetical and spiritual maturation through instruction and frequent participation in the eucharist.

46. This pattern remains the ideal for both churches, since it corresponds the most exactly possible to the appropriation of the scriptural and apostolic tradition accomplished by the early Christian churches which lived in full communion with each other.

47. The baptism of infants, which has been practiced from the beginning, became in the Church the most usual procedure for introducing new Christians into the full life of the Church. In addition, certain local changes took place in liturgical practice in consideration of the pastoral needs of the faithful. These changes did not concern the theological understanding of the fundamental unity, in the Holy Spirit, of the whole process of Christian initiation.

48. In the East, the temporal unity of the liturgical celebration of the three sacraments was retained, thus emphasizing the unity of the work of the Holy Spirit and the fullness of the incorporation of the child into the sacramental life of the Church.

In the West, it was often preferred to delay confirmation so as to retain contact of the baptized person with the bishop. Thus, priests were not ordinarily authorized to confirm.

49. The essential points of the doctrine of baptism on which the two churches are agreed are the following:

1. The necessity of baptism for salvation;

2. The effects of baptism, particularly new life in Christ and liberation from original sin;

3. Incorporation into the Church by baptism;

4. The relation of baptism to the mystery of the Trinity;

5. The essential link between baptism and the death and resurrection of the Lord;

6. The role of the Holy Spirit in baptism;

7. The necessity of water, which manifests baptism's character as the bath of new birth;

50. On the other hand, differences concerning baptism exist between the two churches:

1. The fact that the Catholic Church, while recognizing the primordial importance of baptism by immersion, ordinarily practices baptism by infusion;

2. The fact that in the Catholic Church a deacon can be the ordinary minister of baptism.

51. Moreover, in certain Latin churches, for pastoral reasons, for example in order to better prepare confirmands at the beginning of adolescence, the practice has become more and more common of admitting to first communion baptized persons who have not yet received confirmation even though the disciplinary directives which called for the traditional order of the sacraments of Christian initiation have never been abrogated. This inversion, which provokes objections or understandable reservations both by Orthodox and Roman Catholics, calls for deep theological and pastoral reflection because pastoral practice should never lose sight of the meaning of the early tradition and its doctrinal importance. It is also necessary to recall here that baptism conferred after the age of reason in the Latin Church is now always followed by confirmation and participation in the eucharist.

52. At the same time, both churches are preoccupied with the necessity of assuring the spiritual formation of the neophyte in the faith. For that, they wish to emphasize on the one hand that there is a necessary connection between the sovereign action of the Spirit, who realizes through the three sacraments the full incorporation of the person into the life of the Church, the latter's response and that of his community of faith and, on the other hand, that the full illumination of the faith is only possible when the neophyte, of whatever age, has received the sacraments of Christian initiation.

53. Finally, it is to be recalled that the Council of Constantinople, jointly celebrated by the two churches in 879-880, determined that each see would retain the ancient usages of its tradition, the Church of Rome preserving its own usages, the Church of Constantinople its own, and the thrones of the East also doing the same (cf. Mansi XVII, 489 B).

Bari
June 10, 1987
Second Session, Fourth Plenary Meeting

A RESPONSE TO THE JOINT INTERNATIONAL COMMISSION FOR THEOLOGICAL DIALOGUE BETWEEN THE ORTHODOX CHURCH AND THE ROMAN CATHOLIC CHURCH REGARDING THE BARI DOCUMENT: "FAITH, SACRAMENTS, AND THE UNITY OF THE CHURCH"

U.S. Theological Consultation, 1988

Several years ago, the official Eastern Orthodox-Roman Catholic Consultation in the United States, established by the Standing Conference of Canonical Orthodox Bishops (SCOBA) and the National Conference of Catholic bishops (NCCB), at its 26th meeting (May 23-25, 1983), prepared a response to the first common statement of the Joint International Commission for Theological Dialogue between the Orthodox Church and the Roman Catholic Church, namely "The Mystery of the Church and of the Eucharist in the Light of the Mystery of the Holy Trinity," the Munich Statement (dated July 6, 1982). Our response was sent to the presiding hierarchy of the Joint Commission and was subsequently published in various theological journals.

In the United States Consultation we have followed the work of the International Commission with great interest. In fact, two of the Roman Catholic members of our own Consultation are also members of the International Commission (Msgr. Frederick McManus and Rev. John Long). At the 33rd meeting in our series of consultations that began in 1965, we completed and submitted to the International Commission an agreed statement entitled: "Apostolicity as God's Gift in the Life of the Church" (dated November 1, 1986). This statement was formulated especially with the future agenda of the International Consultation in mind since apostolicity is one of the themes scheduled for study at the International Commission's future meetings.

Since the International Commission recently made public its second common statement: "Faith, Sacraments, and the Unity of the Church," the Bari Statement (August 1, 1987), we in the United States Consultation have analyzed the document at several meetings and in private study. We now wish to submit to the International Commission a common response to this latest text.

We would also like to take this opportunity to encourage the International Commission to invite theological faculties and societies, ecumenical associations, diocesan and national ecumenical commissions around the world to respond to its future statements. We also urge the Commission to distribute its texts more widely and in a more official way, with an accompanying letter by the co-chairmen situating the document. The reception and response processes not only will supply local reflections to the International Commission but also will provide opportunities to Orthodox and Roman Catholics to share their Christian faith. Given the importance of its work, the International Commission should seriously consider a future revision of its statements and their publication together for circulation to a much wider audience, perhaps with commentary.

That a second joint statement of the International Commission has been published, despite some delays and setbacks as reported in the press, is a consoling sign of the continuing graces being poured out upon our churches by the Holy Spirit. As does the Munich Statement, this text moves us farther away from our long history of mutual estrangement. We recognize that this common statement does not pretend to be an exhaustive treatment of all the theological issues on these subjects, but addresses rather issues that might hinder mutual understanding and prevent eventual full communion. We hail this achievement and unite our prayers with those of the members of the Joint International Commission as they prepare to meet in June 1988 in New Valamo, Finland, to study together the theology of ordination.

Our response to the Bari Statement has two parts: first, some brief remarks regarding its methodology, and some questions for clarification; second, a list of needed corrections to the English-language translation of the document made in light of a close study of the French text.

Part One: Our Reactions to the Bari Statement

1. First of all, three preliminary remarks. (a) In our judgment, Sacred Scripture is used too sparingly in the document. Specifically, more atten-

tion should have been given to the way that "faith" is described in the New Testament. (b) We applaud the serious effort to avoid polemical or scholastic terms. (c) As was the case with the Munich text, it is not clear for what groups of readers this document is intended.

2. Regarding the theology of faith and of communion (*koinonia*) there is much to be praised in the document. Faith is appropriately described as a "synergy of the grace of God and human freedom." That the Church is the locus for the flowering of faith and that the Church's faith constitutes the norm and the criterion of the personal act of faith are carefully stated (no. 5). The importance of the liturgy for nurturing faith is well described. However, the theological explanation of faith in the text is often confusing and incomplete. The term "faith" sometimes is used in such a broad way that it is seen as an equivalent for the notion of the kerygma, the entire Christian message, or even restrictively to a summary of religious truths that Christians include in their recitation of the symbol or creed. Often the text seems to reify faith, to reduce it to an inert deposit which needs only to be handed on (nos. 5, 14, 21, 27). Special clarification also should be given to the document's use of the expression "true faith."

When it is stated that "Faith embraces the totality of doctrine and church practice relating to salvation" (no. 7) this seems too comprehensive. The document is not clear when it states that "faith must be taken as a preliminary condition, already complete in itself, which precedes sacramental communion" (no. 3).

3. Particularly successful in our judgment is the way that the local church is related to the Church universal (cf. nos. 19 and 23). This reflects a sensitive formulation of modern eucharistic ecclesiology. These sections touch on the importance of inculturation and contextualization of preaching and theology; they stress that local churches "...have used varied formulas and different languages which, according to the genius of different cultures, bring into relief particular aspects and implications of the unique salvation event" (no. 19). The text does not, however, take into account the fact that recent official Roman Catholic documents have been preferring the expression "particular church" rather than "local church" so as not to give undue prominence to the geographical factor.

4. What is touched upon briefly in the Munich Document about faith's relationship to concrete social issues (*e.g.* II, 4, para. 3) is happily further strengthened in the Bari text by reference to the importance of charitable works of ministers and their response to social problems (no. 35). We would welcome continued development of these themes in future documents.

5. There is sometimes a certain overemphasis on the role of bishops and presbyters in the document to the neglect of the ministry of the entire people of God. In nos. 34-36 it would be well to mention the important task of theologians and the role of the whole Church in the process of reception. The bishops' teaching is not performed in isolation from the rest of the Church. Hence we applaud the clarification mentioned in no. 36 that, although the bishop is guarantor and judge of the unity of faith, he is so in communion with his people.

6. An attempt is made in nos. 25-33 to distinguish legitimate from illegitimate developments in the Church. The text implies that this task of distinguishing between them is not difficult, whereas the history of the Church has in fact shown that the process of discernment is gradual and sometimes painful. The three criteria for distinguishing (nos. 29-31) are too vague. Is it clear that everything that meets these three criteria "can be considered a legitimate expression of faith" (no. 32)?

7. Throughout the document, the "sovereign action of the Holy Spirit" (no. 52) is stressed, but the relationship of Son and Spirit has not been explored systematically. There are occasional echoes of the very balanced formulations of the Munich Statement (*e.g.* in the first two sentences of no. 15), but there could have been more precision elsewhere.

8. We commend the statement's affirmation that baptism is the beginning of "a process which continues all through Christian existence" (no. 12). We also welcome the effort to relate historical changes in liturgical practice to the pastoral needs of the Church (nos. 47-49).

9. The text places such a heavy emphasis on the eucharist as to suggest that baptism itself does not already achieve entry into divine communion and participation in the eschatological community (no. 37). Baptism should be given the due prominence which early Christian tradition accorded it.

10. The Bari Statement appeals frequently to the authoritative witness of the liturgy (see especially no. 14). We believe, however, that greater attention to the history of the liturgy of Christian initiation would be desirable. Here we might offer two examples: (a) As the sources indicate, the primitive Eastern (*e.g.* Syrian) pattern of initiation was different in certain respects (*e.g.* in the place of anointing) from that presented as "early" and "ideal" by the statement (nos. 39, 40, 46). We believe that this pattern, suggesting as it does a pneumatologically conditioned christology, has important implications for the relationship of Son and Spirit, a subject which we mentioned earlier in point 7 above. (b) In the early Church the bishop may indeed have presided in the baptismal liturgy, but as the historical evidence suggests others performed many of the sacramental actions. This may have important implications for an issue raised in no. 50, point 2.

Part Two: Improvements Needed in the English Translation

The English translator(s) should be commended of the use of inclusive, non-sexist language throughout.

No. 2: The French word *communément* should be translated here not as "commonly" but as "in common."

No. 5: Correct the English "Faith is not the product of an elaboration or of a logical necessity" to read "Faith is not the product of a logical elaboration and necessity" (*La foi n'est pas le produit d'une élaboration et d'une nécessité logiques*).

No. 9: Correct the English "exists in the single Church" to read "exists in the one Church" (*dans l'unique Eglise*).

No. 10: Correct the English "...an attitude towards the milieu of existence" to read: "regarding existence and the world" (*à l'endroit de l'existence et du monde*).

No. 14: Regarding what is said of the principle: *Lex credendi lex orandi*, the English translation states that it is "the criterion for the expression of the true faith." Correct to read "criterion for" without the "the." (There are other criteria!)

No. 15: Correct the English "The Holy Spirit edifies the Church" to read "The Holy Spirit builds up the Church" (*édifie*).

No. 21: Correct "In this sense the true faith is presupposed..." to read "In this sense true faith is supposed."

Nos. 21-23: "Communion" (*koinonia*) is better translated here and throughout as "sharing" (to avoid confusion with the act of receiving the eucharist).

Nos. 24 and 25: Because of the possible misunderstanding of the word "identity," use an alternate translation for "Identity of faith..." to read "Sameness of faith..." (*l'identité de la foi*).

No. 28: Correct the English "the content of the doctrine itself" to read "the very content of the doctrine" (*le contenu même de la doctrine*).

No. 29: Correct "in accord and essential continuity" to read "in essential accord and continuity" (*en accord et continuité essentielles*).

No. 37: It is better to avoid the English word "membership" because of the difficulties establishing who is and who is not a "member." Better to say "belonging to the eschatological community."

Also, avoid the expression "specific character" because of possible misunderstanding of the word "character." Better to say with the French "specificity."

Also, do not say "baptism with water and the Spirit" but rather "baptism in water and in the Spirit" to retain the biblical allusion.

No. 38: Correct "The Catholic Church also preserves it" to read "The Catholic Church also maintains (*maintient*) that unity."

Also, as in the previous draft of the Bari Statement, the citation from the new Roman Ritual of Initiation is quite inaccurate in the French and consequently the English text. The 1973 text says in no. 2: "Thus the three sacraments of Christian initiation closely combine to bring the faithful to the full stature of Christ and to enable them to carry out the mission of the entire people of God in the Church and in the world." This is not exactly what the Bari text says. In fact it is misleading when it says "the mission which, in the world, belongs to the entire assembly..."

No. 43: There is a mistake in the French original which is corrected in the English text: not "*ou par l'un des deux*" but rather "*par les deux.*"

No. 50: Avoid in English the word "ordinarily" because of possible confusion with the word "ordinary" in what follows. Better to say "usually."

No. 51: Correct the misspelling in the French text: *latines* not *latine.*

No. 51: Translate "common" (*répandu*) by the English word "widespread."

Also, the French verb *rappeler* (used here in this section twice) first translated as "called for" seems inaccurate: "Disciplinary directives which called for the traditional order..." Better to say "which recalled the traditional order..." This is how the word is translated later in this section.

No. 52: This section bears the marks of hurried composition. The second sentence is almost incomprehensible (the two items being connected by the preposition "between" are not clear, probably because a word is omitted before the French word for "response"). It is suggested that this section might be rewritten as follows:

> At the same time both churches are very concerned that the neophyte receive the necessary spiritual formation in the faith. Both churches share two convictions that follow: (a) that there is a vital connection between the sovereign action of the Holy Spirit effecting (by means of the three sacraments) a person's full incorporation in the life of the Church and the response to the gift of faith by an individual believer or by the community of faith; and (b) that full illumination

into the faith is possible only when the neophyte (at whatever age it happens) has received the sacraments of Christian initiation.

No. 53: The last sentence in the document appeals to Mansi XVII, 489 B. In an earlier draft the text was cited verbatim but here is rather confusedly summarized. The word/translation "thrones" probably refers to "[episcopal] sees."

Crestwood, NY
June 2, 1988
36th Meeting

Section 3

The Sacrament of Order in the Life of the Church

INTRODUCTION TO SECTION THREE

Unity in faith, unity in sacraments—for Catholics and Orthodox these two closely interrelated aspects of unity are inseparable from consideration of the place of ordained ministry in the life of the Church. The high degree of agreement of Catholics and Orthodox on this subject is evident, for example, in the U.S. Consultation's response to the ministry section of the Lima Document *Baptism, Eucharist and Ministry* (pp. 69-75). Both churches insist upon the sacramental nature of the ordained ministry and regard it as an integral part of the apostolic tradition. Both consider as normative "the three-fold ministry" of bishop, presbyter and deacon; "the historic succession of office holders in the episcopal ministry; the exclusive conferral of ordination by those entrusted with the *episkopê* of the community; and the presidency of the eucharist exclusively by an ordained minister." The chief outstanding difference lies not in their understanding of the ordained ministry *per se* but in their interpretation of the "Petrine office." Nevertheless, Catholics and Orthodox have found it important to address the subject of the ordained ministry together if only because exploration of the subject may bring them closer together on other issues as well.

The U.S. Consultation's agreed statement on "The Pastoral Office" (May 1976) was formulated "in the interest of furthering the mutual recognition of the pastoral office exercised in each of our churches." The statement first outlines the historical trajectory of the understanding and function of the ordained ministry in the Catholic and the Orthodox Churches. (As the earlier agreed statement on the Church also suggests, this attentiveness to historical considerations has been a hallmark of the U.S. Consultation's work.) In its important second section, the statement sets forth in very direct terms the churches' common understanding of the pastoral office. Finally, in its third section, the statement addresses certain recent trends and disputed questions affecting both traditions. These include the question of clerical celibacy, marriage after ordination, ordination of women, and life-style of those called to pastoral office.

During the long hiatus which followed the Joint International Commission's Munich Statement (1982) and the U.S. Consultation's response to it (1983), the U.S. Consultation took up the study of apostolicity. It did so for at least two reasons:

—Particularly in its Bari Statement, the Joint International Commission had spoken of "the one authentic faith received from the apostles" (¶25), the articulation of this faith in the form of creeds which express "in compact form the essentials of the apostolic tradition" (¶20), and the place of this faith and its creedal articulation in Christian initiation. It also spoke of the special role of ordained ministers in maintaining, guaranteeing and promoting growth of communion in faith and sacraments. The U.S. Consultation believed that at this point it could best contribute to the ongoing work of the International Commission by addressing the subject of apostolicity in a synthetic fashion.

—In the judgment of the U.S. Consultation, the time was ripe at least for its own member-theologians, who by this point had worked together amicably and fruitfully for a number of years, to address together the subject of primacy and the "Petrine office." A study of apostolicity would be a natural first step towards this objective.

The resulting agreed statement, "Apostolicity as God's Gift in the Life of the Church," was completed in November 1986 and submitted to the co-presidents of the Joint International Commission for their consideration. Several points in this carefully formulated text call for comment:

—The apostolicity of the Church has both an historical and an eschatological aspect. This means that "here and now the life of the Church—whether expressed in authoritative teaching, in judgment and discipline, or in the eucharist itself—is being molded, corrected and governed by what has been received from the past *and* by what is awaited at the last day" (¶7).

—In the life of the Church and of each Christian, apostolicity is continually experienced within the mystery of Christian initiation, in the baptismal act of receiving and giving back the Church's apostolic faith. "Apostolicity therefore is by no means unique to or limited to the realm of hierarchical ministry." Just as the faithful through baptism share in Christ's royal priesthood, so also they "become bearers of the Church's apostolicity" (¶9).

116

—How, finally, do Orthodox and Catholics understand church structures "which attest to and assure the unity of the churches in their apostolic confession"? (¶11) Here the statement cautions against assessments which would polarize Eastern and Western conceptions. As it points out, "there is no need to claim that what may characterize one tradition in a particular way exhausts the content of that tradition or, in turn, must be absent from another tradition as a matter of course" (¶14).

During the years intervening between the Joint International Commission's plenary session on Crete (1984) and the eventual adoption of "Faith, Sacraments, and the Unity of the Church" in Bari (1987), its subcommissions had worked on what would become the Commission's third agreed statement, "The Sacrament of Order in the Sacramental Structure of the Church, with Particular Reference to the Importance of Apostolic Succession for the Sanctification and Unity of the People of God." The fifth plenary session of the Commission, meeting at the New Valamo Monastery in Finland in 1988, was able to adopt the statement relatively swiftly. Though soon overshadowed by other more urgent developments in Orthodox-Catholic relations, the Valamo Statement was a major theological accomplishment.

Building upon the Munich Statement, the Valamo Statement emphasizes the close link between the work of Christ and the work of the Spirit (section I). Christ and his ministry is present in the Church even now by the power of the Spirit, who "constitutes the earnest of the perfect realization of God's design for the world" (¶3). Ecclesial ministry therefore must be understood in an eschatological perspective. It is spoken of as sacramental because it is "bound to the eschatological reality of the kingdom" (¶11), just as the Church itself is "the sacrament *par excellence*, the anticipated manifestation of the final realities, the foretaste of God's kingdom" (¶22). After discussing the place of the priesthood in the divine economy of salvation (section II), the Valamo Statement goes on to examine in greater detail the ministry of the bishop, presbyter and deacon (section III). These are not viewed in isolation, however. As the statement emphasizes, "the various ministries converge in the eucharistic synaxis" (¶24). If the Church is above all a eucharistic organism in which and by which the *eschaton* is anticipated in the time and space of this world, it follows that its ministry must be seen above all in reference to the eucharist.

It is in this perspective, according to the statement, that the distinctive ministry of the bishop must be understood: "Since it culminates in the celebration of the eucharist in which Christian initiation is completed, through which all become one body of Christ, the ministry of the bishop is, among all the charisms and ministries which the Spirit raises up, a ministry for gathering in unity" (¶25). While focusing in this section on the bishop's ministry of unity within the local church, the Valamo Statement affirms that "this unity of the local church is inseparable from the universal communion of the churches" (¶26). Certain aspects of this affirmation are developed at greater length in the fourth and final section of the statement, which is devoted to apostolic succession. Among other things the statement here surveys the specific means by which communion among the churches has been maintained in the course of church history, focusing on the council of bishops and on the place of the first bishop within the conciliar structure. In conclusion the Valamo Statement notes: "It is in this perspective of communion among local churches that the question could be addressed of primacy in the Church in general and in particular, the primacy of the bishop of Rome, a question which constitutes a serious divergence among us and which will be discussed in the future" (¶55).

Following its practice of reacting jointly to the agreed statements of the Joint International Commission, the U.S. Consultation in 1989 responded to the Valamo Statement. While noting several points in need of clarification or further exploration, most notably the relationship between bishop and presbyter, in general it judged the theology and thrust of the statement very favorably. In conclusion it noted that the issue of primacy, raised in the last paragraph of the Valamo Statement, "is a matter that surely will be treated in the next planned statement on the 'Ecclesiological and Canonical Consequences of the Sacramental Structure of the Church: Conciliarity and Authority in the Church,' scheduled for discussion at Munich in June 1990" (¶27). Unfortunately the Joint International Commission has not yet been able to complete that statement.

The U.S. Consultation's agreed statement on "The Pastoral Office" (¶8), the Joint International Commission's Valamo Statement (¶30), and the U.S. Consultation's reaction to that statement (¶19) all call attention to the conviction of both the Catholic and the Orthodox Churches that ordination is unrepeatable. In the words of the Valamo Statement, "the gift conferred consecrates the recipient once for all to the service of the Church." Catholic and Orthodox theologians have explained this nonrepeatability of ordination in different ways, however. In 1988, following its seventh meeting, the Joint Committee of Orthodox and Catholic Bishops released a summary of its discussions on "Ordination" (October 1988). As the document indicates, for both churches "'reordination' is impossible." Among other things this means that, "for both Orthodox Christians and Roman Catholics, when a member of the clergy who has been ordained in a church that shares with them an understanding of the priesthood and by a bishop in an unquestionable apostolic succession is received into either the Orthodox or the Roman Catholic Church, his ordination should be recognized." At the same time, the document prudently notes that, "until such time when the practice of the Orthodox Church will be unified, these cases will be decided by each autocephalous Orthodox Church."

Following up themes and issues explored in its 1986 statement on apostolicity, the U.S. Consultation in 1989 issued "An Agreed Statement on Conciliarity and Primacy in the Church." It reiterates and expands upon a point made in many other agreed statements: "Each local church, recognized in its celebration of the Eucharist, is a full sacramental realization of the one Church of Christ, provided it remains within the full apostolic faith and is bound in love and mutual recognition to the other communities who profess that faith" (¶4). It prefaces this, however, by calling attention to the ecclesiological significance of baptism and of the profession of the apostolic faith which is inseparable from baptism (¶2). The statement goes on to acknowledge that the same Spirit who distributes and orders charisms within the local church "also manifests his presence in the institutions which keep local communities in an ordered and loving community with one another" (¶5). The two most important expressions of this have been the gathering of bishops in synods and the primacy of one bishop among his episcopal colleagues (¶6). After examining synods and primacy more closely, the statement points to differences in the way these two institutions function within the Catholic and the Orthodox Churches. By emphasizing their interdependence, however, it also suggests that these differences may not be as difficult to reconcile as the churches once thought.

THE PASTORAL OFFICE: A JOINT STATEMENT

U. S. Theological Consultation, 1976

Introduction

1. Both the Orthodox and the Roman Catholic Churches acknowledge that the pastoral office, exercised by bishops and priests, is an essential element of the structure of the Church founded by Jesus Christ.

The members of this dialogue, while recognizing this fact, also understand that certain changes have taken place in the exercise and in the understanding of this office both in the early Church and later in the separated churches.

2. In the interest of furthering the mutual recognition of the pastoral office exercised in each of our churches this Consultation has judged it useful:

(a) To record the results of its discussions of the understanding and function of pastoral office in the history of the Orthodox and the Roman Catholic Churches;

(b) To formulate a statement concerning important elements of our common understanding of pastoral office;

(c) To single out recent discussions on the subject of pastoral office which seem to require the serious attention of both churches.

I. Historical Considerations

According to the New Testament, the witnesses to the resurrection formed the original Church on the basis of their common faith in Christ. Within this group, chosen witnesses were given special authority by the risen Lord to exercise pastoral leadership. While this leadership seems to have been exercised in a variety of concrete ways in the New Testament period, the tendency towards a presbyteral form of government, presided over by a bishop, was apparently more common.

At the outset of the second century this movement towards a more "mono-episcopal" form of local church government continues to develop.

120

In the course of the second and third centuries the bishop gradually emerges everywhere as the center of unity of his own local church and the visible point of contact with other local churches. He is responsible for faith and order locally.

During this period the presbyterate comes to share in the exercise of more aspects of the pastoral office in subordination to the bishop. This subordinate role is seen especially in presbyteral ordination, which is reserved to bishops.

In accord with the development whereby the presbyterate is explicitly included in the pastoral office of the bishop under virtually all aspects, the presbyter is viewed as having the same relationship to Christ as the bishop. Both are seen directly to represent Christ before the community and, at the same time, to represent the Church, as confessing believers, in their official acts.

However, the tendency in the West towards the dissociation of pastoral office from its ecclesial context provided a difference of perspective on the conditions for the valid exercise of the functions of pastoral office. Thus, while Orthodoxy never accepted in principle the concept of "absolute ordination," this notion did find acceptance in the West in the late Middle Ages.

However, the Second Vatican Council's stress on the pastoral dimension of priestly office corrected the weakness of western theology of priesthood. Furthermore, the fathers of the council refocused attention on two major traditional themes: (a) the sacramental nature of episcopal consecration; and (b) the collegial or corporate character of each of these orders, a theme which harmonizes with the traditional Orthodox perspective.

II. Our Common Understanding of the Pastoral Office in the Orthodox and Catholic Traditions

Although the historical perspective points out many divergent practices through the centuries, the members of the Consultation recognize the following as important elements towards the development of a consensus.

1. In the rites of ordination of bishop and presbyter a commission is bestowed by the Holy Spirit to build up the Church (Eph. 4:12) on the cornerstone of Christ and the foundation of the apostles (Eph. 2:20).

121

2. Presiding at the eucharist belongs to those ordained to pastoral office: bishops and presbyters. This exclusive connection between ordination to the pastoral office and the celebration of the eucharist affirms that the pastoral office is realized most directly in this celebration of the faith. In the eucharist the Lord builds up his Church by uniting it with his saving worship and communicating his personal presence through his sacramental body and blood (1 Cor. 10:16-17).

3. The offices of bishop and presbyter are different realizations of the sacrament of order. The different rites for ordination of bishop and presbyter show that a sacramental conferral of office takes place by the laying on of hands with the ordination prayer which expresses the particular significance of each office.

4. While both bishop and presbyter share the one ministry of Christ, the bishop exercises authoritative leadership over the whole community. The presbyter shares in the pastoral office under the bishop.

5. Ordination in apostolic succession is required for the bestowal of pastoral office because pastoral office is an essential element of the sacramental reality of the Church: Ordination effectively proclaims that pastoral office is founded on Christ and the Spirit who give the grace to accomplish the task of exercising the ministry of the apostles.

6. The fundamental reason why pastoral office is required for the celebration of the eucharist lies in the relationship of pastoral office to Church and the relationship of eucharist to Church. Pastoral office is a constitutive element of the structure of Church and the eucharist is the place where the Church most perfectly expresses and realizes itself. Consequently, the requirement of correspondence between the comprehensive ecclesial reality and the eucharist dictates the exercise of pastoral office.

7. Bishops and presbyters can only represent Christ as bishops and presbyters when they exercise the pastoral office of the Church. Therefore, the Church can recognize only an ordination which involves a bishop with a pastoral office and a candidate with a concrete title of service.

8. We have a common understanding of these effects of sacramental ordination: (a) the ordained is claimed permanently for the service of the Church and so cannot be "reordained"; (b) in the exercise of his office, he is distinct but not separated from the community; (c) he is not dependent

merely on his subjective capabilities for the exercise of his service, since he receives the special bestowal of the Spirit in ordination.

Catholic theologians have explained these elements in terms of *character,* priestly *character.* Similar elements are included in the Orthodox understanding of priesthood as a *charisma.* Both character and charisma stress the relationship of the ordained to the gift of the Holy Spirit on which the exercise of his ministry in service to the community depends.

III. Recent Trends and Disputed Questions in Both Traditions

Roman Catholic and Orthodox theologians today have addressed themselves to several major topics related to the theology of pastoral office.

1. Some Roman Catholic theologians are challenging the traditional presentation of the pastoral office as direct representation of Christ. They interpret pastoral office as directly representing the faith of the Church and, consequently, Christ who is the living source of the faith. From this viewpoint the peculiarity of pastoral office is situated in the public guardianship of the common matter of all believers: the mission of Christ.

2. The traditional exclusion of women from ordination to the pastoral office affects both Catholic and Orthodox theologians, but in a differing way. Concerning this issue, Catholic theologians are examining biblical data, traditional practice, theological and anthropological data. Since they have not reached a consensus, the question remains disputed among them.

Some Catholic theologians share the position of those Orthodox theologians who reaffirm the traditional practice of excluding women from the pastoral office and base this on the necessity of the iconic representation of Christ in the person of bishops and presbyters.

3. Two of the issues touching the life-style of those called to pastoral office come under serious consideration in both traditions: (a) the compatibility of ordination with occupations which are not directly part of the pastoral office, and (b) the existing practice of celibacy.

(a) Both Catholic and Orthodox theologians see a long tradition of ordained persons exercising certain occupations compatible with the pastoral office which are also seen to serve the sanctification of society.

(b) In the Orthodox Church questions are raised concerning a married episcopate and marriage after ordination. Among Catholics of the Latin rite the celibacy issue focuses on the possibility of also committing the pastoral office to a married clergy.

4. Faced with the important issue of mutual recognition of ministries, both Orthodox and Roman Catholic theologians are searching for criteria leading to such a goal.

Conclusion

The members of the Consultation draw the following conclusions: despite differing emphases, both churches agree on the nature and forms of pastoral office; theologians of both traditions perceive that they have common as well as distinct questions to be resolved.

Washington, DC
May 19, 1976
14th Meeting

APOSTOLICITY AS GOD'S GIFT IN THE LIFE
OF THE CHURCH

U.S. Theological Consultation, 1986

1. In the creed we confess the Church to be "one, holy, catholic, and *apostolic.*" What is meant by this term? Modern scholarship, reflected in many joint and common statements of the ecumenical dialogue, has advanced discussion of this question in several important areas. For example, historico-critical study of the Bible has called attention to the ways in which the word *apostolos* is used in the New Testament as well as to the distinctive role of the Twelve and to the place of Peter in the New Testament. So also, historians of doctrine have called attention to the importance of the struggle against gnosticism in the second century for the development of the concept of apostolic succession.

2. In 1985 the North American Orthodox-Roman Catholic Bilateral Consultation took up the study of apostolicity. Our papers and discussions prompted the following reflections, which we offer now particularly with the hope that they will help to advance the work of the International Orthodox-Roman Catholic Consultation as it moves forward in its own discussion of apostolicity.

3. It is not our intention simply to repeat or even to summarize the many scholarly foundational studies on apostolicity, though at times we shall call attention to points raised in them. Rather, we wish to examine certain other aspects of this subject, for we are convinced that, as Orthodox and Roman Catholics, we share a perception of apostolicity and of its implications for church structures which in some sense has united us even during periods of mutual antagonism. By trying to articulate this shared perception, we hope to carry our own discussion of apostolicity beyond the points of agreement and convergence already reached by others involved in ecumenical dialogue.

4. Biblical scholarship has drawn our attention to the fact that the New Testament understanding of apostolicity is not so one-dimensional as both our traditions have sometimes appeared to presume. The differing

theological emphases found there—St. Paul's claim to apostolic title or the tendency in Luke-Acts to identify the apostles with the Twelve—suggest that there is a continuing need for theological reflection on apostolicity, a task to which we today are also called.

5. In biblical language apostles are those who have been sent out to perform a task in the name of another. They are endowed with the authority and freedom to act authentically on behalf of the one who sent them. Apostles in the New Testament are witnesses to the risen Christ who are explicitly commissioned by him to spread the gospel of his resurrection to the world and to promote, in his name, the active presence and power of God's kingdom. We call the Church apostolic first of all because the Church continues to share this mission in history, continues to be authorized by the risen Lord, through its continuing structures, as his legitimate representative.

6. For Orthodox and Roman Catholics, therefore, that the Church is apostolic is not simply a statement but an object of faith. The creed says: "I *believe* one holy, catholic and apostolic Church." Like the Christ-event, this apostolicity is a gift from God given once for all; its content is not of our making. As biblical scholars have observed, the apostles were unique and irreplaceable in their witness to God's decisive intervention in human history. At the same time, this apostolic gift has an eschatological dimension, particularly—but not exclusively—when the Twelve are identified as apostles. The apostle appears as a uniquely authoritative figure not only at the foundation of the Church but also as a companion of the eschatological Christ at the judgment of the last day. This eschatological dimension does not only mean that the Church, founded on the Twelve, awaits its perfect form at the end of God's plan for history. It also means that the Church shares now in the finality, the irrevocable fullness, of God's action within the changes of history, precisely because the Twelve have passed on to the Church their witness to the presence of God's kingdom in the risen Lord and their role as authoritative heralds of his coming in history.

7. These two dimensions of apostolicity—the historical and the eschatological—cannot be separated, and certainly in our lived experience as Orthodox and Roman Catholics they have always been held together. Indeed, one of the characteristics of God's gift of apostolicity is that it manifests the events of the *end* to the present time. This is seen clearly in

the pattern of the eucharist, where the Holy Spirit brings the reality of the resurrected Christ to the Church, and it is visible also in the tradition of iconography, which brings to bear upon the present life of the Church both the historical past and the power of the world to come. Apostolicity thus is not reduced to simple reference to the past, nor is it referred only to the reality of a future age. It means that here and now the life of the Church—whether expressed in authoritative teaching, in judgment and discipline, or in the eucharist itself—is being molded, corrected, and governed by what has been received from the past *and* by what is awaited at the last day.

8. We frequently speak of our faith as apostolic, by this usually stressing that its content has been received from the apostles. This understanding of the apostolic faith took on particular importance in the Church's struggle against gnosticism in the second century, when it came to be described as a deposit left by the apostles and handed down with the communities founded by them. But there has never been any need to understand this deposit as an inert object, relayed in purely mechanical fashion from generation to generation by duly authorized ministers. Rather, it remains a living confession. We see the paradigm of this in Peter's response to Christ's question, "Who do men say that I am?... Who do you say that I am?" The apostolic faith of Peter appears not only in the content of the confession—"Thou art the Christ, the son of the living God"—but also in the very act of confessing.

9. It is primordially within the mystery of Christian initiation that apostolicity is continually experienced in the life of the Church and in the life of each Christian. The baptismal act of receiving and giving back the Church's confession of faith (*traditio/redditio*) marks each Christian's entry into and appropriation of the apostolic life and faith of the Church. As an essential element in the life of the whole Church and of every Christian, apostolicity therefore is by no means unique to or limited to the realm of hierarchical ministry. For just as we share by baptism in the royal and prophetic priesthood, so also by this baptismal confession we too become bearers of the Church's apostolicity.

10. In our consultation attention was drawn to at least two corollaries which may follow from this understanding of apostolic faith: (a) The apostolicity of ministry is generally seen as derived from the continuity of

127

the community as a whole in apostolic life and faith; the succession of ministers in office is normally agreed to be subordinate to that ecclesial apostolicity. (b) Apostolicity seems to consist more in fidelity to the apostles' proclamation and mission than in any one form of handing on community office. These observations alert us once again to the danger of reducing apostolicity simply to forms and institutional structures. Yet we also must resist any temptation to locate apostolicity in what is merely individual or in what falls outside the mediated nature of the divine economy—as happened and still happens, for example, in the gnostic claim to immediate experience. Apostolicity is experienced not in atemporal isolation but rather in the Church's social nature as a community of faith and in its historical continuity and permanence—even in concrete forms and patterns once given the Church's life by its relation to the civilization of the Greco-Roman world.

11. Within this social and historical experience of the apostolic Church, how do we as Orthodox and Roman Catholics conceive of those structures which attest to and assure the unity of the churches in their apostolic confession? Here historians have called attention to certain differences of approach which may characterize our churches. Yet we are uncomfortable with any assessment that would too sharply polarize differences, as though at every point—even those on which at first glance we would appear to be united—we were in fact divided by hopelessly irreconcilable mentalities.

12. In the Eastern Churches there has frequently been an emphasis on the fullness of each church's apostolicity and, indeed, "petrinity," and there has been criticism of the Roman Church for tending to localize these qualities in a single see. The Roman Church, on the other hand, has strongly emphasized the need to express the unity of the Church's apostolic faith through concrete structures and practice and has criticized the Eastern Churches for losing sight of this need. Such differences of approach should not, however, be presented as evidence of an irreducible opposition between "local church" and "universal Church." This dilemma is an artificial one which arises at least in part when we are unwilling to see the same qualities present in both the local and the universal, albeit realized in different ways. The image of Peter within the apostolic college is reflected in the life of each local church; it is also reflected in the visible

communion of all the local churches. There is no intrinsic opposition between these two approaches.

13. In examining the Church's historical relationship to civil society, scholars have also contrasted a "principle of accommodation" in the East to a "principle of apostolicity" in the West. Yet at a time when East and West were united in one Christian Roman Empire, neither approach necessarily excluded the other, for both pointed and aspired to universality. It was in Rome after all, the imperial capital, that Peter and Paul, "first enthroned of the apostles, teachers of the *oikumenê*," bore witness to the apostolic faith even until death (Troparion of the feast of SS. Peter and Paul in the Byzantine rite). And in the East, it was not an abstract principle of conformity to civil structures that prevailed. Rather, the concrete structures of a universal empire were used to express the Church's universality. Also instructive here are ways in which the themes of diversity-in-unity and ordered harmony are developed in the many Byzantine treatises on the "pentarchy." What is envisioned is by no means simply an institutional unity, but an organic unity.

14. These points are offered in the hope that they will clarify and facilitate our common approach not only to the question of apostolicity but also to the question of primacy. Taken together, they call us to exercise particular caution in our use of theological language. When distinctions have been made or noted—as was done above, for example, in distinguishing the content and the act of apostolic faith—we must resist the temptation to leave them in a state of opposition. Unless the distinguished elements are recombined in their proper relationship and proportion, the integrity of the underlying theological reality is lost and the spiritual experience of this reality in both our traditions is travestied. There is no need to claim that what may characterize one tradition in a particular way exhausts the content of that tradition or, in turn, must be absent from another tradition as a matter of course.

15. The historical study of apostolicity also calls us to examine carefully the ways in which we present our respective histories. This has particular importance when we are speaking of that historical continuity we each claim as bearers of the apostolic faith, or when we recount those particular incidents in our histories—for example, the monothelite controversy in the seventh century—which may reflect different under-

standings of apostolicity. In such contexts we can easily forget the achievements of our common theological reflection and retreat once again—consciously or unconsciously—into what is less than the fullness of truth. We must not be too quick to identify this kind of retreat with that fearless confession of the apostolic faith "in season and out of season" which binds us all as Orthodox and Catholic Christians.

Brighton, MA
November 1, 1986
33rd Meeting

THE SACRAMENT OF ORDER IN THE SACRAMENTAL STRUCTURE OF THE CHURCH WITH PARTICULAR REFERENCE TO THE IMPORTANCE OF APOSTOLIC SUCCESSION FOR THE SANCTIFICATION AND UNITY OF THE PEOPLE OF GOD

Joint International Commission, 1988

1. Having expressed our idea of the mystery of the Church as a communion of faith and sacraments, preeminently manifested in the eucharistic celebration, our commission now addresses the crucial question of the place and role of ordained ministry in the sacramental structure of the Church. We will deal, then, with the sacrament of order as well as with ordination to each of the three degrees of episcopate, presbyterate and diaconate. We rely on the certitude that in our churches apostolic succession is fundamental for the sanctification and the unity of the people of God.

2. Our churches affirm that ministry in the Church makes actual that of Christ himself. In the New Testament writings, Christ is called apostle, prophet, pastor, servant, deacon, doctor, priest, *episkopos*. Our common tradition recognizes the close link between the work of Christ and that of the Holy Spirit.

3. This understanding prevents us seeing in the economy Christ in isolation from the Spirit. The actual presence of Christ in his Church is also of an eschatological nature, since the Spirit constitutes the earnest of the perfect realization of God's design for the world.

4. In this perspective the Church appears as the community of the New Covenant which Christ through the Holy Spirit gathers about himself and builds up as his body. Through the Church, Christ is present in history; through it he achieves the salvation of the world.

5. Since Christ is present in the Church, it is his ministry that is carried out in it. The ministry in the Church therefore does not substitute for the ministry of Christ. It has its source in him. Since the Spirit sent by Christ

gives life to the Church, ministry is only fruitful by the grace of the Spirit. In fact, it includes many functions which the members of the community carry out according to the diversity of the gifts they receive as members of the body of Christ. Certain among them receive through ordination and exercise the function proper to the episcopate, to the presbyterate and to the diaconate. There is no Church without the ministries created by the Spirit; there is no ministry without the Church, that is to say, outside and above the community. Ministries find their meaning and grounds for existence *(raison d'être)* only in it.

I. Christ and the Holy Spirit

6. The Spirit, which eternally proceeds from the Father and reposes on the Son, prepared the Christ event and achieved it. The incarnation of the Son of God, his death and his resurrection were accomplished in fact according to the will of the Father, in the Holy Spirit. At the baptism, the Father through the manifestation of the Spirit inaugurates the mission of the Son. This Spirit is present in his ministry: the announcing of the Good News of salvation, the manifesting of the coming of the kingdom, the bearing witness to the Father. Likewise, it is in the same Spirit that, as the unique priest of the New Covenant, Christ offers the sacrifice of his own life and it is through the Spirit that he is glorified.

7. Since Pentecost, in the Church which is his body, it is in the Spirit alone that those who are charged with ministry can carry out the acts which bring the body to its full stature. In the ministry of Christ as in that of the Church, it is the one and the same Spirit which is at work and which acts with us all the days of our life.

8. In the church ministry should be lived in holiness, with a view towards the sanctification of the people of God. So that the whole Church and especially its ordained ministers might be able to contribute to "the perfecting of the saints for the work of ministry for building up the body of Christ," different services are made possible by many charisms (Eph. 4:11-12; cf. 1 Cor. 12:4-28; Rom. 12:4-8).

9. The newness of the Church's ministry consists in this: Christ, servant of God for humanity, is present through the Spirit, in the Church, his body, from which he cannot be separated. For he himself is the "first

born among many brothers." It is according to this sacramental way that one must understand the work of Christ in history from Pentecost to the Parousia. The ministry of the Church as such is sacramental.

10. For this reason Christ's presence in the Church is also eschatological. Wherever the Spirit is at work, he actually reveals to the world the presence of the kingdom in creation. Here is where ecclesial ministry is rooted.

11. This ecclesial ministry is by nature sacramental. The word sacramental is meant to emphasize here that every ministry is bound to the eschatological reality of the kingdom. The grace of the Holy Spirit, earnest of the world to come, has its source in the death and resurrection of Christ and is offered, in a sacramental manner, by means of sensible realities. The word sacramental likewise shows that the minister is a member of the community whom the Spirit invests with proper functions and power to assemble it and to preside in the name of Christ over the acts in which it celebrates the mysteries of salvation. This view of the sacramentality of ministry is rooted in the fact that Christ is made present in the Church by the Spirit whom he himself has sent to the Church.

12. This nature of ecclesial ministry is further shown in the fact that all ministries are intended to serve the world so as to lead it to its true goal, the kingdom of God. It is by constituting the eschatological community as body of Christ that the ministry of the Church answers the needs of the world.

13. The community gathered in the Spirit around Christ exercising his ministry for the world has its foundation in Christ who is himself the cornerstone, and in the community of the Twelve. The apostolic character of churches and their ministry is understood in this light.

14. On the one hand, the Twelve are witness of the historic life of Jesus, of his ministry and of his resurrection. On the other, as associated with the glorified Christ, they link each community with the community of the last days. Thus the ecclesial ministry will be called apostolic because it is carried out in continuity and in fidelity to what was given by Christ and handed on in history by the apostles. But it will also be apostolic because the eucharistic assembly at which the minister presides is an anticipation of the final community with Christ. Through this double relationship the Church's ministry remains constantly bound to that of the Twelve, and so to that of Christ.

II. The Priesthood in the Divine Economy of Salvation

15. The entire divine economy of salvation culminates in the incarnation of the Son, in his teaching, his passion, his glorious resurrection, his ascension and his second coming. Christ acts in the Holy Spirit. Thus, once and for all, there is laid the foundation for re-establishing the communion of man with God.

16. According to the Epistle to the Hebrews, Christ by his death has become the one mediator of the New Covenant (Heb. 9:15) and having entered once for all into the Holy Place with his own blood (Heb. 9:12), he is forever in heaven the one and eternal High Priest of this New Covenant, "so as to appear now in the presence of God on our behalf" (Heb. 9:24) to offer his sacrifice (Heb. 10:12).

17. Invisibly present in the Church through the Holy Spirit, whom he has sent, Christ then is its unique High Priest. In him, priest and victim, all together, pastors and faithful, form "a chosen race, a royal priesthood, a holy nation, a people he claims as his own" (1 Pt. 2:9; cf. Rv. 5:10).

18. All members of the churches, as members of the body of Christ, participate in this priesthood, called to become "a living sacrifice holy and acceptable to God" (Rom. 12:1; cf. 1 Pt. 2:5). Head of the Church, Christ has established, to make himself present, apostles chosen among the people, whom he endowed with authority and power by strengthening them through the grace of the Holy Spirit. The work and mission of the apostles are continued in the Church by the bishops with the priests and deacons who assist them. By ordination, the bishops are established as successors of the apostles and direct the people along the ways of salvation.

19. Grouped around the glorified Lord, the Twelve give witness to the presence of the kingdom already inaugurated and which will be fully manifested at the second coming. Christ has indeed promised them that they would sit on twelve thrones, judging with the Son of Man the twelve tribes of Israel (Mt. 19:28).

20. As historic witnesses of what the Lord accomplished, the ministry of the Twelve is unique and irreplaceable. What they laid down was founded once and for all, and no one in the future could build except on the foundation thus established (Eph. 2:20; Rv. 21:14).

21. But the apostles remain at the same time the foundations of the Church as it endures through the ages, in such a way that the mission they received from the Lord always remains visible and active, in expectation of the Lord's return (cf. Mt. 18:18 and, earlier, 16:19).

22. This is why the Church, in which God's grace is at work, is itself the sacrament *par excellence,* the anticipated manifestation of the final realities, the foretaste of God's kingdom, of the glory of the God and Father, of the eschaton in history.

23. Within this sacrament which is the Church, the priesthood conferred by ordination finds its place being given for this Church. In fact, it constitutes in the Church a charismatic ministry (*leitourgêma*) *par excellence.* It is at the service of the Church's life and continued existence by the Holy Spirit, that is to say, of the unity in Christ, of all the faithful living and dead, of the martyrs, the saints, the just of the Old Testament.

III. The Ministry of the Bishop, Presbyter and Deacon

24. In the celebration of the eucharist, the entire assembly, each according to his or her status, is *litourgos* of the *koinonia,* and is so only through the Spirit. "There are varieties of ministries, but the same Lord.... To each is given the manifestation of the Spirit for the common good" (1 Cor. 12:5, 7). The various ministries converge in the eucharistic synaxis, during which they are conferred. However, their diversity is ordered to the entire life of the community: fidelity to the Word of God, abiding in harmony and fraternal charity, witness before "those outside," growth in holiness, constancy in prayer, care for the poorest.

25. Since it culminates in the celebration of the eucharist in which Christian initiation is completed, through which all become one body of Christ, the ministry of the bishop is, among all the charisms and ministries which the Spirit raises up, a ministry of presiding for gathering in unity. In fact, bearing the variety of gifts of the Spirit, the local church has at its center the bishop whose communion realizes the unity of all and expresses the fullness of the Church.

26. This unity of the local church is inseparable from the universal communion of the churches. It is essential for a church to be in communion with the others. This communion is expressed and realized in and

through the episcopal college. By his ordination, the bishop is made minister of a church which he represents in the universal communion.

27. Episcopal ordination, which according to the canons is conferred by at least two or three bishops, expresses the communion of the churches with that of the person selected: It makes him a member of the communion of bishops. In ordination the bishops exercise their function as witnesses to the communion in the apostolic faith and sacramental life not only with respect to him whom they ordain, but also with respect to the church of which he will be bishop. What is fundamental for the incorporation of the newly elected person in the episcopal communion is that it is accomplished by the glorified Lord in the power of the Holy Spirit at the moment of the imposition of hands.

Here we are only considering ordination under its sacramental aspect. The problems raised by the manner of electing a bishop will be studied later.

28. Episcopal ordination confers on the one who receives it by the gift of the Spirit, the fullness of the priesthood. During the ordination the concelebration of the bishops expresses the unity of the Church and its identity with the apostolic community. They lay hands and invoke the Holy Spirit on the one who will be ordained as the only ones qualified to confer on him the episcopal ministry. They do it, however, within the setting of the prayer of the community.

29. Through his ordination the bishop receives all the powers necessary for fulfilling his function. The canonical conditions for the exercise of his function and the installation of the bishop in the local church will be further discussed by the commission.

30. The gift conferred consecrates the recipient once for all to the service of the Church. This is a point of the traditional doctrine in East and West which is confirmed by the fact that in the event of disciplinary sanctions against a bishop followed by canonical reintegration, there is no reordination. On this subject, as on all the essential points concerning ordination our churches have a common doctrine and practice, even if on certain canonical and disciplinary requirements, such as celibacy, customs can be different because of pastoral and spiritual reasons.

31. But ecclesial ministry is exercised through a variety of functions. These are exercised in interdependence; none could replace another. This

is especially true of the fundamental ministries of the bishop, the presbyter and the deacon, and of the functions of the laity, all of which together give structure to the eucharistic community.

32. Throughout the entire history of our churches women have played a fundamental role, as witnessed not only by the most holy Mother of God, but also by the holy women mentioned in the New Testament, by the numerous women saints whom we venerate, as well as by so many other women who up to the present day have served the Church in many ways. Their particular charisms are very important for the building up of the body of Christ. But our churches remain faithful to the historical and theological tradition according to which they ordain only men to the priestly ministry.

33. Just as the apostles gathered together the first communities, by proclaiming Christ, by celebrating the eucharist, by leading the baptized towards growing communion with Christ and with each other, so the bishop, established by the same Spirit, continues to preach the same Gospel, to preside at the same eucharist, to serve the unity and sanctification of the same community. He is thus icon of Christ the servant among his brethren.

34. Because it is at the eucharist that the Church manifests its fullness, it is equally in the presiding at the eucharist that the role of the bishop and of the presbyter appears in its full light.

35. In the eucharistic celebration, in fact, believers offer themselves with Christ as a royal priesthood. They do so thanks to the ministerial action which makes present in their midst Christ himself who proclaims the word, makes the bread and the cup become through the Spirit his body and blood, incorporating them in himself, giving them his life. Moreover, the prayer and the offering of the people incorporated in Christ are, so to speak, recapitulated in the thanksgiving prayer of the bishop and his offering of the gifts.

36. The eucharist thus realizes the unity of the Christian community. It also manifests the unity of all the churches which truly celebrate it and further still the unity, across the centuries, of all the churches with the apostolic community from the beginnings up to the present day. Transcending history, it reunites in the Spirit the great assembly of the apostles,

of martyrs, of witnesses of all periods gathered around the Lamb. Indeed, as the central act of episcopal ministry it makes clearly present the world to come: the Church gathered in communion, offering itself to the Father, through the Son, in the Holy Spirit.

37. He who presides at the eucharist is responsible for preserving communion in fidelity to the teaching of the apostles and for guiding it in the new life. He is its servant and pastor. The bishop is also the guide of the entire liturgical life of his local church and, following his example, this church becomes a community of prayer. He presides at its praise and at its intercession, and he himself prays unceasingly for all those entrusted to him by the Lord, knowing that he is responsible for each one before the tribunal of God.

38. It also rests with him to see to that there be given to his people, by preaching and catechesis, the authentic content of the word of God given to the apostles "once and for all." He is in fact the primary one responsible for the preaching of the word of God in his diocese.

39. To him also belongs the task of leading this people towards proclaiming to all human beings salvation in Jesus Christ, and towards a witness which embodies that proclamation. Therefore, it is for him to govern his church in such a way that it always remains faithful to its Christian vocation and to the mission deriving therefrom. In all this, however, he remains a member of the Church called to holiness and dependent on the salvific ministry of this Church, as St. Augustine reminds his community: "For you I am a bishop, with you I am a Christian." At his ordination the bishop makes his own the faith of the whole Church by solemnly confessing it and thus becomes father to the extent that he has fully become its son by this confession. It is essential for the bishop to be the father of his people.

40. As successors of the apostles, bishops are responsible for communion in the apostolic faith and fidelity to the demands of a life lived according to the Gospel.

41. It is in presiding over the eucharistic assembly that the role of the bishop finds its accomplishment. The presbyters form the college grouped around him during that celebration. They exercise the responsibilities the bishop entrusts to them by celebrating the sacraments, teaching the word

of God and governing the community, in profound and continuous communion with him. The deacon, for his part, is attached to the service of the bishop and the priest and is a link between them and the assembly of the faithful.

42. The priest, ordained by the bishop and dependent upon him, is sent to fulfill certain definite tasks; above all he is sent to a parish community to be its pastor: He presides at the eucharist at the altar (consecrated by the bishop), he is minister of the sacraments for the community, he preaches the Gospel and catechizes; it is his duty to keep in unity the charisms of the people (*laos*) of God; he appears as the ordinary minister of the local eucharistic community, and the diocese is thus a communion of eucharistic communities.

43. The diaconate is exercised at the service of the bishop and the priest, in the liturgy, in the work of evangelization and in the service of charity.

IV. Apostolic Succession

44. The same unique ministry of Christ and his apostles remains in action in history. This action is, through the Spirit, a breakthrough to "the world to come," in fidelity to what the apostles transmitted about what Jesus did and taught.

45. The importance of this succession comes also from the fact that the apostolic tradition concerns the community and not only an isolated individual, ordained bishop. Apostolic succession is transmitted through local churches ("in each city," according to the expression of Eusebius of Caesarea; "by reason of their common heritage of doctrine," according to Tertullian in the *De Praescriptione* 32, 6). It is a matter of a succession of persons in the community, because the *Una Sancta* is a communion of local churches and not of isolated individuals. It is within this mystery of *koinonia* that the episcopate appears as the central point of the apostolic succession.

46. According to what we have already said in the Munich Document, "apostolic succession, therefore, means something more than a mere transmission of powers. It is succession in a church which witnesses to the apostolic faith, in communion with the other churches which witness to

the same apostolic faith. The 'see' (*cathedra*) plays an essential role in inserting the bishop into the heart of ecclesial apostolicity" (Munich Document II, 4). More precisely, the term *cathedra* is used here in the sense of the presence of the bishop in each local church.

47. "On the other hand, once ordained, the bishop becomes in his church the guarantor of apostolicity and the one who represents it within the *communion* of churches, its link with the other churches. That is why in his church every eucharist can only be celebrated *in truth* if presided over by him or by a presbyter *in communion* with him. Mention of him in the anaphora is essential" (*ibid.*).

48. "Attachment to the apostolic communion joins all the bishops together, linking the *episkopê* of the local churches to the college of the apostles" (*ibid.*, III, 4). The bishops are thus rooted in the "once for all" of the apostolic group through which the Holy Spirit gives witness to the faith. Indeed, as the foundation of the Church, the Twelve are unique. Even so, it was necessary that other men should make visible their irreplaceable presence. In this way the link of each community would be maintained with both the original community and the eschatological community.

49. Through his ordination each bishop becomes successor of the apostles, whatever may be the church over which he presides or the prerogatives (*presbeia*) of this church among the other churches.

50. Incorporated into the number of those to whom the particular responsibility for the ministry of salvation has been entrusted, and so placed in the succession of the apostles, the bishop ought to pass on their teaching as well as model his whole life on them. Irenaeus of Lyons puts it thus: "It is where the charisms of God have been planted that we should be instructed in the truth, that is, among those in whom are united succession in the Church from the apostles, unassailable integrity of conduct and incorruptible purity of doctrine" (*Adv. Haer.* IV, 26, 5). Among the essential functions of the bishop is that of being in his church through the Spirit a witness and guarantor of the faith and an instrument for maintaining it in apostolic fidelity. Apostolic succession is also a succession in the labors and sufferings of the apostles for the service of the Gospel and in the defense of the people entrusted to each bishop. According to the words of the First Letter of St. Peter, the apostolic succession is

also a succession in the presence of mercy and understanding, of defense of the weak, of constant attention to those entrusted to their charge, with the bishop thus being a model for the flock (cf. 1 Pt. 5:1-4; 2 Cor. 4:8-11; 1 Tim. 4:12; Tt. 2:7).

51. Furthermore it belongs to the episcopal ministry to articulate and organize the life of the church with its service and offices. It is his task also to watch over the choice of those who are to carry out responsibilities in his diocese. Fraternal communion requires that all the members, ministers or lay people, listen to each other for the good of the people of God.

52. In the course of its history, the Church in East and West has known various forms of practicing communion among bishops: by exchange of letters, by visits of one church to another, but principally by synodal or conciliar life. From the first centuries a distinction and a hierarchy was established between churches of earlier foundation and churches of more recent foundation, between mother and daughter churches, between churches of larger cities and churches of outlying areas. This hierarchy or *taxis* soon found its canonical expression, formulated by the councils, especially in the canons received by all the churches of the East and West. These are, in the first place, canons 6 and 7 of the First Council of Nicea (325), canon 3 of the First Council of Constantinople (second ecumenical council, 381), canon 28 of Chalcedon (fourth ecumenical council, 451), as well as canons 3, 4 and 5 of Sardica (343) and canon 1 of the Council of Saint Sophia (879-880). Even if these canons have not always been interpreted in the same way in the East and in the West, they belong to the heritage of the Church. They assigned to bishops occupying certain metropolitan or major sees a place and prerogatives recognized in the organization of the synodal life of the Church. Thus was formed the pentarchy: Rome, Constantinople, Alexandria, Antioch and Jerusalem, even if in the course of history there appeared apart from the pentarchy other archbishops, metropolitans, primates and patriarchs.

53. The synodal character of episcopal activity showed itself especially in questions under discussion which interested several local churches or the churches as a whole. Thus in each region different types of synods or local and regional councils and conferences of bishops were organized. Their forms could change according to different places and times, but their guiding principle is to manifest and make efficacious the life of the

Church by joint episcopal action, under the presidency of the one whom they recognized as the first among them. In fact, according to canon 34 of the Apostolic Canons, belonging to the canonical tradition of our churches, the first among the bishops only takes a decision in agreement with the other bishops and the latter take no important decision without the agreement of the first.

54. In ecumenical councils, convened in the Holy Spirit at times of crisis, bishops of the Church, with supreme authority, decided together about the faith and issued canons to affirm the tradition of the apostles in historic circumstances which directly threatened the faith, unity and sanctifying work of the whole people of God, and put at risk the very existence of the Church and its fidelity to its founder, Jesus Christ.

55. It is in this perspective of communion among local churches that the question could be addressed of primacy in the Church in general and in particular, the primacy of the bishop of Rome, a question which constitutes a serious divergence among us and which will be discussed in the future.

Uusi Valamo, Finland
June 26, 1988
Fifth Plenary Meeting

A JOINT REACTION BY THE ORTHODOX-ROMAN CATHOLIC CONSULTATION IN THE U.S.A. TO THE INTERNATIONAL ORTHODOX-ROMAN CATHOLIC COMMISSION'S TEXT: "THE SACRAMENT OF ORDER IN THE SACRAMENTAL STRUCTURE OF THE CHURCH WITH PARTICULAR REFERENCE TO THE IMPORTANCE OF APOSTOLIC SUCCESSION FOR THE SANCTIFICATION AND UNITY OF THE PEOPLE OF GOD"

U. S. Theological Consultation, 1989

1. As members of the official Orthodox-Roman Catholic Consultation in the United States of America established in 1965 by the Standing Conference of Canonical Orthodox Bishops (SCOBA) and the National Conference of Catholic Bishops (NCCB), we have followed with interest the work of the Joint International Commission for Theological Dialogue between the Roman Catholic Church and the Orthodox Church at its meetings held in Patmos and Rhodes (1980), Munich (1982), Crete (1984) and Bari, Italy (1986 and 1987). We have also noted the progress reached at the fifth plenary session held from June 19 to 27, 1988, at Valamo, Finland, where there was published the latest of three common statements exploring important points of agreement and difference in the doctrinal life of our churches.

2. We have followed a practice of responding jointly to the various agreed statements prepared by the International Commission. At our 26th meeting (May 23-25, 1983) we submitted to the presiding hierarchy of the Joint International Commission our official response to the Munich Document: "The Mystery of the Church and of the Eucharist in the Light of the Mystery of the Holy Trinity" (dated July 6, 1982).

3. At our 33rd meeting (November 1, 1986) we submitted to the Joint International Commission an agreed statement entitled: "Apostolicity as God's Gift in the Life of the Church." This statement of ours was not a

direct response to a text of the international group but contained a series of suggested formulations since apostolicity was known to be a major issue in planned discussions on the sacrament of order.

4. After the International Commission published its second common statement, the Bari Document, entitled: "Faith, Sacraments, and the Unity of the Church" (August 1, 1987), we analyzed this text at several meetings and on June 2, 1988, at our 36th meeting, approved a joint official response which was then sent to the International Commission.

5. Now meeting at our 39th session (October 26-28, 1989), after detailed discussion of the International Commission's statement: "The Sacrament of Order in the Sacramental Structure of the Church with Particular Reference to the Importance of Apostolic Succession for the Sanctification and Unity of the People of God" (dated June 26, 1988), we wish to submit this official reaction.

6. In general, our Consultation judged the theology and thrust of the Valamo statement favorably. We also noted that care had been given to providing a clear and literate English translation, though we did find several problems (*e.g.,* lack of consistency in translating *presbyteros,* which appears sometimes as priest and sometimes as presbyter).

Introduction [nos. 1-5]

7. It is not clear that the International Commission has identified its audience. There are places even in the Introduction where terms are used that may not be comprehended except by specialists. For example, when the document speaks of the disadvantage of contemplating Christ "in the economy" in isolation from the Spirit (no. 3) many readers could miss the Pauline allusion to *oikonomia,* the term used by St. Paul to identify God's design for salvation. Similarly, when Eph. 1:14 is alluded to where it is stated that "...the Spirit constitutes the *earnest* [*arrabon*] of the perfect realization of God's design for the world" (no. 3), this reference could be cited.

I: Christ and the Holy Spirit [nos. 6-14]

8. In this section the Valamo text builds upon the theology expressed in the Munich Document which emphasizes the close link between the work of Christ and that of the Holy Spirit. The section is given the

comprehensive title "Christ and the Holy Spirit," but the main purpose of these nine numbers is to try to explain the divine persons' relationship to ecclesial ministry and to explain why ecclesial ministry is both "sacramental" and "apostolic."

9. We observe, however, that the Valamo Document is inconsistent in its use of the term ministry/minister. At points, for example in nos. 5 and 24, all the baptized faithful are seen as exercising diverse ministries. At other points a distinction is implied between this general ministry of all the faithful and that of the ordained (*e.g.*, no. 8). In other cases, ministry/minister can mean only the ordained, and in at least one instance (no. 11) it can mean only the one who assembles the community and presides in the celebration of the sacraments, *i.e.* presbyters and bishops but not deacons.

10. This inconsistency makes it difficult to know how to understand the term in a given context. For example, in nos. 7 and 8, if only the ordained minister is implied, then the text seems to set the ordained minister over against the people of God, suggesting anachronistically that the New Testament usage of *diakonia* is referring exclusively to the ministry of the ordained.

II: The Priesthood in the Divine Economy of Salvation [nos. 15-23]

11. In Section II there follow nine paragraphs about the priesthood. We found helpful the statement that "the Church, in which God's grace is at work, is itself the sacrament *par excellence*, the anticipated manifestation of the final realities, the foretaste of God's kingdom, of the glory of the God and Father, of the *eschaton* in history" (no. 22). This statement supports the theological teaching of the Church as "sacrament." It also distinguishes between Church and kingdom of God, a distinction frequently neglected in preaching.

12. The heading uses the term "priesthood" although in the following section there is an effort rather to employ only the specific terms bishops, presbyters and deacons. The word "priesthood" (*sacerdoce*) seems to be used to provide a generic term that comprehends the priesthood of Jesus Christ, the priesthood of all believers, as well as the priesthood of the bishop and presbyter. There is, however, no systematic effort in the text to

deal with the fact that the New Testament does not apply the Old Testament vocabulary of priesthood to bishops and presbyters.

13. In our view the attempt to explain the multiple relationships: Christ—the Twelve—apostles—successors to apostles, is not successful. What is meant by the assertion that "Christ has established, *to make himself present*, apostles..." (no. 18), or "it was necessary that other men should *make visible* their [apostles'] irreplaceable *presence*" (no. 48)? The notion of representation in connection with ordained ministry needs to be further explored. (Here we note that the text in no. 33 should read the bishop is "icon of Christ," not, as the English translation states, he is "the icon of Christ.")

14. We would also have wished that the Valamo text had been more attentive to the New Testament differentiation between the terms "the Twelve" and "apostle(s)" and to the fact that the New Testament sometimes uses *episkopos* and *presbyteros* interchangeably. The text (nos. 13-14 and 20-21) seems to identify the Twelve with the apostles without further ado. Ephesians 2:20 is cited in support of the role of the Twelve (no. 20). On the whole, the document reflects an oversimplified view of the structures present in the early Church especially in the New Testament period. Discussion of such questions as primacy would benefit from closer attention to the historical development of the episcopacy.

III. The Ministry of the Bishop, Presbyter and Deacon [nos. 24-43]

15. This section aims to treat three historical forms of ordained ministry: that of the bishop, presbyter and deacon, but in fact presbyters and deacons are treated only very briefly (presbyters only in nos. 41-42 and deacons only in no. 43).

16. The ministry of the bishop, it is stated, "culminates in the celebration of the eucharist where Christian initiation is completed" (no. 25). During the eucharist, the text continues, the bishop exercises a unique ministry unlike that of any other ministry, namely presiding to gather the community in unity. Here we see the influence of eucharistic ecclesiology. Many Christians in their liturgical experience relate the celebration of the eucharist also to the presbyter. However, the text does later acknowledge

that it is often the presbyter who exercises many of the functions earlier associated with the bishop, when it notes: "it is equally in the presiding at the eucharist that the role of the bishop *and of the presbyter* appears in its full light" (no. 34) and even refers to the presbyter as "the ordinary minister of the local eucharistic community" (no. 42).

17. In its brief treatment of the presbyterate, the document appears to define it only in relationship to the episcopate (no. 41, 42). It is correct to state that it is "in the presiding at the eucharist that the role... of the presbyter appears in its full light" (no. 34). But it should be added that through his ordination the presbyter also acquires a new relationship to the community, as a counselor to the bishop and elder among the people, in union with the bishop. This relationship is an expression of conciliarity in the local church.

18 Our consultation heartily endorses the assertion in no. 26 that the "unity of the local church is inseparable from the universal communion of the churches" and that "it is essential for a church to be in communion with the others." We also appreciate the assertion that "the bishop is made minister of a church which he represents in the universal communion." However, some treatment of auxiliary and/or titular bishops, who do not preside over local churches, would have been useful at this point. This section does not mention situations in which several bishops preside over the same geographical area.

19. In no. 30 the conviction is expressed that ordinations, whether to the episcopate or the presbyterate, may not be repeated. Instead of appealing as the West does to the indelible *character* of an ordination, the unrepeatable nature of ordination is well expressed as follows: "The gift conferred consecrates the recipient once for all to the service of the Church" (no. 30). One can also be grateful that here Orthodox and Roman Catholics have officially stated that "on this subject [the inadmissibility of reordination], as on all the essential points concerning ordination, our churches have a common doctrine and practice, even if on certain canonical and disciplinary requirements, such as celibacy, customs can be different because of pastoral and spiritual reasons" (no. 30).

20. There is one brief paragraph (no. 32) about the role of women in the Church. Here the text speaks of the value of "their [women's] particular charism" without further specification. The text, however, continues: "our churches remain faithful to the historical and theological tradition

according to which they ordain only men to the priestly ministry." No reference is made to the possible ordination of women to the diaconate as has since been suggested, for instance, at the recent Inter-Orthodox Rhodes Conference on Women and the Question of Ordination (October 30—November 7, 1988). In view of the importance of such issues within our churches and in ecumenical dialogues, further discussion will be needed.

21. We are pleased to note reference to an additional responsibility of the bishop, one in accord with contemporary stress on orthopraxis, namely that the bishop is responsible for "fidelity to the demands of a life lived according to the Gospel" (no. 40). The document likewise contains the valuable insight that: "Apostolic succession is also a succession in the labors and sufferings of the apostles for the service of the Gospel and in the defense of the people entrusted to each bishop" (no. 50).

IV. Apostolic Succession [nos. 44-55]

22. The final twelve paragraphs deal with apostolic succession, although three of the numbers are merely citations by the International Consultation of its own recent Munich text. This section was read with particular interest by the United States Consultation inasmuch as we had highlighted this importance in our 1986 document entitled "Apostolicity as God's Gift in the Life of the Church."

23. The Valamo Document states that the same unique ministry of Christ and his apostles remains in action in history. "This action is, through the Spirit, a breakthrough to the 'world to come,' in fidelity to what the apostles transmitted about what Jesus did and taught" (no. 44). Although the text does not show much historical nuancing when it states that the "bishop becomes successor of the apostles," it does imply that all bishops are equal in dignity notwithstanding the *presbeia* or prerogatives of their specific church (no. 49).

24. Several other emphases are well taken. Particularly interesting is the assertion that: "the importance of this [apostolic] succession comes also from the fact that the apostolic tradition concerns the community and not only an isolated individual, ordained bishop" (no. 45). The text also stresses that apostolic succession "is a matter of a succession of persons in the community...and not of isolated individuals."

25. Still these statements do not completely address an important issue cited in our earlier submission to the International Consultation, "Apostolicity as God's Gift in the Life of the Church," which stated: "As an essential element in the life of the whole Church and of every Christian, apostolicity therefore is by no means unique to or limited to the realm of hierarchical ministry" (U.S. text, ¶9). While it could be argued that the Valamo text is open to what we stated, namely that "the apostolicity of ministry is generally seen as derived from the continuity of the community as a whole in apostolic life and faith" (U.S. text ¶10), the international text is less successful, we feel, in explaining what we noted, namely that "apostolicity seems to consist more in fidelity to the apostles' proclamation and mission than in any one form of, handing on community office" (U.S. text ¶10).

26. A useful statement is included about "the synodal character of episcopal activity" (no. 53) as well as a succinct but comprehensive description of ecumenical councils: "In ecumenical councils, convened in the Holy Spirit at times of crisis, bishops of the Church, with supreme authority, decided together about the faith and issued canons to affirm the tradition of the apostles in historic circumstances which directly threatened the faith, unity and sanctifying work of the whole people of God, and put at risk the very existence of the Church and its fidelity to its founder Jesus Christ" (no. 54).

27. In the concluding paragraph the International Commission indicates unfinished business specifically relating to primacy in the Church and in particular to the primacy of the Bishop of Rome, "a question which constitutes a serious divergence among us and which will be discussed in the future" (no. 55). This is a matter that surely will be treated in the next planned statement on the "Ecclesiological and Canonical Consequences of the Sacramental Structure of the Church: Conciliarity and Authority in the Church" scheduled for discussion at Munich in June 1990. From what we have seen in this present analysis, the Joint International Commission for Theological Dialogue has been moving toward greater maturity and comprehensiveness in the formulation of its agreed statements.

Brighton, MA
October 28, 1989
39th Meeting

149

ORDINATION

Joint Committee of Orthodox and Catholic Bishops, 1988

At their last two meetings (Milwaukee, November 10-11, 1987, and Boston, September 6-8, 1988), members of the Joint Committee of Orthodox and Roman Catholic Bishops have heard presentations and discussed in several sessions the perpetuity of the effects of ordination. They also reviewed the recently released statement of the Joint International Commission for Theological Dialogue between the Roman Catholic Church and the Orthodox Church: "The Sacrament of Order in the Sacramental Structure of the Church with Particular Reference to the Importance of Apostolic Succession for the Sanctification and Unity of the People of God." The Joint Committee of Orthodox and Roman Catholic Bishops now issues this summary of its discussions.

Three general points of agreement on orders were noted:

(1) the three sacred orders of diaconate, presbyterate, and episcopate have a sacramental nature; (2) these orders are exclusively conferred by bishops with unquestionable apostolic succession; and (3) ordination implies a setting apart. Roman Catholic theology has emphasized an indelible sacramental character to explain this distinctive status as a special configuration to Christ the High Priest. Thus the sacrament of orders adds an essential specification to the indelible characters resulting from baptism and confirmation—sacraments more recently described as relating all the faithful to the mission and witness of Christ.

From the Orthodox point of view, the distinctive status resulting from ordination is intended to last permanently. A cleric, however, may be the subject of deposition because of serious sin which creates a permanent canonical hindrance to performing his sacred function. In such a case, even though he may be penitent, he cannot be restored to clerical status. On the other hand, there are some offenses of a canonical nature for which the penalty of deposition is foreseen but that are not necessarily an obstacle to canonical reintegration to holy orders, if they are not an impediment to ordination itself.

150

With either the Roman Catholic understanding of character or the Orthodox understanding of the creation of a permanent hindrance due to sin, "reordination" is impossible. Even in cases when a Roman Catholic cleric may lose clerical status either through cause or petition, the sacred ordination never becomes invalid. For both Orthodox Christians and Roman Catholics, when a member of the clergy who has been ordained in a church that shares with them an understanding of the priesthood and by a bishop in an unquestionable apostolic succession is received into either the Orthodox or the Roman Catholic Church, his ordination should be recognized. It should be noted, however, that until such time when the practice of the Orthodox Church will be unified, these cases will be decided by each autocephalous Orthodox Church.

Following the Seventh Meeting in Boston
October 1, 1988

AN AGREED STATEMENT ON CONCILIARITY AND PRIMACY IN THE CHURCH

U.S. Theological Consultation, 1989

For the past three years, the Orthodox-Roman Catholic Consultation in the United States of America has been studying questions related to the theology and practice of councils and to the exercise of primacy in our churches. Our papers and discussions prompted the following reflections, which we now offer in the hope that they will advance the work of the international Orthodox-Roman Catholic dialogue, and the wider relations among the churches, as they have advanced our own understanding of these issues.

1. In both Orthodox and Roman Catholic theology, the Church is the mystery of God-given unity among human beings, who are bound together by their faith in the risen Lord and by the transforming gift of the Holy Spirit into the divine and human fellowship (*koinonia*) we call the body of Christ (1 Cor. 12:13). Joined by the Holy Spirit to the Son in his loving obedience to the Father's will, the Church manifests redeemed creation within the embrace of the triune reality of God, calling God "Abba! Father!" by the gift of the Spirit of his Son (Gal. 4:6), as it strives towards the fullness of his kingdom.

2. Individual human persons become sharers in this mystery through sharing in the Church's profession of the apostolic faith and through baptism "in the name of the Father and of the Son and of the Holy Spirit" (Matt. 28:19). "Born" there into the Church's life "by water and the Holy Spirit" (John 3:5), they may now "consider themselves dead to sin and alive to God in Christ Jesus" (Rom. 6:11). So the Church, in its most extensive and inclusive sense, genuinely comprises all those who profess the apostolic faith and are baptized in the name of the Holy Trinity, recognizing them as "fellow citizens with the saints and members of the household of God" (Eph. 2:19).

3. When it gathers, under the life-giving impulse of the Holy Spirit, to celebrate in the eucharist the Son's "obedience unto death" (Phil. 2:8) and to be nourished by participation in his risen life, the Church most fully expresses

what, in God's order of salvation, it is: an assembly of faithful human persons who are brought into communion by and with the persons of the Holy Trinity, and who look forward to the fulfillment of that communion in eternal glory. So the clearest human reflection of the Church's divine vocation is the Christian community united to celebrate the eucharist, gathered by its common faith, in all its variety of persons and functions, around a single table, under a single president (*proestos*), to hear the Gospel proclaimed and to share in the sacramental reality of the Lord's flesh and blood (Ignatius, Eph. 5:2-3; Philad. 4), and so to manifest those gathered there as "partakers of the divine nature" (2 Pet. 1:4). "If you are the body of Christ and his members," proclaims St. Augustine, "your divine mystery is set on the table of the Lord; you receive your own mystery... Be what you see and receive what you are" (Serm. 272).

4. The mystery of Christ's Church, in its fullness, is therefore most directly and clearly encountered in the eucharistic community. Each local church, recognized in its celebration of the eucharist, is a full sacramental realization of the one Church of Christ, provided it remains within the full apostolic faith and is bound in love and mutual recognition to the other communities who profess that faith. The church in each place expresses its participation in the universal Church through its celebration of the one eucharist and in its concern for the worldwide spread of the Gospel and for the welfare and right faith of its sister communities, as well as in its prayer for their needs and the needs of the world.

5. United with Christ and within itself by the divine gifts of faith and love and by the other charisms and sacramental events which enliven it, the Church is also "set in order," as St. Basil reminds us, "by the Holy Spirit" (*On the Holy Spirit* 39). This ordering of charisms within the community is the basis of the Church's structure, and the reason why permanent offices of leadership have been divinely established within the eucharistic body, since apostolic times, as a service of love and a safeguard of unity in faith and life. Thus the same Spirit who unites the Church in a single universal body also manifests his presence in the institutions which keep local communities in an ordered and loving communion with one another.

6. The two institutions, mutually dependent and mutually limiting, which have exercised the strongest influence on maintaining the ordered communion of the churches since apostolic times, have been the gather-

153

ing of bishops and other appointed local leaders in synods, and the primacy or recognized preeminence of one bishop among his episcopal colleagues.

(a) Synods—whether held at the provincial, national or universal level, whether standing bodies (such as the *synodos endêmousa* of the Ecumenical Patriarchate), regularly convened gatherings, or extraordinary meetings called to meet some historic crisis—are the faithful community's chief expression of the "care for all the churches" which is central to every bishop's pastoral responsibility, and of the mutual complementarity of all the body's members.

(b) Primacy—whether that of the metropolitan within his province, or that of a patriarch or presiding hierarch within a larger region—is a service of leadership that has taken many forms throughout Christian history, but that always should be seen as complementary to the function of synods. It is the primate (*protos*) who convenes the synod, presides over its activities, and seeks, together with his colleagues, to assure its continuity in faith and discipline with the apostolic Church; yet it is the synod which, together with the primate, gives voice and definition to the apostolic tradition. It is also the synod which, in most churches, elects the primate, assists him in his leadership, and holds him to account for his ministry in the name of the whole Church (Apostolic Canons 34).

7. The particular form of primacy among the churches exercised by the bishops of Rome has been and remains the chief point of dispute between the Orthodox and Roman Catholic Churches, and their chief obstacle to full ecclesial communion with each other. Disagreement has often centered on the way in which the leadership exercised by Peter in expressing and confirming the faith of the other disciples (Matt. 16:17f.; Lk. 22:32; John 21:15-19) is to be realized in church life. The Orthodox have emphasized that the role of Peter within the apostolic college is reflected principally in the role of the bishop within the local church. Roman Catholics have claimed for the bishops of Rome, since the fourth century, not only the first place in honor among their episcopal colleagues but also the "Petrine" role of proclaiming the Church's apostolic tradition and of ensuring the observation of canonical practices.

As our Consultation has suggested in its earlier statement, "Apostolicity as God's Gift in the Life of the Church" (1986; ¶12), "There is no intrinsic opposition between these two approaches." The Orthodox do accept the notion of universal primacy, speaking of it as a "primacy of honor" accorded to a *primus inter pares*; at the same time, they cannot accept an understanding of the role of the primate which excludes the collegiality and interdependence of the whole body of bishops, and in consequence continue to reject the formulation of papal primacy found in Vatican I's constitution *Pastor Aeternus*. Engaged since the Second Vatican Council in further development of the doctrine of papal primacy within the context of a collegially responsible episcopate (see especially *Lumen Gentium* 22-23), the Roman Catholic Church is presently seeking new forms of synodal leadership which will be compatible with its tradition of effective universal unity in faith and practice, under the headship of the bishop of Rome.

8. The fullest synodal expression of the Church's universal reality is the gathering of bishops from various parts of the world in "ecumenical council," to deal with questions of urgent and universal importance by clarifying and defining the "ecumenical" faith and practice of the apostolic tradition (see the statement of the International Dialogue between the Roman Catholic Church and the Orthodox Church, "The Sacrament of Order in the Sacramental Structure of the Church" [New Valamo, 1988] ¶54). The Orthodox and Roman Catholic Churches agree in recognizing the seven great councils of the early Church as ecumenical in character and import. Because the circumstances of their convocation, their preparation and membership, and the process of their subsequent recognition by the churches vary, history offers us no single juridical model of conciliar structure as normative. Still, the acceptance of the binding authority of certain councils by the apostolic churches in worldwide communion—however and whenever that acceptance becomes clear—constitutes for the whole body of Christ an event of charismatic unity at the highest level. It is in the reception of a common faith, especially as that faith is formulated by the ecumenical councils, that the churches experience most authentically the unity in the Lord that is the foundation of eucharistic communion.

Brighton, MA
October, 1989
39th Meeting

Section 4

New Challenges to Orthodox-Catholic
Dialogue: Recent Changes in Eastern Europe
and the Present Search for Full Communion

INTRODUCTION TO SECTION FOUR

The sudden collapse of communism in Eastern Europe in the late eighties and early nineties caught the world by surprise. Politicians and diplomats, church leaders and theologians all scrambled to adjust to volatile new situations in which religious, ethnic, nationalistic and economic factors were closely intertwined. Particularly portentous for Orthodox-Catholic relations was the reemergence of the Eastern Catholic Churches in Romania, Slovakia, Poland and the former Soviet Union. With the rise of Soviet hegemony in Eastern Europe following World War II, these churches had been brutally suppressed. Bishops and leading churchmen had been arrested and sent to prison camps; state-orchestrated "reunion synods" in Lviv (1946) and elsewhere had declared the liquidation of the Union of Brest (1596) and similar unions; state authorities had seized church properties and converted them to secular purposes or turned them over to the Orthodox. Now, however, Eastern Catholics were emerging from their underground existence, seeking confirmation of their canonical status from Catholic authorities, demanding legal recognition from the state, and clamoring for the return of church properties seized at the time of the suppression.

The complicity of the Orthodox church leadership in the suppression of the late forties would be hard to deny, but it is not hard to understand. In the Soviet Union the Orthodox Church itself had very nearly been liquidated during the twenties and thirties, when hundreds of bishops and tens of thousands of other clergy and faithful were executed or sent to prison camps, and it had gained a measure of legal recognition only during World War II, when Stalin had needed the church's support in the war effort. Elsewhere in Eastern Europe as well, the new realities of communist rule would have made resistance to the suppression difficult even had church leaders been so inclined. However understandable these circumstances, the reemerging Eastern Catholics had little reason to be favorably disposed towards the Orthodox—all the more so because Orthodox church leaders still showed little inclination to acknowledge any role in the wrongs which Eastern Catholics had suffered.

The involvement of state officials and local politicians further aggravated relations between Eastern Catholics and Orthodox. In some places they favored Orthodox interests by trying to stall the process of legalization and hinder the transfer of properties claimed by the Eastern Catholics; in other places they favored Eastern Catholic interests. Charges and counter-charges of vigilante tactics and coercion, often easier to believe than to substantiate, became commonplace and in some places still continue. Further complicating the situation from 1990 onward, as the Soviet Union itself began to break up, was the rise of Orthodox separatist movements in Ukraine.

These new tensions in Eastern Europe had a chilling effect on Orthodox-Catholic relations at all levels. Symptomatic of the changed atmosphere was the Orthodox response to Pope John Paul II's invitation to participate in the 1991 Special Synod of Bishops on "The New Evangelization of Europe." Most of the invited Orthodox churches declined to send representatives. One of the few Orthodox who were present, Metropolitan Spyridon of Venice, who was representing the Ecumenical Patriarchate of Constantinople, did not mince words in ascribing this veritable boycott to renewed Catholic proselytism and "uniatism" in Eastern Europe; and he warned that "the road of reconciliation between the Catholic and Orthodox Churches, painstakingly constructed during the past decades, now seems seriously compromised."

As these remarks suggest, in the view of the Orthodox "uniatism" lies at the root of the new crisis in relations. The use of this term, now generally regarded as derogatory, is expressive of the centuries of conflicting claims, mistrust and pain which characterized Catholic-Orthodox relations until the sixties. For the Orthodox, at least, discussion of the crisis should not take as its point of departure the forced suppressions of the Eastern Catholic Churches in the late forties, as though a return to the *status quo ante* were the obvious and only appropriate solution. Discussion should rather go back to Brest and the subsequent "unions" which brought so many Eastern Christians living under Polish or Hapsburg rule into the Roman communion but at the price of their spiritual and canonical unity with their Orthodox brothers and sisters. On the other hand, the Eastern Catholics, no matter how they explain their historical past, insist on the particular identity they have gained over the course of centuries, which often has not been respected either by the Orthodox or by their fellow Catholics.

The issue of "uniatism" was never wholly absent even in the heyday of the "dialogue of charity." For example, the third Pan-Orthodox Rhodes Conference (1964), while authorizing dialogue with the Roman Catholic Church, at the same time was sharply critical of "uniatism," viewing it as the major obstacle to closer relations; and several Orthodox Churches objected strongly to the presence of Eastern Catholics on the Joint International Commission. To be sure, the Second Vatican Council's Decree on Ecumenism and its Constitution on the Church created an improved atmosphere; Catholic rediscovery of the *koinonia* ecclesiology of the early Church, with its emphasis on subsidiarity and episcopal collegiality, facilitated dialogue as "sister churches." At the same time, in the view of a number of Orthodox theologians, the council's Decree on the Eastern Churches not only did not resolve the issue of "uniatism" but in fact exacerbated it. Before the council, in line with the universalist ecclesiology of the times, it was quite natural to speak of "Eastern Rite Catholics" as though they differed from Latin Rite Catholics only in the externals of worship. The council, however, had affirmed that the Eastern Catholics precisely constituted *churches,* whose vocation was to provide a bridge to the separated churches of the East by witnessing to the possibility of communion with Rome without loss of cultural and ecclesial identity. Was there not—the Orthodox would ask—an inconsistency here? If, as subsequent dialogue would emphasize, the Orthodox Churches themselves are truly "sister churches," already nearly at the point of full communion with the Roman Catholic Church, why were these "bridge churches" needed? Do they not rather constitute a continuing denial of the ecclesial reality of the Orthodox Churches on the part of the Catholic Church?

Such ecclesiological questions had not been explicitly addressed in the course of theological dialogue between Orthodox and Catholics. In the late seventies and early eighties it had seemed better to begin with what unites rather than what divides. But these questions had not gone away, and the great changes which began to transform Eastern Europe in the late eighties brought them again to the fore, along with a host of practical problems relating to property and pastoral activities.

At the insistence of its Orthodox members, the Joint International Commission in 1988 established a special subcommission alongside its regular subcommissions to study the question of "uniatism." At its first meeting, in Vienna in January 1990, the subcommission reiterated the position long held by both sides, that the relationship between Orthodox and Catholics must be based on "an ecclesiology of sister churches," and it began the difficult task of establishing a common position on "uniatism." Also in January 1990, high-level discussions between the Russian Orthodox Church and the Roman Catholic Church led to "Recommendations for the Normalization of Relations between Orthodox and Catholics of the Eastern Rite in the Western Ukraine." While these recommendations had little or no immediate practical success, they too contributed to the work of the Commission.

By the time the sixth plenary session of the Joint International Commission met in Munich/Freising in June 1990, relations between Catholics and Orthodox in Eastern Europe had deteriorated to the point that, on the insistence of the Orthodox membership, the Commission agreed to turn its attention exclusively to the issue of "uniatism." Without following its own accepted procedures for preparing materials for discussion, it released a brief document announcing this decision in which it acknowledged "uniatism" as "an urgent problem to be treated with priority over all other subjects to be discussed in the dialogue." It went on to define "uniatism" in this context to mean "the effort which aims to bring about the unity of the Church by separating from the Orthodox Church communities or Orthodox faithful without taking into account that, according to ecclesiology, the Orthodox Church is a sister church which itself offers the means of grace and salvation. In this sense...we reject 'uniatism' as a method of unity opposed to the common Tradition of our Churches." (¶6b) Returning to its normal procedures, the Commission entrusted preparation of a draft text for consideration at its next plenary session to three joint subcommissions and then to its joint coordinating committee, which completed this task at Arricia (near Rome) in June 1991. Like the Freising document, the Arricia draft text enjoyed a wide circulation. It was this text which eventually would form the basis for the Joint International Commission's fourth agreed statement, "Uniatism, Method of Union of the Past, and the Present Search for Full Communion" (Balamand, 1993).

In the United States during these years, both the Theological Consultation and the Joint Committee of Orthodox and Catholic Bishops closely followed the deteriorating ecclesiastical situation in Eastern Europe and the desperate efforts of the Joint International Commission to restore an atmosphere conducive to dialogue. Their joint statements, communiqués and other documents from this period reveal the impact which international tensions had on concerned Orthodox and Catholics in the United States. Typical in many ways is the "Joint Communiqué of the Orthodox-Roman Catholic Consultation in the United States on Current Tensions between Our Churches in Eastern Europe" (October 1990). Expressing both hope and apprehension, it calls for development of effective procedures to deal with specific points of tension as well as "deeper exploration of basic ecclesiological issues and of their practical implications." It calls attention to the new atmosphere in which the churches now meet: "Inspired by the example of the first millennium, our churches have begun to meet and work together as sister churches on the basis of an ecclesiology of communion" (¶4). And, on the basis of the Consultation's own experience in North America, it expresses confidence "that genuine theological dialogue, in a spirit of mutual respect and love, is in fact possible" (¶5). The Consultation's 1992 joint statement on "Tensions in Eastern Europe Related to 'Uniatism'" develops many of these themes and adds several recommendations that may appear typically "American": Needed, among other things, are practical mechanisms for the mutual resolution of conflicts, objective and dispassionate information-gathering and reporting, and shared scholarly research. The statement also calls for clearer differentiation between the several meanings which words like "uniatism" have and for deeper exploration of what "mutual recognition as sister churches" might mean in practice.

Briefer but no less significant are the contributions of the Joint Committee of Orthodox and Catholic Bishops. The bishops' 1991 "Statement" of support for historical Christianity in Eastern Europe and the former Soviet Union expresses concern that misguided efforts by some in the West, both Protestant and Catholic, will treat the newly opened lands of the East as mission territory ripe for "conversion," disregarding the deep historical roots and actual presence of the Christian churches already there. As for relations between Catholics and Orthodox, the bishops'

1992 "Communiqué" on Eastern Europe acknowledges that "iniquities have been perpetrated by both churches" and calls for repentance and mutual forgiveness on both sides. At the same time, it notes the fear expressed by many Orthodox that at the present juncture the Catholic Church may be "changing its mind in regard to basic presuppositions upon which the Orthodox Church and the Roman Catholic Church meet as equal churches, manifesting the fullness of catholicity of the One, Holy Catholic and Apostolic Church."

In June 1993 the Joint International Commission, meeting at Balamand, Lebanon, completed and released its long-awaited statement on "Uniatism, Method of Union of the Past, and the Present Search for Full Communion." The statement begins with a review of ecclesiological principles, emphasizing the importance of the concepts of *koinonia* and "sister churches" and eschewing what has been called "ecclesiological and soteriological exclusivism." However the purpose of the statement is preeminently practical. Roughly half the text is devoted to rules and guidelines intended "to lead to a just and definitive solution to the difficulties which the Oriental [Eastern] Catholic Churches present to the Orthodox Church" (¶17). The Commission's hope is that, "by excluding for the future all proselytism and all desire for expansion by Catholics at the expense of the Orthodox Church," it has "overcome the obstacles which impelled certain autocephalous Orthodox Churches to suspend their participation in the theological dialogue" (¶35). To this end, the Commission reaffirms a position already set forth in Vienna, Munich/Freising and Ariccia, that "the method which has been called 'uniatism'" is to be rejected "because it is opposed to the common tradition of our churches" (¶2); it "can no longer be accepted either as a method to be followed or as a model of the unity our Churches are seeking" (¶11). At the same time, the Commission acknowledges the Eastern Catholic Churches' "right to exist and to act in answer to the spiritual needs of their faithful" (¶3). These churches have the rights and obligations which are connected with this communion [with the See of Rome]. The principles determining their attitude towards the Orthodox are those which have been stated by the Second Vatican Council and have been put into practice by the popes who have clarified the practical consequences flowing from these principles.... These churches, then, should be inserted, on

164

both local and universal levels, into the dialogue of love... and enter into the theological dialogue, with all its practical implications. (¶16)

The Balamand Statement met with a variety of reactions from many quarters. Some of these, as the U.S. Consultation notes in its Response to the statement, "have been positive but others negative and even abusive" (¶3). Some of these negative reactions suggest unfamiliarity with the continuing work of the Joint International Commission and with the place of the Balamand Statement within this work. Others reveal how unaware many Orthodox and Catholics are of the changed atmosphere for theological dialogue which has developed since the sixties. Particularly in Eastern Europe, many are suspicious of ecumenism generally and have difficulty conceiving of Catholic-Orthodox relations in anything other than the confrontational terms of an earlier period. In general, however, the statement's practical rules and guidelines have gotten a relatively favorable reception among both Catholics and Orthodox, notwithstanding some apprehension that they may be unrealistic and unworkable. On the other hand, the statement's presentation of ecclesiological principles has found less favor, particularly among those Orthodox who have been critical of ecumenism generally. Issues singled out for criticism include the statement's presentation of the historical record of Orthodox-Catholic relations, its references to the practice of rebaptism, and the concept of "sister churches."

In its response to the Balamand Statement (October 1994), the U.S. Consultation characterized it as "a strong and positive contribution to the theological dialogue between our churches" (¶17). The Consultation particularly applauded the practical rules and guidelines which constituted the second part of the statement. It also took into consideration some of the criticisms leveled against the ecclesiological principles enunciated in the first part of the statement. In this connection, the Consultation suggested ways in which the Balamand Statement's presentation of the historical record could be more nuanced (¶¶/-8); it observed that "such an important issue as rebaptism demands deeper historical and theological investigation" along the lines laid down in the 1987 Bari Statement (¶9); and it noted the need to explore more fully "the precise significance and manifold implications" of the concept of "sister churches" and itself offered some observations on the subject (¶12). In addition, noting the many times that the Balamand Statement speaks of religious freedom and liberty, the Consultation observed that "where concern for the solidarity and spiritual health of the community as a whole is absent, the exercise of 'freedom' and 'liberty' can lead all to easily to the fragmentation of society and to the alienation of persons from each other and from God" (¶14).

It remains to be seen what practical effect the Balamand Statement will have on Orthodox-Catholic relations in Eastern Europe and whether the Joint International Commission will be able to take up its work on theological issues any time in the near future. Further dialogue on ecclesiological issues posed by "uniatism" may still have to take place. While the crisis over "uniatism" did deflect the Joint International Commission from its original agenda for dialogue, in the long run it may help bring a note of realism to its work. Certainly it has shown how fragile ecumenical dialogue can be if it is not rooted in the actual life and experience of the churches.

A JOINT COMMUNIQUE OF THE ORTHODOX-ROMAN CATHOLIC CONSULTATION IN THE UNITED STATES ON CURRENT TENSIONS BETWEEN OUR CHURCHES IN EASTERN EUROPE

U. S. Theological Consultation, 1990

1. During its 41st meeting, held in Brighton, Massachusetts, October 18-20, 1990, the Orthodox-Roman Catholic Consultation in the United States took note of recent developments in Eastern Europe which have manifold and immediate implications for relations between our churches. The consultation also took note of the Statement issued on this subject by the Joint International Commission for Theological Dialogue between the Roman Catholic Church and the Orthodox Church, meeting in Munich-Freising, June 6-15, 1990.

2. In the past months a new atmosphere of political freedom in Eastern Europe has given our churches unexpected and indeed unprecedented opportunities for cooperation, common witness and deeper unity. At the same time rapid political and social changes have been accompanied by serious tensions which, many fear, may threaten our churches' continued progress to unity.

3. With the Joint Commission we deplore all forms of violence, intimidation and coercion in violation of the religious liberty of persons, communities and churches. We also encourage continued efforts by the appropriate ecclesiastical authorities to develop adequate and effective procedures for dealing with specific points of tension.

4. Above all, we call attention to the need for deeper exploration of basic ecclesiological issues and of their practical implications. Especially since the Pan-Orthodox conferences (1961-68), the Second Vatican Council (1962-65) and the mutual lifting of anathemas (1965), our churches have come to recognize that some of the methods and models of union employed by both sides in the past in fact have deepened disagreement and division. Inspired by the example of the first millennium, our churches have begun to meet and work together as sister churches, on the

167

basis of an ecclesiology of communion. Our consultation believes that further reflection on ecclesiological principles and continued practical efforts, in a spirit of Christian love and forgiveness, to overcome past hostility are of vital importance at this critical point in relations between our churches.

5. It is difficult for us in North America, living in circumstances very different from those in Eastern Europe, fully to appreciate the complexity of the religious, cultural, political and social situation there. Yet our experience in this consultation leads us to believe that genuine theological dialogue, in a spirit of mutual respect and love, is in fact possible, and that such dialogue can help our churches respond effectively to the many painful practical issues that still divide us. Our Christian hope—indeed the prayer of Jesus "that all may be one"—demands that we continue, on a sound theological basis, our work together for Christian unity.

Brighton, MA
October 20, 1990
41st Meeting

STATEMENT ON EASTERN EUROPE

Joint Committee of Orthodox and Catholic Bishops, 1991

With gratitude to God we welcome the disintegration of communism in Eastern Europe and particularly in the Soviet Union, where Christian people, the majority of whom are Orthodox, but not exclusively so, have suffered relentless religious persecution and oppression for the past 74 years. We gratefully recognize the fact that the Christian Church has nevertheless survived this persecution. Unfortunately, attempts to restore democracy have also given rise to types of proselytizing that do not respect the nature of the cultures and do not accept the historical Christianity already present there. This Christianity is in need of the moral support and material help of Christian people throughout the world.

Baltimore
September 19, 1991
Tenth Meeting

169

JOINT STATEMENT OF THE UNITED STATES ORTHODOX-ROMAN CATHOLIC CONSULTATION ON TENSIONS IN EASTERN EUROPE RELATED TO "UNIATISM"

U. S. Theological Consultation, 1992

The most recent (43rd) meeting of the U.S. Orthodox-Roman Catholic Consultation at the Holy Cross Greek Orthodox School of Theology, Brookline, Massachusetts, May 26-28, 1992, focused upon the question of "Uniatism" and reviewed a number of recent statements regarding religious conflicts in Eastern Europe. Included among these texts were: the joint text of the Roman Catholic Church and Russian Orthodox Church (January 17, 1990), the Freising Statement of the Joint International Commission for Theological Dialogue between the Roman Catholic Church and the Orthodox Church (June 15, 1990), our Consultation's previous joint communiqué on "Current Tensions between Our Churches in Eastern Europe" (October 20, 1990), the Ariccia draft statement of its Coordinating Committee on "Uniatism as a Method of Union in the Past and the Present Search for Full Communion" (June 15, 1991), the statement of the U.S. Orthodox and Roman Catholic Bishops' Commission (September 19, 1991), and the "Message of the Primates of the Most Holy Orthodox Churches" from the fourteen primates of patriarchates and autocephalous and autonomous churches (March 15, 1992). We, the members of this Consultation, formulate this joint statement of concern.

1. Our own experience of cooperation and dialogue in North America has generally been a harmonious and fruitful one. This experience convinces us that resolution of the present difficulties will be possible only through prayer and a deepened dialogue in truth and love.

2. We recognize that it is not always possible for us to judge the accuracy of reports on abuses of justice or proselytism in distant parts of the world. We decry publication of unverified alleged events or incidents that only fan the feelings of fear and prejudice as well as inflammatory

170

reactions to verified incidents. We also decry one-sided or prejudicial reporting on religious developments in Eastern Europe and elsewhere, which, through emotionalism or sensationalism, would tend to undercut efforts toward genuine cooperation and reconciliation. We therefore appeal to world-wide human rights' agencies and the media to lend their service for a balanced presentation of events, and we commit ourselves to the task of sharing and attempting to verify such information as we receive.

3. We recognize that, because of the burden of past history and the painful actions of governments and churches, there exist among Christians in many parts of the world, especially Eastern Europe, a high degree of resentment, antipathy, suspicion and even fear of other Christian communities. If such attitudes are to be overcome, it is essential that our churches together formulate and implement practical recommendations, such as those presented in the Ariccia working draft, the January 1990 agreement between the Roman Catholic Church and the Russian Orthodox Church, and elsewhere, effectively addressing the specific issues that divide us.

4. Therefore, we encourage mutual consultation at all levels, particularly before any activities are undertaken which might even inadvertently give offense to others. Such consultation would help all parties to avoid needless misunderstandings.

5. In reviewing the various documents which have dealt with recent tensions between our churches, we find that expressions like "Uniatism" have been used and understood in diverse ways. We believe that such expressions require more careful analysis. Among other things, a distinction should be made between "Uniatism" understood as an inappropriate, indeed unacceptable, model or method for church union, and "Uniatism" understood as the existence of convinced Eastern Christians who have accepted full communion with the See of Rome as part of their self-understanding as a church. "Uniatism" in the former sense is no longer accepted by either of our churches.

6. We are convinced that in countries previously under Communist oppression, as well as elsewhere, a healthy interaction between the Orthodox Church and the Roman Catholic Church or even between the Orthodox Church and the Eastern Catholic Churches could lead to

important developments in theological renewal, liturgical reform, and useful formulation of Christian social and political doctrine.

7. We recognize the importance of participating jointly in and sharing the results of theological, ecclesiastical, and historical research among clergy, seminarians and laity, especially in countries where freedom of the press and easy access to international scholarship have been systematically hindered.

8. The present difficulties offer theologians opportunities to explore, from a new perspective, certain theological themes which have been discussed repeatedly in recent ecumenical dialogues. We are challenged, to give only two examples, to explain what "mutual recognition as sister churches" means in practice, and to explore structures needed for achieving communion among the worldwide community of local churches.

Brookline, MA
May 28, 1992
43rd Meeting

COMMUNIQUE ON EASTERN EUROPE

Joint Committee of Orthodox and Catholic Bishops, 1992

The members of the Joint Committee of Orthodox and Roman Catholic Bishops gathered for their eleventh meeting, September 30—October 2, 1992, in Tenafly, New Jersey. They reaffirmed their commitment to these annual dialogues and their conviction that through dialogue, mutual understanding, good will and trust, they are following the teachings of the Lord. The theological dialogue at all levels is under severe strain because of recent events in Eastern Europe. The Roman Catholic bishops listened with concern as the Orthodox bishops expressed their deepest reservations with the recent letter of the Congregation for the Doctrine of the Faith, "Some Aspects of the Church Understood as Communion." In their view, the letter is a sign that the Roman Catholic Church is changing its mind in regard to basic presuppositions upon which the Orthodox Church and the Roman Catholic Church meet as equal churches, manifesting the fullness of catholicity of the one, holy, catholic and apostolic Church.

As the bishop members of this dialogue committee study the history of the relationship between the two churches since the schism, they recognize that iniquities have been perpetrated by both churches (for example, the problems associated with Brest and Lviv). In this context it is important to study the recent developments in Eastern Europe and the former Soviet Union. Having recognized that transgressions and deceptions have been committed, leaders and faithful of both churches must repent and express mutual forgiveness. In this spirit, the example of Patriarch Athenagoras and Pope Paul VI, whose vision continues to inspire Catholics and Orthodox alike, must not be surrendered.

With the arrival of His Holiness Patriarch Pavle of Serbia in the United States, the bishops turned their thoughts to the tragic events occurring in the territory of the former Yugoslavia. They condemn the past and present manipulation of religion for advancing geopolitical and ethnic interests, which have rekindled so many deep prejudices and enmities. The bishops appealed to all in the United States to pray for the reconciliation of the peoples of that troubled region. As winter approaches, thousands of lives are endangered. The bishops expressed their support for urgent humanitarian effort in meeting the needs of all who suffer there. They applauded the actions of Orthodox and Catholic leaders, and other religious leaders, toward terminating the terrible carnage taking place in these areas.

Tenafly, New Jersey
October 2, 1992
11th Meeting

UNIATISM, METHOD OF UNION OF THE PAST, AND THE PRESENT SEARCH FOR FULL COMMUNION

Joint International Commission, 1993

Introduction

1. At the request of the Orthodox Churches, the normal progression of the theological dialogue with the Catholic Church has been set aside so that immediate attention might be given to the question which is called "uniatism."

2. With regard to the method which has been called "uniatism," it was stated at Freising (June 1990) that "we reject it as a method for the search for unity because it is opposed to the common tradition of our churches."

3. Concerning the Oriental Catholic Churches, it is clear that they, as part of the Catholic communion, have the right to exist and to act in answer to the spiritual needs of their faithful.

4. The document prepared at Ariccia by the joint coordinating committee (June 1991) and finished at Balamand (June 1993) states what is our method in the present search for full communion, thus giving the reason for excluding "uniatism" as a method.

5. This document is composed of two parts:

1) Ecclesiological principles and

2) Practical rules.

Ecclesiological Principles

6. The division between the churches of the East and of the West has never quelled the desire for unity wished by Christ. Rather this situation, which is contrary to the nature of the Church, has often been for many the occasion to become more deeply conscious of the need to achieve this unity, so as to be faithful to the Lord's commandment.

7. In the course of the centuries various attempts were made to reestablish unity. They sought to achieve this end through different ways, at times conciliar, according to the political, historical, theological and spiritual situation of each period. Unfortunately, none of these efforts

175

succeeded in reestablishing full communion between the church of the West and the church of the East, and at times even made oppositions more acute.

8. In the course of the last four centuries, in various parts of the East, initiatives were taken within certain churches and impelled by outside elements, to restore communion between the church of the East and the church of the West. These initiatives led to the union of certain communities with the See of Rome and brought with them, as a consequence, the breaking of communion with their mother churches of the East. This took place not without the interference of extra-ecclesial interests. In this way Oriental Catholic Churches came into being. And so a situation was created which has become a source of conflicts and of suffering in the first instance for the Orthodox but also for Catholics.

9. Whatever may have been the intention and the authenticity of the desire to be faithful to the commandment of Christ: "that all may be one" expressed in these partial unions with the See of Rome, it must be recognized that the reestablishment of unity between the church of the East and the church of the West was not achieved and that the division remains, embittered by these attempts.

10. The situation thus created resulted in fact in tensions and oppositions.

Progressively, in the decades which followed these unions, missionary activity tended to include among its priorities the effort to convert other Christians, individually or in groups, so as "to bring them back" to one's own church. In order to legitimize this tendency, a source of proselytism, the Catholic Church developed the theological vision according to which she presented herself as the only one to whom salvation was entrusted. As a reaction, the Orthodox Church, in turn, came to accept the same vision according to which only in her could salvation be found. To assure the salvation of the "separated brethren" it even happened that Christians were rebaptized and that certain requirements of the religious freedom of persons and of their act of faith were forgotten. This perspective was one to which that period showed little sensitivity.

11. On the other hand certain civil authorities made attempts to bring back Oriental Catholics to the church of their fathers. To achieve this end they did not hesitate, when the occasion was given, to use unacceptable means.

12. Because of the way in which Catholics and Orthodox once again consider each other in their relationship to the mystery of the Church and discover each other once again as sister churches, this form of "missionary apostolate" described above, and which has been called "uniatism," can no longer be accepted either as a method to be followed nor as a model of the unity our churches are seeking.

13. In fact, especially since the Pan-Orthodox Conferences and the Second Vatican Council, the rediscovery and the giving again of proper value to the Church as communion, both on the part of Orthodox and of Catholics, has radically altered perspectives and thus attitudes. On each side it is recognized that what Christ has entrusted to his Church—profession of apostolic faith, participation in the sacraments, above all the one priesthood celebrating the one sacrifice of Christ, the apostolic succession of bishops—cannot be considered the exclusive property of one of our churches. In this context, it is clear that any rebaptism must be avoided.

14. It is in this perspective that the Catholic Churches and the Orthodox Churches recognize each other as sister churches, responsible together for maintaining the Church of God in fidelity to the divine purpose, most especially in what concerns unity. According to the words of Pope John Paul II, the ecumenical endeavor of the sister churches of East and West, grounded in dialogue and prayer, is the search for perfect and total communion which is neither absorption nor fusion but a meeting in truth and love (cf. *Slavorum Apostoli*, no. 27).

15. While the inviolable freedom of persons and their obligation to follow the requirements of their conscience remain secure, in the search for reestablishing unity there is no question of conversion of people from one church to the other in order to ensure their salvation. There is a question of achieving together the will of Christ for his own and the design of God for his Church by means of a common quest by the churches for a full accord on the content of the faith and its implications. This effort is being carried on in the current theological dialogue. The present document is a necessary stage in this dialogue.

16. The Oriental Catholic Churches who have desired to reestablish full communion with the See of Rome and have remained faithful to it, have the rights and obligations which are connected with this communion. The principles determining their attitude towards Orthodox

177

Churches are those which have been stated by the Second Vatican Council and have been put into practice by the popes who have clarified the practical consequences flowing from these principles in various documents published since then. These churches, then, should be inserted, on both local and universal levels, into the dialogue of love, in mutual respect and reciprocal trust found once again, and enter into the theological dialogue, with all its practical implications.

17. In this atmosphere, the considerations already presented and the practical guidelines which follow, insofar as they will be effectively received and faithfully observed, are such as to lead to a just and definitive solution to the difficulties which these Oriental Catholic Churches present to the Orthodox Church.

18. Towards this end, Pope Paul VI affirmed in his address at the Phanar in July 1967: "It is on the heads of the churches, of their hierarchy, that the obligation rests to guide the churches along the way that leads to finding full communion again. They ought to do this by recognizing and respecting each other as pastors of that part of the flock of Christ entrusted to them, by taking care for the cohesion and growth of the people of God, and avoiding everything that could scatter it or cause confusion in its ranks" (*Tomos Agapis*, no. 172). In this spirit Pope John Paul II and Ecumenical Patriarch Dimitrios I together stated clearly: "We reject every form of proselytism, every attitude which would be or could be perceived to be a lack of respect" (December 7, 1978).

Practical Rules

19. Mutual respect between the churches which find themselves in difficult situations will increase appreciably in the measure that they will observe the following practical rules.

20. These rules will not resolve the problems which are worrying us unless each of the parties concerned has a will to pardon, based on the Gospel and, within the context of a constant effort for renewal, accompanied by the unceasing desire to seek the full communion which existed for more than a thousand years between our churches. It is here that the dialogue of love must be present with a continually renewed intensity and perseverance which alone can overcome reciprocal lack of understanding

and which is the necessary climate for deepening the theological dialogue that will permit arriving at full communion.

21. The first step to take is to put an end to everything that can foment division, contempt and hatred between the churches. For this the authorities of the Catholic Church will assist the Oriental Catholic Churches and their communities so that they themselves may prepare for full communion between Catholic and Orthodox Churches. The authorities of the Orthodox Church will act in a similar manner towards their faithful. In this way it will be possible to take care of the extremely complex situation that has been created in Eastern Europe, at the same time in charity and in justice, both as regards Catholics and Orthodox.

22. Pastoral activity in the Catholic Church, Latin as well as Oriental, no longer aims at having the faithful of one church pass over to the other; that is to say, it no longer aims at proselytizing among the Orthodox. It aims at answering the spiritual needs of its own faithful and it has no desire for expansion at the expense of the Orthodox Church. Within these perspectives, so that there will no longer be a place for mistrust and suspicion, it is necessary that there be reciprocal exchanges of information about various pastoral projects and that this cooperation between bishops and all those with responsibilities in our churches can be set in motion and develop.

23. The history of the relations between the Orthodox Church and the Oriental Catholic Churches has been marked by persecutions and sufferings. Whatever may have been these sufferings and their causes, they do not justify any triumphalism; no one can glory in them or draw an argument from them to accuse or disparage the other church. God alone knows his own witnesses. Whatever may have been the past, it must be left to the mercy of God, and all the energies of the churches should be directed towards obtaining that the present and the future conform better to the will of Christ for his own.

24. It will also be necessary—and this on the part of both churches—that the bishops and all those with pastoral responsibilities in them scrupulously respect the religious liberty of the faithful. These, in turn, must be able to express freely their opinion by being consulted and by organizing themselves to this end. In fact, religious liberty requires that, particularly in situations of conflict, the faithful are able to express their opinion and to

decide without pressure from outside if they wish to be in communion either with the Orthodox Church or with the Catholic Church. Religious freedom would be violated when, under the cover of financial assistance, the faithful of one church would be attracted to the other, by promises, for example, of education and material benefits that may be lacking in their own church. In this context, it will be necessary that social assistance, as well as every form of philanthropic activity be organized with common agreement so as to avoid creating new suspicions.

25. Furthermore, the necessary respect for Christian freedom—one of the most precious gifts received from Christ—should not become an occasion for undertaking a pastoral project which may also involve the faithful of other churches, without previous consultation with the pastors of these churches. Not only should every form of pressure, of any kind whatsoever, be excluded, but respect for consciences, motivated by an authentic exigency of faith, should be one of the principles guiding the pastoral concern of those responsible in the two churches and should be the object of their common reflection (cf. Gal. 5:13).

26. That is why it is necessary to seek and to engage in an open dialogue, which in the first place should be between those who have responsibilities for the churches at the local level. Those in charge of the communities concerned should create joint local commissions or make effective those which already exist, for finding solutions to concrete problems and seeing that these solutions are applied in truth and love, in justice and peace. If agreement cannot be reached on the local level, the question should be brought to mixed commissions established by higher authorities.

27. Suspicion would disappear more easily if the two parties were to condemn violence wherever communities of one church use it against communities of a sister church. As requested by His Holiness Pope John Paul II in his letter of May 31, 1991, it is necessary that all violence and every kind of pressure be absolutely avoided in order that freedom of conscience be respected. It is the task of those in charge of communities to assist their faithful to deepen their loyalty towards their own church and towards its traditions and to teach them to avoid not only violence, be that physical, verbal or moral, but also all that could lead to contempt

for other Christians and to a counter-witness, completely ignoring the work of salvation which is reconciliation in Christ.

28. Faith in sacramental reality implies a respect for the liturgical celebrations of the other church. The use of violence to occupy a place of worship contradicts this conviction. On the contrary, this conviction sometimes requires that the celebration of other churches should be made easier by putting at their disposal, by common agreement, one's own church for alternate celebration at different times in the same building. Still more, the evangelical ethos requires that statements or manifestations which are likely to perpetuate a state of conflict and hinder the dialogue be avoided. Does not St. Paul exhort us to welcome one another as Christ has welcomed us, for the glory of God (Rom. 15:7)?

29. Bishops and priests have the duty before God to respect the authority which the Holy Spirit has given to the bishops and priests of the other church and for that reason to avoid interfering in the spiritual life of the faithful of that church. When cooperation becomes necessary for the good of the faithful, it is then required that those responsible for an agreement among themselves, establish for this mutual assistance clear principles which are known to all, and act subsequently with frankness, clarity, and with respect for the sacramental discipline of the other church.

In this context, to avoid all misunderstanding and to develop confidence between the two churches, it is necessary that Catholic and Orthodox bishops of the same territory consult with each other before establishing Catholic pastoral projects which imply the creation of new structures in regions which traditionally form part of the jurisdiction of the Orthodox Church, in view to avoid parallel pastoral activities which would risk rapidly degenerating into rivalry or even conflicts.

30. To pave the way for future relations between the two churches, passing beyond the outdated ecclesiology of return to the Catholic Church connected with the problem which is the object of this document, special attention will be given to the preparation of future priests and of all those who, in any way, are involved in an apostolic activity carried on in a place where the other church traditionally has its roots. Their education should be objectively positive with respect to the other church. First of all, everyone should be informed of the apostolic succession of the other church and the authenticity of its sacramental life. One

should also offer all a correct and comprehensive knowledge of history aiming at a historiography of the two churches which is in agreement and even may be common. In this way, the dissipation of prejudices will be helped, and the use of history in a polemical manner will be avoided. This presentation will lead to an awareness that faults leading to separation belong to both sides, leaving deep wounds on each side.

31. The admonition of the Apostle Paul to the Corinthians (1 Cor. 6:1-7) will be recalled. It recommends that Christians resolve their differences through fraternal dialogue, thus avoiding recourse to the intervention of the civil authorities for a practical solution to the problems which arise between churches or local communities. This applies particularly to the possession or return of ecclesiastical property. These solutions should not be based only on past situations or rely solely on general juridical principles, but they must also take into account the complexity of present realities and local circumstances.

32. It is in this spirit that it will be possible to meet in common the task of reevangelization of our secularized world. Efforts will also be made to give objective news to the mass-media, especially to the religious press, in order to avoid tendentious and misleading information.

33. It is necessary that the churches come together in order to express gratitude and respect towards all, known and unknown—bishops, priests or faithful, Orthodox, Catholic whether Oriental or Latin—who suffered, confessed their faith, witnessed their fidelity to the Church, and, in general, towards all Christians, without discrimination, who underwent persecutions. Their sufferings call us to unity and, on our part, to give common witness in response to the prayer of Christ "that all may be one, so that the world may believe" (John 17:21).

34. The International Joint Commission for Theological Dialogue between the Catholic Church and the Orthodox Church, at its plenary meeting in Balamand, strongly recommends that these practical rules be put into practice by our churches, including the Oriental Catholic Churches who are called to take part in this dialogue, which should be carried on in the serene atmosphere necessary for its progress, towards the reestablishment of full communion.

182

35. By excluding for the future all proselytism and all desire for expansion by Catholics at the expense of the Orthodox Church, the commission hopes that it has overcome the obstacles which impelled certain autocephalous churches to suspend their participation in the theological dialogue and that the Orthodox Church will be able to find itself altogether again for continuing the theological work already so happily begun.

Balamand, Lebanon
June 23, 1993
Seventh Plenary Meeting

A RESPONSE OF THE ORTHODOX-ROMAN CATHOLIC CONSULTATION IN THE UNITED STATES TO THE JOINT INTERNATIONAL COMMISSION FOR THEOLOGICAL DIALOGUE BETWEEN THE ORTHODOX CHURCH AND THE ROMAN CATHOLIC CHURCH REGARDING THE BALAMAND DOCUMENT (DATED JUNE 23, 1993): "UNIATISM, METHOD OF UNION OF THE PAST, AND THE PRESENT SEARCH FOR FULL COMMUNION"

U.S. Theological Consultation, 1994

1. Since the early 1980s, the Orthodox-Roman Catholic Consultation in the United States, established by the Standing Conference of Canonical Orthodox Bishops in the Americas (SCOBA) and the National Conference of Catholic Bishops (NCCB), has closely followed the work of the Joint International Commission for Theological Dialogue between the Orthodox Church and the Roman Catholic Church. The U.S. Consultation has responded to documents published by the International Commission as part of its original plan for theological dialogue set down at Rhodes in 1980: "The Mystery of the Church and of the Eucharist in the Light of the Mystery of the Holy Trinity" (Munich 1982), "Faith, Sacraments and the Unity of the Church" (Bari 1987) and "The Sacrament of Order in the Sacramental Structure of the Church" (Valamo 1988).

2. More recently, as the International Commission has interrupted its original plan in order to give immediate attention to the question of "uniatism," the U.S. Consultation has also studied this question, reflecting not only on the preliminary document released by the International Commission in Freising (1990), the draft prepared for the Commission in Ariccia (1991) and widely diffused, and related texts, but also on our own North American experience. Three brief statements already have been issued: "A Joint Communiqué of the Orthodox-Roman Catholic Consultation in the United States on Current Tensions between our Churches in Eastern Europe" (Brighton, MA, 1990), "Joint Statement of the

United States Orthodox-Roman Catholic Consultation on Tensions in Eastern Europe Related to 'Uniatism'" (Brookline, MA, 1992), and "A Statement of the Catholic Members of the U.S. Orthodox-Roman Catholic Consultation" (Douglaston, NY, 1992).

3. Now that the final expression of the International Commission's work has appeared in the document "Uniatism, Method of Union of the Past, and the Present Search for Full Communion" (Balamand, 1993), we in the U.S. Consultation have analyzed the document and taken note of reactions to it by various Catholics and Orthodox, some of which have been positive but others negative and even abusive. We now wish to submit our common response and reflections to the Joint International Commission and to others of the wider community of faith.

4. Our Consultation rejoices that the International Commission has been able to complete the work it set out for itself on the difficult question of "uniatism." With the Commission, we hope that "by excluding for the future all proselytism and all desire for expansion by Catholics at the expense of the Orthodox Church" (¶35), enough has been achieved in reestablishing trust between Orthodox and Roman Catholics after the events which led to the interruption of the theological work of the Commission in 1990 so that all members of the Commission can now return to that work. The theological dialogue itself must be deepened if it is to progress, and further issues relating to the ecclesial status of the Eastern Catholic Churches, only touched upon at Balamand, need to be relocated within this deepening of the properly theological task facing the Joint International Commission.

5. We applaud the Commission's efforts in the second part of the document to formulate various practical rules and guidelines intended "to lead to a just and definitive solution to the difficulties which the Oriental Catholic Churches present to the Orthodox Church" (¶17). These rules and guidelines call for:

— reciprocal exchanges of information about various pastoral projects (¶22);

—avoidance of those forms of philanthropic activity that might be construed as attempts to buy new adherents to the detriment of the other church (¶24);

—open dialogue at the local level (¶26);

—avoidance of all forms of violence (¶27);

—mutual respect for each other's places of worship and even sharing of facilities when circumstances require (¶28);

—respect for the spiritual life and sacramental discipline of the other church (¶29a);

—consultation before the establishment of new pastoral projects which might unnecessarily parallel or even undermine those of the other church in the same territory (¶29b);

—dissipation of inherited prejudicial readings of the historical record, especially in the preparation of future priests (¶30);

—resolving differences through fraternal dialogue, thus avoiding recourse to the civil authorities or to merely legal principles when seeking solutions to property disputes or other pressing practical problems (¶31);

—objectivity in the presentation of events and issues in the mass media (¶32).

6. In our estimation, however, most important of the practical rules and guidelines is the Document's emphasis on the need for "a will to pardon" (¶20). We are all aware that the history of relations between our two churches often has been a tragic one, filled with persecutions and sufferings, but we must not remain prisoners of this past. At the present critical moment in the life of our churches, particularly in those parts of the world which only now are emerging from many decades of insidious pressures and overt persecution at the hands of atheistic forces, the energies of our churches must be directed toward assuring that "the present and the future conform better to the will of Christ for his own." As for "whatever may have been the past, it must be left to the mercy of God" (¶23). But how can our churches and our faithful truly acquire this will to pardon? The Balamand Document offers a very helpful proposal:

It is necessary that the churches come together in order to express gratitude and respect towards all, known and unknown...who suffered, confessed their faith, witnessed their fidelity to the Church, and in general, towards all Christians, without discrimination, who underwent persecutions (¶33).

7. The Balamand Document very appropriately seeks to present certain historical events such as the genesis of the Eastern Catholic Churches and their impact on relations between Catholics and Orthodox (¶¶6-11) in an even-handed way, without rendering specific judgments. However, its presentation is rather schematic and contains some incomplete formulations. Future theological and historical statements on these and related items will call for more nuanced presentations.

8. The Document's historical account does not highlight the important role which the Protestant Reformation played in the West and its impact on Roman Catholic ecclesiology. Mention of this would help to explain how attitudes of exclusivism, justly criticized in the Document, developed among Roman Catholics not primarily in response to the Orthodox but to other crises and controversies.

9. While the Document's rejection of rebaptism is clear (¶¶10 and 13), the question of rebaptism will need further articulation in subsequent studies. In the text the juxtaposition of rebaptism and "the religious freedom of persons" (¶10) is somewhat confusing. Such an important issue as rebaptism demands deeper historical and theological investigation. The groundwork for this has been laid in the International Commission's Bari Document (1987) which was devoted to the intimate connection between "Faith, Sacraments and the Unity of the Church." If, as that agreed statement suggests (cf. ¶¶20 and 21), mutual recognition of sacraments is inseparable from mutual recognition of faith, do our churches in fact find the same essential content of the faith present in each other, notwithstanding inevitable differences in verbal formulation?

10. The Balamand Document's goal is preeminently practical: to create a "serene atmosphere" for renewed progress in dialogue "toward the reestablishment of full communion" (¶34) by rejecting the proselytism and expansionist practices and policies (¶35) associated with "uniatism." In our judgment, its greatest strength lies in the rules and guidelines presented in its second part. With the International Commission, we would strongly recommend "that these practical rules be put into practice by our churches, including the Oriental Catholic Churches who are called to take part in this dialogue" (¶34). We also appreciate the effort made in its first part to set forth the ecclesiological principles which serve as a basis for these practical rules. We would hope that our churches will also take

them seriously. It is likewise our hope that the International Commission will be able to return to consideration of these ecclesiological principles in the near future in the context of its theological study.

11. We are aware that the International Commission did not intend the Balamand Document to be a complete presentation of ecclesiology. Nevertheless, the Document does draw our attention to several promising avenues for discussion. For example, it presupposes the "communion ecclesiology" which many theologians have found to be the most promising way of conceiving the complexity of the Church. This approach, in our estimation, changes the context of past disputes and creates new possibilities for fresh examination of the issues which historically have divided us, even though more work in this area obviously is needed before full agreement is reached.

12. We also note the Document's use of the concept of "sister churches" (cf. ¶14). The use of this venerable term in modern Orthodox-Catholic dialogue has helped to place relations between our churches on a new footing. We hope that, when the International Commission resumes work on ecclesiology, it will be able more fully to explore its precise significance and manifold implications. The concept of sister churches includes the notion of mutual respect for each other's pastoral ministry. As the Balamand Document states, "bishops and priests have the duty before God to respect the authority which the Holy Spirit has given to the bishops and priests of the other church and for that reason to avoid interfering in the spiritual life of the faithful of that church" (¶29). The concept also includes the notion of the co-responsibility of our churches for "maintaining the Church of God in fidelity to the divine purpose, most especially in what concerns unity" (¶14). This, we believe, is a point which should be developed further. The Document's forceful treatment of proselytization needs to be balanced by a proper understanding of mission. Bishops are responsible not simply for the pastoral care of their own faithful but also for the good estate and upbuilding of the whole Church and for the evangelization of the world.

13. In ecumenical efforts there often is a tension between the views and actions of "higher authorities" (¶26) and ecumenists on the one hand, and those of many Christians at the grass-roots level on the other. The Balamand Document as a whole expects higher authorities to act vigorously in enforcing policies it deems advisable even while emphasizing the importance of the activities of the local church (¶26). In particular, it

points to the necessity of "a will to pardon" at *every* level of church life. In a balanced and even-handed way, it seeks to put an end to the present tensions occasioned by the existence of the Eastern Catholic Churches. On the one hand, as the Document points out repeatedly: "... 'uniatism' can no longer be accepted either as a method to be followed or as a model of the unity our churches are seeking" (¶12), "because it is opposed to the common tradition of our churches" (¶2). At the same time, as the document also states, "concerning the Oriental Catholic Churches, it is clear that they, as part of the Catholic communion, have the right to exist and to act in answer to the spiritual needs of their faithful" (¶3).

14. The Balamand Document speaks frequently of the "religious freedom of persons" (¶10) and "the religious liberty of the faithful" (¶24), of "freedom of conscience" (¶27) and "respect for consciences" (¶25), acknowledging "the inviolable freedom of persons and their obligation to follow the requirements of their consciences" (¶15). The language employed in modern presentations of this theme is familiar enough in the Western world in its concern for human rights, and is certainly not alien to either of our churches. In developing this theme, however, our churches have called attention to the need for a coherent understanding of community and therefore to the need to locate individual rights and responsibilities within the common good. When the document speaks of "the faithful" and of their religious liberty "to express their opinion and to decide without pressure from outside if they wish to be in communion either with the Orthodox Church or with the Catholic Church" (¶24), this distinction becomes crucial. Neither the Orthodox nor the Catholic understanding sees the "faithful" only as referring to an individual Christian apart from community. Rather, we both urge that personhood can only ultimately be grasped in relation to the "body" and, through the body, to the tri-personal life of God. Where concern for the solidarity and spiritual health of the community as a whole is absent, the exercise of "freedom" and "liberty" can lead all too easily to the fragmentation of society and to the alienation of persons from each other and from God.

15. Important in this connection is the Balamand Document's rejection of the premise that only one of our churches is the unique possessor of the means of grace in such a way that conversion to that church from the other is necessary for salvation. The Document asserts that "on each

side it is recognized that what Christ has entrusted to his Church...cannot be considered the exclusive property of one of our churches" (¶13). To be sure, there may be cases in which conscience leads an Orthodox or a Catholic Christian to enter the other church (cf. ¶14). This, however, does not mean that our churches should set out to "win converts" by cultivating inappropriate fears and anxieties.

16. At the same time, the assertion that "what Christ has entrusted to his Church...cannot be considered the exclusive property of one of our churches" (¶13) does not necessarily imply that the fullness of the faith resides indifferently in each of our churches, as some critics of the Balamand Document have incorrectly charged. There are still a number of serious issues that divide us. Yet the assertion does imply that the deficiencies and errors which we may see in one another's understanding of doctrine and church structures are not failures that would altogether exclude the other from the mystery of the Church.

17. The Document speaks of itself as "a necessary stage" (¶15) in the current theological dialogue. We may hope and expect that it will be superseded as the International Commission continues its work, beginning with "Ecclesiological and Canonical Consequences of the Sacramental Structure of the Church: Conciliarity and Authority in the Church." Even the practical rules and guidelines are described as "leading to" rather than constituting a definitive solution to the problems raised up by "uniatism" (¶17). As the document stresses, a "climate for deepening our dialogue" (¶20) must be created, beginning with a "will to pardon." Our best energies must be put into the task of creating that climate. While pointing out some shortcomings of the Balamand Document, we nevertheless regard it to be a strong and positive contribution to the theological dialogue between our churches.

Brighton, MA
October 15, 1994
48th Meeting

Section 5

Pastoral Care for Orthodox-Catholic Marriages

INTRODUCTION TO SECTION FIVE

Soon after the members of the U. S. Theological Consultation reached agreement in 1969 with their first joint statement on the eucharist, they began work on a second agreed statement at their next meeting, on May 20, 1970. This work was revised at the Consultation's eighth meeting on November 4, 1971, and issued as "An Agreed Statement on Mixed Marriage." Records from the early years of the Consultation, going back to its second meeting in 1966, when substantive discussions were recorded for the first time, show that both the eucharist and mixed marriages were discussed frequently. True to the consensus of those who met regularly then, the Consultation balanced theological discussion of what divides Orthodox and Catholics with consideration of practical problems. It displayed an ardent desire to address especially those areas of pastoral care, reception of the eucharist and mixed marriages, that touched the lives of the faithful in the United States most often.

The Theological Consultation's 1971 agreement on marriage launched a long examination of the theology of marriage and of the practical difficulties that arise from differences in this area. There followed a series of agreed statements, all of which are included in this section. Perhaps more evident in this final section than anywhere else in this collection is the way that subsequent statements build upon the consensus reached in prior agreements.

During the next quarter century when the topic of Orthodox-Catholic marriages was discussed in dialogue, the number of mixed marriages for the Orthodox in the U.S. increased significantly. For example, in 1984 it was estimated that 50 percent of the marriages of members of the Greek Archdiocese were with non-Orthodox and 50 percent of these were with Catholics. In 1994, new statistics suggested that 80 percent of marriages in the Archdiocese were mixed and that 80 percent of these were with Catholics. Catholics too increased their rate of mixed marriage. Unfortunately, during this period, for a variety of reasons, no implementation of the agreements could occur to the satisfaction of both sides.

The content of the first four documents appearing here, the successive joint agreements of the Theological Consultation in 1971, 1974, 1978,

193

and 1980 on certain aspects of Orthodox-Catholic marriages, is clear enough. One can see that the members of the Theological Consultation focused on the pastoral difficulties confronting these couples in the several decisions that they face: the site of the marriage, the upbringing of children, and the development of a spiritual life together. In addition, these agreed statements touch on the major theological issues relating to marriage that have divided Orthodox and Catholics.

For both churches, mixed marriages are not encouraged; nevertheless, the churches realize that they need to be given considerable pastoral attention because they are an increasing reality in pluralistic societies. This presents a number of practical and theological problems.

—For small minorities in American society, like the Orthodox, whose numbers may actually decrease in proportion to the general population due to intermarriage, the survival of a vibrant tradition is at stake.

—Each church insists that it is the responsibility of the faithful to raise their children in that church. In the case of an Orthodox-Catholic marriage, this policy creates a conflictual situation.

—In the Orthodox view, the marriage of an Orthodox Christian can be performed only by an Orthodox priest as the minister of the sacrament, while in the Catholic view the contracting partners are the ministers of the sacrament. For Catholics, the requirement that a Catholic priest officiate may be dispensed for a serious reason.

—If an Orthodox were to marry in a Catholic church and before a Catholic priest, he or she would have to be reconciled to the Orthodox Church to receive the sacraments. In some of the Orthodox churches this might involve a second marriage ceremony in an Orthodox church. The Catholic Church, however, firmly rejects the practice of two marriage ceremonies.

—The Orthodox Church permits divorce under certain circumstances and allows remarriage, in some cases even for a second time; but the Catholic Church does not allow the dissolution of consummated sacramental marriages. This creates an obstacle for a Catholic wishing to marry a divorced Orthodox Christian even if that person has permission to remarry from the Orthodox Church. Normally the Orthodox partner must submit to the annulment process of the Catholic Church.

Despite these very real differences, there is considerable common ground. Both churches consider marriage a sacrament, a vocation from God in which the presence of Christ is mediated through the action of the Holy Spirit. Both churches believe the intimate human love that is the foundation of marriage is made sacred and elevated into the trinitarian life of God through the action of the Church. In the view of both churches, sacramental marriage requires the mutual consent of the believing Christian partners and God's blessing imparted through the official ministry of the Church. Although the Orthodox Church and the Catholic Church have different ways of addressing the pastoral challenge of marriages that have failed, both uphold the enduring nature of marriage but in diverse ways. In addition, both churches affirm the value of human life, and for both the right to life implies the right to a decent life and to full human development.

After a number of meetings, papers and agreed statements relating to mixed marriage, work on the subject had proceeded as far as the Theological Consultation could take it. In 1981 the Greek Orthodox Archdiocese and the Catholic Archdiocese of New York began a locally based dialogue taking advantage of the considerable talent and resources in the region. Several participants on both sides in the New York dialogue were members of the Theological Consultation. Building upon the four agreed statements of the national dialogue relating to marriage, the local dialogue produced its own "Agreed Statement on Orthodox-Catholic Marriages," which addressed certain points of pastoral practice which the participants deemed to be particularly important in caring for these marriages. By then, in early 1986, representatives of the Catholic Archdiocese of Newark and the Catholic Dioceses of Brooklyn and Rockville Center had joined representatives of the Orthodox Church in America and the Antiochian Orthodox Christian Archdiocese in the dialogue, now known as the Metropolitan New York/New Jersey Orthodox-Catholic Dialogue. The dialogue's agreed statement concluded with a list of ten specific recommendations to the two churches.

Representatives of the New York/New Jersey Dialogue presented their agreed statement to the Joint Committee of Orthodox and Catholic Bishops in 1986. At their 1987 meeting, the bishops took another look at the ten recommendations of the New York/New Jersey dialogue. Certain concerns and difficulties were raised by the bishops, and these were forwarded as questions to the Theological Consultation. The theologians addressed these concerns at their next meeting in 1988. Their responses were noted, drafted, circulated for revision, and then returned to the bishops in time for their meeting later in the same year. The bishops reviewed the replies and also studied papers by canonists concerning the ten recommendations of the New York/New Jersey agreed statement. The discussion among the bishops was carefully noted, and the bishops agreed that a response to the New York/New Jersey dialogue should be drafted and agreed upon by their co-chairmen, who would sign it and send it to that dialogue. This response was completed in March 1989.

At their meeting in 1989, the members of the Joint Committee of Bishops listened to two Scripture scholars reflect on New Testament passages relating to marriage and especially to the permanence of marriage. Then, after some deliberation, the bishops agreed to ask two scholars from the Theological Consultation to review the agreed statements and other materials produced from these discussions of mixed marriages and draft a text for them to consider at their next meeting in 1990. Throughout that meeting, the drafters and staff worked to incorporate the bishops' suggestions and emendations. The final product was the bishops' "Pastoral Statement on Orthodox-Roman Catholic Marriages." (It should be noted, of course, that such joint statements are not considered binding on the churches but rather represent at this stage the collective wisdom of the participants. Publication is not promulgation but distribution. Nevertheless, this Pastoral Statement represents agreement between Orthodox and Catholics at a high level. Like the other agreed statements appearing here, it is a major contribution to the published record of relations between Orthodox and Catholics.)

On the Catholic side, the 1990 statement was discussed at the next meeting of the NCCB's Bishops' Committee for Ecumenical and Interreligious Affairs. Its members agreed that the chairman should take the two recommendations of the 1990 statement to the next meeting of the Administrative Committee of the National Conference of Catholic Bishops. This he did in 1991. The approximately fifty Catholic bishop members of the NCCB Administrative Committee agreed unanimously to the recommendation that materials be prepared jointly with the Orthodox for Orthodox-Catholic couples and that these materials should reflect the sentiments of the agreed statement of the Joint Committee of Bishops. Secondly, they voted their sympathy with the second recommendation on certain aspects of the liturgical ceremony for a marriage between an Orthodox Christian and a Catholic.

On the Orthodox side, the 1990 agreement was discussed at successive meetings of SCOBA. Reservations on the part of certain members of SCOBA were expressed. SCOBA accepted the 1990 statement in principle, but it wanted to monitor carefully whatever would result from it. In the interval, no progress was made on the joint preparation of materials for Orthodox and Catholic couples. Finally, in early 1994, a critique of the 1990 statement, largely the views of Orthodox theologians and pastors, was presented to the bishops of the dialogue.

Despite the lack of progress in the joint preparation of materials, the collection of documents on marriage still constitutes a remarkable achievement. The documents reveal points of agreement on the theology of marriage which would have been unimaginable only a few decades ago. In addition, their concern for appropriate pastoral care for Orthodox-Catholic married couples augurs well for the future. At a time when the language of sister churches increasingly is being used by Orthodox and Catholic theologians, it may be hoped that Orthodox and Catholic pastors will be able to work together to address the pastoral needs of Orthodox-Catholic couples.

AN AGREED STATEMENT ON MIXED MARRIAGE

U.S. Theological Consultation, 1971

The recent dialogue between the Orthodox and Catholic Churches has led to a deeper appreciation of their common tradition of faith. This exploration has helped us to reassess some specific theological and pastoral problems in the area of Christian marriage. We recognize the practical difficulties which couples continue to face when they enter a mixed marriage as long as their churches are divided on matters of doctrine and styles of Christian life. Because of these difficulties both of our churches discourage mixed marriages.

I. Pastoral Problems

1. We recognize that under the conditions of modern life these mixed marriages will continue to take place. For this reason counseling of couples entering such unions by pastors of both churches is imperative. In this counseling the sincerely held religious convictions of each party, based upon their church's tradition, must be respected, especially as regards the nature of marriage and the style of life in marriage.

2. One area in which counseling by the pastors is desirable concerns the Christian upbringing of the children. We recognize the responsibility of each partner to raise their children in the faith of their respective churches. We encourage the pastors of both churches to counsel these couples in the hope of helping to resolve the problem which this responsibility creates. Specific decisions should be made by the couple only after informed and serious deliberation. Whether the decision is made to raise the children in the Orthodox or Catholic tradition, both partners should take an active role in the Christian upbringing of the children and in establishing their marriage as a stable Christian union. The basis for this pastoral counsel is not religious indifferentism, but our conviction of a common participation in the mystery of Christ and his Church.

3. Each partner should be reminded of the obligation to respect the religious convictions and practice of the other and mutually to support and encourage the other in growing into the fullness of the Christian life.

II. Theological Problems

1. According to the view of the Orthodox Church the marriage of an Orthodox can only be performed by an Orthodox priest as the minister of the sacrament. In the view of the Catholic Church the contracting partners are the ministers of the sacrament, and the required presence of a Catholic major cleric as witness of the Church can be dispensed with for weighty reasons. In view of this, we recommend that the Catholic Church, as a normative practice, allow the Catholic party of a proposed marriage with an Orthodox to be married with the Orthodox priest officiating. This procedure should, however, take place only after consultation by the partners with both pastors.

2. We plan the further study of the Orthodox and Catholic traditional teaching concerning marriage.

Barlin Acres, MA
November 4, 1971
Eighth Meeting

AN AGREED STATEMENT ON RESPECT FOR LIFE

U.S. Theological Consultation, 1974

We, the members of the Orthodox-Roman Catholic Bilateral Consultation in the United States, after extensive discussions on the sanctity of marriage, feel compelled to make a statement concerning the inviolability of human life in all its forms.

We recognize that human life is a gift of God entrusted to mankind and so feel the necessity of expressing our shared conviction about its sacred character in concrete and active ways. It is true that the Christian community's concern has recently seemed to be selective and disproportionate in this regard, *e.g.,* in the anti-abortion campaign. Too often human life has been threatened or even destroyed, especially during times of war, internal strife, and violence, with little or no protestation from the Christian leadership. Unfortunately, the impression has frequently been given that churchmen are more concerned with establishing the legitimacy of war or capital punishment than with the preservation of human life. We know that this has been a scandal for many, both believers and unbelievers.

We feel constrained at this point in history to affirm that the "right to life" implies a right to a decent life and to full human development, not merely to a marginal existence.

We affirm that the furthering of this goal for the unborn, the mentally retarded, the aging, and the underprivileged is our duty on a global as well as a domestic scale.

We deplore in particular the U.S. Supreme Court's decision failing to recognize the rights of the unborn—a decision which has led to widespread indiscriminate early abortion.

We affirm our common Christian tradition with regard to the right of the unborn to life.

We acknowledge our responsibility to mediate the love of Christ, especially to the troubled expectant mother, and thus make possible the transmission and nurturing of new life and its fully human development.

200

We urge our churches and all believers to take a concrete stand on this matter at this time and to exemplify this evangelical imperative in their personal lives and professional decisions.

Washington, DC
May 24, 1974
Tenth Meeting

AN AGREED STATEMENT ON THE SANCTITY OF MARRIAGE

U.S. Theological Consultation, 1978

Introduction

At a time when the sacred character of married life is radically threatened by contrary lifestyles, we the members of the Orthodox-Roman Catholic Consultation feel called by the Lord to speak from the depth of our common faith and to affirm the profound meaning, the "glory and honor," of married life in Christ.

I. The Sacramental Character of Marriage

For Christians of both the Orthodox and Roman Catholic Churches marriage is a sacrament. Through the prayers and actions of our wedding rites we profess the presence of Christ in the Spirit and believe that it is the Lord who unites a man and a woman in a life of mutual love. In this sacred union, husband and wife are called by Christ not only to live and work together, but also to share their Christian life so that each with the aid of the other may progress through the Holy Spirit in the life of holiness and so achieve Christian perfection. This relationship between husband and wife is established and sanctified by the Lord. As a sacred vocation, marriage mirrors the union of Christ and the Church (Eph. 5:23).

Christ affirmed and blessed the oneness and profound significance of marriage. Christian tradition, following his teaching, has always proclaimed the sanctity of marriage. It has defined marriage as the fundamental relationship in which a man and woman, by total sharing with each other, seek their own growth in holiness and that of their children, and thus show forth the presence on earth of God's kingdom.

II. Enduring Vocation

The special character of the human relationship established through marriage has always been recognized in the Christian tradition. By sancti-

202

fying the marital bond, the Church affirms a permanent commitment to personal union, which is expressed in the free giving and acceptance of each other by a man and a woman. The sacrament of marriage serves as an admirable example of the union which exists between God and the believer. The Old Testament uses marriage to describe the covenant relationship between God and his people (Hosea). The Letter to the Ephesians sees marriage as the type of relationship which exists between Christ and his Church (Eph. 5:31-35). Consequently both the Orthodox and Roman Catholic Churches affirm the permanent character of Christian marriage: "What God has joined together, let no man put asunder" (Mt. 19:6).

However, the Orthodox Church, out of consideration of the human realities, permits divorces, after it exhausts all possible efforts to save the marriage, and tolerates remarriages in order to avoid further human tragedies. The Roman Catholic Church recognizes the dissolution of sacramental nonconsummated marriages either through solemn religious profession or by papal dispensation. To resolve the personal and pastoral issues of failed marriages which have been consummated an inquiry is often undertaken to uncover whether there exists some initial defect in the marriage covenant which would render the marriage invalid.

III. The Redeeming Effect of Marital Love

A total sharing of a life of love and concern is not possible apart from God. The limitations of human relationships do not allow for a giving and receiving which fulfill the partners. However, in the life of the Church, God gives the possibility of continual progress in the deepening of human relationships. By opening the eyes of faith to the vision that these relationships have as their goal, God offers a more intimate union with himself. Through the liberating effect of divine love, experienced through human love, believers are led away from self-centeredness and self-idolatry. The Gospel indicates the direction that this love must ultimately take: toward intimate union with the One who alone can satisfy the fundamental yearning of people for self-fulfillment.

Given this vision of reality, Christian tradition recognizes that the total devotion of the married partners implies as its goal a relationship with God. It teaches, moreover, that the love which liberates them to seek union with God and which is the source of sanctification for them is made possible through the presence of the Spirit of God within them.

Through the love manifested in marriage, an important witness is given to the world of the love of God in Christ for all people. The partners in Christian marriage have the task, as witnesses of redemption, to accept as the inner law of their personal relationship that love which determines the relationship between Christ and the Church: "Husbands, love your wives as Christ loved the Church and gave himself up for her" (Eph. 5:25). Through this love which liberates believers from selfish interests and sanctifies their relationships, the Christian husband and wife find the inspiration in turn to minister in loving service to others.

IV. Theological Clarifications on Christian Marriage

In the teaching of the Orthodox and Roman Catholic Churches a sacramental marriage requires both the mutual consent of the believing Christian partners and God's blessing imparted through the ministry of the Church.

At present there are differences in the concrete ways in which this ministry must be exercised in order to fulfill the theological and canonical norms for marriage in our two churches. There are also differences in the theological interpretation of this diversity. Thus the Orthodox Church accepts as sacramental only those marriages sanctified in the liturgical life of the church by being blessed by an Orthodox priest.

The Catholic Church accepts as sacramental the marriages which are celebrated before a Catholic priest or even a deacon, but it also envisions some exceptional cases in which, by reason of a dispensation or the unavailability of a priest or deacon, Catholics may enter into a sacramental marriage in the absence of an ordained minister of the Church.

An examination of the diversities of practice and theology concerning the required ecclesial context for Christian marriage that have existed in both traditions demonstrates that the present differences must be considered to pertain more to the level of secondary theological reflection than to that of dogma. Both churches have always agreed that the ecclesial context is constitutive of the Christian sacrament of marriage. Within this fundamental agreement various possibilities of realization are possible as history has shown and no one form of this realization can be considered to be absolutely normative in all circumstances.

V. Plans for Further Study

The members of the Orthodox-Roman Catholic Consultation give thanks to God for this common faith in the sanctity of marriage which we share in our sister churches. We recognize, however, that pastoral problems remain to be studied in depth, such as the liturgical celebration of weddings between Orthodox and Roman Catholic partners and the religious upbringing of children in such families. We continue to explore these questions out of a common vision of marriage and with confidence in the guidance of the Holy Spirit.

New York, NY
December 8, 1978
19th Meeting

JOINT RECOMMENDATIONS ON THE SPIRITUAL FORMATION OF CHILDREN OF MARRIAGES BETWEEN ORTHODOX AND ROMAN CATHOLICS

U.S. Theological Consultation, 1980

Introduction

1. In this consultation's "Agreed Statement on Mixed Marriages" reference was made to the spiritual formation of children of marriages involving Orthodox and Roman Catholic partners. The consultation affirms the position taken in that statement but now presents a more detailed explanation of its reasons for it.

Christian Marriage and the Spiritual Formation of Children

2. Our understanding of the spiritual formation of children is based on our common understanding of Christian marriage as a sacrament, as expressed in our "Agreed Statement on the Sanctity of Marriage" (New York, December 8, 1978). Christian marriage is a vocation from God in which the liberating effect of divine love is experienced through human love. This love expresses itself in permanent commitment to mutual fidelity, help and support in all aspects of life, spiritual as well as physical. It also expresses itself in the generation of new life—that is, in the procreation and nurture of children—again, on both the spiritual and physical levels. A primary responsibility of parents therefore is the spiritual formation of their children, a task which is not limited to church membership and formal religious education but extends to all aspects of their lives.

Church Community and the Spiritual Formation of Children

3. Christian marriage also has a social dimension which extends beyond the partners and their relatives. Through marriage the partners are integrated in a new way into the church community. Just as the marriage partners have a responsibility for the building up of the Church, so the

church community itself has a responsibility to each Christian family to foster its life of faith. In particular the community shares in the responsibility for the spiritual formation of children.

Current Practice

4. Practical difficulties often arise in discharging this responsibility, especially in mixed marriages. Today each of our churches insists that the children of such marriages be raised within its own communion, on the grounds that this is in the best interests of the child's spiritual welfare, thus presuming that one of the parents will relinquish the chief responsibility to the other. Yet if the purpose of the general law is indeed the child's spiritual welfare, its application should be guided by a prudent judgment concerning what is better for the child in the concrete situation.

Practical Recommendations

5. The Orthodox-Roman Catholic couple contemplating marriage should discuss the problem of the spiritual formation of children with both their pastors. Both parents should be urged to take an active role in their children's spiritual formation in all its aspects. Pastors should counsel the parents, and their children as well, against indifference in religious matters, which so often masks itself as tolerance. Since unity in Christ through the Spirit is the ultimate basis and goal of family life, all members of the family should be willing, in a spirit of love, trust, and freedom, to learn more about their faith. They should agree to pray, study, discuss, and seek unity in Christ, and to express their commitment to this unity in all aspects of their lives.

6. Decisions, including the initial and very important one of the children's church membership, rest with both husband and wife and should take into account the good of the children, the strength of the religious convictions of the parents and other relatives, the demands of their consciences, the unity and stability of the family, and other aspects of the specific context. In some cases, when it appears certain that only one of the partners will fulfill his or her responsibility, it seems clear that the children should be raised in that partner's church. In other cases, however, the children's spiritual formation may include a fuller participa-

tion in the life and traditions of both churches, respecting, however, the canonical order of each church. Here particularly the decision of the children's church membership is more difficult to make. Yet we believe that this decision can be made in good conscience. This is possible because of the proximity of doctrine and practice of our churches, which enables each to a high degree to see the other precisely as *Church*, as the locus for the communion of men and women with God and with each other through Jesus Christ in the Holy Spirit.

Conclusion

7. In no way do we mean to minimize differences that still exist between our churches; and we are well aware of the difficulties which these differences may present for those in mixed marriages. Yet we are convinced that such marriages can be a means of spiritual growth both for the partners and for their children.

8. We are also aware that our joint recommendations on the formation of children of marriages between Orthodox and Roman Catholics differ in certain respects from the present legislation and practice of our churches. Yet we believe that our position is theologically and pastorally sound. Therefore we would urge our respective hierarchies to consider ways of reformulating legislation and pastoral guidelines in this area and of communicating this on the parish level, so that the spiritual growth of both the partners and the children of such marriages may better be fostered.

New York, NY
October 11, 1980
22nd Meeting

AGREED STATEMENT ON ORTHODOX-ROMAN CATHOLIC MARRIAGES

Metropolitan New York/New Jersey Orthodox-Roman Catholic Dialogue, 1986

Preamble

This paper is the result of nearly four years of Orthodox-Roman Catholic discussions in the metropolitan New York/New Jersey region. Beginning with an initial meeting in November 1981 between the ecumenical staffs of the Greek Orthodox Archdiocese of North and South America and the Roman Catholic Archdiocese of New York, the dialogue has expanded to include a number of dioceses. Representatives of the Antiochian Orthodox Christian Archdiocese, the Orthodox Church in America, the Roman Catholic Archdiocese of Newark, the Roman Catholic Diocese of Brooklyn, and the Roman Catholic Diocese of Rockville Center have participated in these discussions. In addition, until his assignment away from the region, a representative of the Serbian Orthodox Church in the U.S.A. and Canada participated regularly.

Meeting five times a year, the dialogue group has examined extensively documents and church laws relating to Orthodox-Roman Catholic marriages. After much deliberation, the dialogue group mandated a subcommittee to draft a joint statement with pastoral recommendations. The entire dialogue group revised the drafted statement extensively in a series of three meetings.

All meetings of the Metropolitan New York/New Jersey Orthodox-Roman Catholic Dialogue have been candid and open discussions of the actual situation of Orthodox-Roman Catholic marriages in the region. The dialogue has benefitted from the pastoral experience of many participants as well as from the ecumenical expertise of several participants who also serve on national and international committees, consultations, and dialogues. The ten points, jointly recommended in the conclusion and representing the consensus of this dialogue, are realistic and merit prompt attention. Their implementation would well serve Orthodox-Roman

209

Catholic couples entering marriage and would promote Orthodox-Roman Catholic relations in the United States.

I. Introduction

To articulate a theology of marriage is a complex task which has engaged both the Orthodox and Roman Catholic Churches over the centuries down to the present day. One cannot find in the New Testament a clear and systematic doctrine of the sacrament of marriage. In the New Testament churches, marriage is more often mentioned in the context of anticipating the imminent end of the world and the Parousia.

Christians derive a significant understanding of the theology of marriage from the Old Testament. In Genesis, God is shown to be the author of holy matrimony, in which a man and a woman are united to help each other achieve their salvation. Although the injunction of Gen. 1:28 to increase and multiply and subdue the earth does not completely describe the nature and purpose of marriage, it does indicate an important characteristic of the marital relationship.

In Old Testament references to marriage, the concept of spousal love appears in virtually every passage. Attraction and love are the subject of the Song of Songs in which God's relationship to his people is imaged in the marriage of a man and a woman. The same theme appears in Hosea 2:19-20, Isaiah 54:5, and Ezekiel 16:8. This authentic love of a man and a woman in marriage reflects the compassionate love God has for his people. God's fidelity to his people, despite their faithlessness to him, is striking. The image of husband and wife is also carried into the New Testament to describe God's love for his people. In Eph. 5:32 and Rev. 19:7, the relationship between husband and wife is perceived as the relationship between Christ and the Church.

As the celebration of the marriage rite unfolds in both churches, Old Testament references to the marriages of Abraham and Sarah, Isaac and Rebekah, Jacob and Rachel, and other biblical couples are made. It is easy for a bridal pair in the marriage rites of both churches to understand their marriage as being in continuity with the scriptural foundations of marriage. The joining of hands, the exchanging of rings, and the exchanging of crowns are descriptive of the spiritual union and interdependence that the couple shares.

A couple's free decision to marry must be made in accordance with God's design for marriage. Their decision requires the couple to be constant in their care, sacrifice, protection, and love for one another. Orthodox Christians and Roman Catholics share a common understanding of the glory and honor of married life in Christ. The marriage between an Orthodox and a Roman Catholic is unique because of a common participation in the mystery of Christ and his Church. Marriage is a sacrament through which Christ unites a man and a woman in mutual love for the ultimate sake of the salvation of each.

Although in some societies marriage is especially encouraged and almost expected of everyone, the two churches believe that marriage is not mandatory. It is a divine gift and must flow from God's invitation to accept this particular grace. An authentic Christian marriage carries with it the gift of discerning God's will for the couple and the gift of healing whatever may wound the marriage. In the kingdom to come the marriage union will be brought into the perfect relationship that is fulfilled totally and completely in Christ.

The marital bond is by nature indissoluble. Both the Orthodox and Roman Catholic Churches "affirm the permanent character of Christian marriage: 'What God has joined together, let no man put asunder'" (Mt. 19:6). (See: "An Agreed Statement on the Sanctity of Marriage," 1978, above pp. 202-205.) The revised *Code of Canon Law* for the Latin Church reminds pastors to aid spouses in the unity of conjugal and family life and to see to it that the children of a mixed marriage do not lack spiritual assistance in fulfilling their obligations (canon 1128). If this is carried out, the faithful of both communions are assured that children born of such marriages will be initiated into and spiritually nourished by the sacramental mysteries of Christ. Their formation in authentic Christian doctrine and ways of Christian living would be very similar in either church. Differences in liturgical life and private devotion need not be a stumbling block to family prayer.

Without denying the existence of certain dogmatic differences which, in fact, do impede full sacramental and canonical communion between the two churches, it is clear that certain of these dogmatic differences, real as they are, between Orthodox Christians and Roman Catholics, do not have a major influence on the everyday Christian lives of our people. Since these Christians are privileged to have such a mutual understanding, it is pastorally prudent to emphasize and uphold the sound and consistent teaching of both churches. This should be the first, and perhaps most important, principle to underscore and uphold in pastoral preparation of couples involved in Orthodox-Roman Catholic marriages.

II. Consideration of Canonical Discipline

Both churches have established canonical disciplines regarding impediments to marriage, the formalities of marriage, and matrimonial consent. (See the appendices for comparison of the disciplines of the two churches regarding: I. Impediments, II. Canonical Form, III. Matrimonial Consent, IV. Convalidation, and V. Dissolution and Annulment.)

III. Pastoral Concerns

One of the objectives of this paper is to indicate the problem areas concerning marriages between Orthodox Christians and Roman Catholics which take place in this region and to suggest guidelines for the pastoral care of these marriages within the framework of the theological understanding, canonical discipline, and pastoral experience of the two churches. Toward this end, an effort has been made in this paper to identify and clarify as much as possible those areas of agreement which already do exist. Now this paper will try to indicate common practices and recommendations for future developments in the area of pastoral care, especially in those cases where differences still exist between us.

This Orthodox-Roman Catholic dialogue recognizes a common concern for the problems of family life and the spiritual formation of the young people of both churches. Common Christian witness, personal spirituality, mutual respect, and socio-sexual morality, as well as particular problems such as chemical dependency, child abuse, family violence, and divorce, are not merely Orthodox or Roman Catholic issues. These two communions offer some very specific and similar positions based on shared and complementary traditions.

212

Specific attention can be given to the relationship of the churches in the Americas. The situation here offers some distinct advantages. The political, ethnic, and cultural differences which, in the old countries, often nourished mistrust, and even hatred, are disappearing. In the Americas, Christians are engaged in an effort to construct a society which is pluri-traditional and yet reflects a unity and harmony among us. The variety in the Orthodox communities carries with it a variety of ecclesiastical practices regarding marriages between their own communicants as well as marriages with Roman Catholics. This variety offers a spectrum of solutions which should make it possible to treat individual cases according to the circumstances of each case. The revised *Code of Canon Law* also contributes to this process since it provides much more flexibility than has existed in the past and is explicitly conscious of the particular relationships existing between the two churches. It is with this in mind that the following pastoral guidelines are offered for counseling couples entering into Orthodox-Roman Catholic marriages.

A. General Norms of Premarital Counseling

Marriage within the same faith community is the ideal for both churches. Increasing contacts among people of various religious backgrounds and the growth of genuine love among them clearly show that mixed marriages have become a fact and indeed have become frequent. Attempts to discourage such marriages, for example, by strong family opposition or strict application of canonical discipline, have often resulted in the alienation of one or both partners from church life and have led to instances where persons have given up church practice and may have even lost their faith. The fact that the couple is conscious of their genuine Christian love and wishes to celebrate it in a sacrament should be the occasion for positive pastoral encouragement. The disciplines of the two churches, therefore, should serve as pastoral aids to their people who wish to remain in their respective churches and to pass on an authentic Christian heritage to their children. Marriage is an occasion of joy and an expression of mutual love and commitment. Its positive aspects should be stressed rather than its negative aspects or feelings.

The engaged couple, as a couple, should seek the premarital counseling of the pastors of both churches. Priests of both churches have a pastoral obligation to meet with the couple to discuss the various spiritual aspects and serious responsibilities of their proposed marriage. Each priest has an obligation to encourage the couple to meet with the other pastor. In addition to this personal contact, appropriate reading material and other media aids should be provided for couples planning to marry, especially those materials which emphasize theological positions shared by both churches. In premarital counseling the religious convictions of each partner and the teachings and practices of both churches should be respected.

Both priests ought to counsel against religious indifference and encourage each partner to retain real commitment to his/her own church and to participate fully in its life. Given this commitment, sharing frequently in the liturgical life of the other church according to the discipline of that church is recommended, especially where this would foster the unity of family life.

B. The Planning and Celebration of the Marriage Ceremony

The planning and celebration of the marriage ceremony itself pose certain difficulties because of the differences in canonical discipline in this regard. According to Roman Catholic discipline, given the proper dispensations, marriage can take place in either the Roman Catholic or Orthodox Church. While most Orthodox ecclesiastical provinces require that the marriage take place in the Orthodox Church only, recent synodal decisions of two (the Patriarchate of Moscow and the Church of Poland) recognize the validity of the sacrament of marriage performed by Roman Catholic priests provided that the Orthodox bishop gives his permission. (See: *Diakonia* II: 2/67, p. 202 and III: 1/68, p. 43.)

The priests of both churches are responsible for carrying out the rite of marriage according to their respective disciplines. Both churches permit the presence of both the Roman Catholic and Orthodox priest at the same ceremony. However, the roles that each fulfills may differ according to varying disciplines. These facts should be recognized and explained to the couple so as to assist in promoting mutual understanding, if not mutual agreement. If the couple requests the special presence of a priest of the other church, the invitation should be extended to him through the

214

officiating priest. The following specific regulations of each church should be noted.

In the Orthodox Church (in agreement with the "Guidelines for Orthodox Christians in Ecumenical Relations," of the Standing Conference of Canonical Orthodox Bishops in the Americas, 1973, pp. 19-22):

1. The active participation of the Roman Catholic priest within the marriage rite is not permitted at this time, and this should be made explicit to him at the time of the invitation.

2. The Roman Catholic priest should be invited to wear his liturgical vesture (choir dress or alb).

3. He should be given a place which distinguishes him from the congregation.

4. At the conclusion of the Orthodox ceremony, the Roman Catholic priest will be properly acknowledged and introduced. He then may give a benediction to the couple and address to them words of exhortation and good wishes.

5. Mixed marriages are never celebrated within the context of a eucharistic liturgy.

6. Announcement and publication of the marriage should clearly indicate the distinction between the Orthodox celebrant and the guest Roman Catholic priest, avoiding confusing terms as "assisted" or "participated," but rather indicating that the Roman Catholic priest "was present and gave a blessing."

In the Roman Catholic Church:

1. When the Roman Catholic priest officiates, the active participation of the Orthodox priest within the marriage rite is permitted, for example, reading the Scriptures, giving the homily, offering prayers, and giving a blessing. However, out of respect for the current discipline which does not permit an Orthodox priest to participate in this way, the officiating Roman Catholic should not invite him to do so.

2. The Orthodox priest who accepts an invitation to be present at the marriage rite should be invited to wear the liturgical vesture permitted by his discipline.

3. He should be given a place of honor in the sanctuary.

4. The Roman Catholic priest should acknowledge and welcome the Orthodox priest, preferably at the start of the marriage ceremony; at the conclusion of the ceremony, he should invite the Orthodox priest to offer prayer and words of good wishes to the couple.

5. While Orthodox-Roman Catholic marriages may be celebrated at a eucharistic liturgy, such a choice should be strongly discouraged in view of current prohibitions regarding eucharistic sharing.

6. Announcement and publication of the marriage should clearly indicate the distinction between the Roman Catholic celebrant and the guest Orthodox priest, avoiding confusing terms like "a double ceremony" or "an ecumenical marriage," but rather indicating that the Orthodox priest "was present and offered prayers."

Particular note should be taken of the fact that in the case of Orthodox-Roman Catholic marriages, Roman Catholic discipline (revised *Code of Canon Law,* canon 1127, 1) recognizes the validity of the marriage of an Orthodox and a Roman Catholic performed by an Orthodox priest. Indeed, if a proper dispensation from the canonical form is secured, the marriage is also licit. While Roman Catholic policy allows an Orthodox priest to be a marriage officiant in a Roman Catholic church building, Orthodox practice requires the specific permission of the Orthodox bishop.

Neither the Orthodox Church nor the Roman Catholic Church permits two separate marriage ceremonies. The common consent of two people baptized into Christ creates a new sacramental union whose root significance would be destroyed by the repetition of the wedding ceremony. Both adhere to Christ in faith; both share the Church's sacramental life; both pray in the same Spirit; both are guided by the same Holy Scripture. All this converges to make this most important moment a sacred event for the bride and groom. Three requirements must be observed in Orthodox-Roman Catholic marriages:

1. The marriage rite can be performed only once, and all indication of two distinct religious ceremonies should be avoided.

2. The ceremony should take place in an Orthodox or Roman Catholic church building.

216

3. The rite of the celebration is that of the officiating priest, and it should be made clear that one person is officiating in the name of that church.

It is the recommendation of the Metropolitan New York/New Jersey Orthodox-Roman Catholic Dialogue that some canonical provision be made to resolve the problem which has great pastoral implications for Orthodox Christians marrying in the Roman Catholic Church. When an Orthodox Christian marries a Roman Catholic in a Roman Catholic ceremony, the Orthodox partner usually is separated from the participation in the sacraments of the Orthodox Church. In order to rectify the canonical situation of the Orthodox partner, current discipline requires that the marriage be regularized in the Orthodox Church. Any form of regularization should avoid giving the impression that the marriage which has taken place in the Roman Catholic Church does not have a fundamental sacramental character. Nor should it imply that a "new" ceremony is taking place. The goal is to reintegrate the Orthodox communicant into the full life of his/her own Church and to restore him/her to full canonical standing within the Church. In the hope of alleviating this canonical problem, this dialogue offers some recommendations further on for consideration by the appropriate authorities. (See *Conclusion.*)

C. Counseling those entering into Orthodox-Roman Catholic marriages concerning family life and rearing of children

The religious education of children is the responsibility of both parents. The couple ought to be counseled to give serious consideration prior to the wedding to the religious upbringing of their children. It is recognized that each church desires that every reasonable effort be made on the part of its own member to raise the children within its own community. It is hoped, however, that no prior agreement which would exclude the possibility of raising the children in either the Orthodox or Roman Catholic faith be entered into by either party. Within the context of the agreement which takes place before the marriage, the following norms are to be maintained:

1. A free decision must be made by the couple to raise the children either in the Orthodox or Roman Catholic Church. The practice of raising some of the children in one church and others in the other

church is wrong. It divides the family, fails to reflect the theology and practice of either church, and could lead to an attitude of indifference. It is equally unacceptable to neglect to baptize and catechize children under the presumption that they will "decide for themselves" when they are older. Such a procedure very often results in those children having only a weak and confused faith and spiritual life.

2. Children should be taught to love and respect the church and religious traditions of the other parent. Towards this end they should be able to worship occasionally at the liturgy and to participate in the devotional life of that parent's church. However, every impression should be avoided of rearing the children in a "Christian faith" without identifying them with a concrete ecclesial community and spiritual tradition.

3. Where one partner is uncommitted to his/her faith and apparently will give little encouragement to the religious training of the children or become involved in it, then the children should be reared in the church of the committed parent rather than have no connection with the sacramental life of either church. (See "Joint Recommendations on the Spiritual Formation of Children of Marriages between Orthodox and Roman Catholics," U.S. Orthodox-Catholic Consultation, 1980, above pp. 206-208.)

While exposure to and participation in both traditions is desirable for the sake of the unity of the family, there are a number of points where differences in practice between the Orthodox and Roman Catholic Churches may very well pose problems and ought to be discussed during pastoral counseling, such as:

1. Church attendance,

2. Family worship at home,

3. Fasts (more numerous and probably more strictly observed in the Orthodox Church),

4. Feasts, especially Pascha/Easter and Christmas, which may or may not differ in the date of celebration and in the customs and concomitant demands made by them.

Both priests should counsel the couple on moral issues concerning family life, stressing commonality of beliefs and tradition, in order to bring about as much unity as possible in the faith and morals of the family. Topics in counseling should include mutual respect, marital morality (including premarital and extramarital conduct), accepted means of family planning, family violence, divorce, chemical dependencies. Particular attention should be given to the subjects of Christian witness in a mixed marriage and personal spirituality. Whenever necessary, priests should be ready to recommend professional counseling or therapy in addition to their own pastoral counseling. It is particularly recommended that joint materials concerning Christian marriage and family life and especially the Christian rearing of children be developed and produced jointly for the guidance of the clergy and for the use of people involved in Orthodox-Roman Catholic marriages.

IV. Conclusion

This document has included a number of concrete recommendations which are presented to the two churches for implementation. Some of them are immediately applicable. However, since others may not coincide in detail with current discipline and practices in the respective churches, the following points are presented to the churches for their particular consideration and action:

1. That canonical procedures for marriages between Orthodox and Roman Catholics be made uniform and obligatory in both churches;

2. That the two churches formally recognize the sacramentality of marriage in each other's church;

3. That, in the light of examples given by the present canonical discipline of the Roman Catholic Church and synodal decisions of the Patriarchate of Moscow and the Church of Poland, measures of reciprocity be taken for recognizing the validity and liceity of all Orthodox-Roman Catholic marriages taking place in this country, as long as the proper canonical procedures are observed;

4. That the two churches work toward eliminating the canonical institute of the formal promises to baptize and educate the children in a particular church, as an absolute requirement for Orthodox-Roman Catholic marriages. (See "Joint Recommendations on the Spiritual Formation of Children of Marriages between Orthodox and Roman

Catholics," U.S. Orthodox-Catholic Consultation, 1980, above pp. 206-208.);

5. That there be only one marriage ceremony in which either one or both priests are present, with the rite being that of the officiating priest and with specific parts of the service being offered to the guest priest in accordance with accepted norms;

6. That the marriage be recorded in both churches' registries;

7. That if a church judges that some supplementary liturgical action is needed so that its own member may be readmitted to full sacramental and disciplinary communion, care should be taken that the liturgical form of this celebration not give the impression of being another marriage ceremony, or that the marriage which had already taken place is not being recognized;

8. That both churches seek to safeguard the richness and integrity of each tradition by cautioning the couple and their respective pastors against attempts to absorb one partner into the other's church;

9. That the two churches give full consideration to the marriage and dissolution/annulment requirements and procedures of each church, recognizing that, when the canonical disciplines differ, any unclear case should be brought to the appropriate authorities of both churches who, in common consultation, will seek to arrive at a solution; and

10. That materials for Christian marriage and family life and especially the spiritual formation of children be jointly developed and produced both for the guidance of the clergy and for the use of the people involved in Orthodox-Roman Catholic marriages.

Epilogue

We, the Metropolitan New York/New Jersey Orthodox-Roman Catholic Dialogue, offer this statement as a vision for improving pastoral care for our people in Orthodox-Roman Catholic marriages. In a spirit of cooperation, we have pinpointed the essential areas of difference which are in need of resolution.

We give glory to the triune God for the continuing opportunity to engage in dialogue. Through the prayers of the Holy Mother of God and all the saints, may this statement be another step towards achieving Christian unity.

January 6, 1986
[signatures]

APPENDIX:
CANONICAL PROCEDURES

Orthodox Canonical Procedures

Introductory Note:

This summary does not purport to be a complete treatise either on the Orthodox · law of marriage or on that of mixed marriage; its purpose is to serve the needs of the participants of the current dialogue, especially with reference to Orthodox-Roman Catholic marriages. In many instances, the canons provide only very general norms. Canon law was normally supplemented by civil legislation, the provisions of which were subsequently incorporated into the constitutions of the autocephalous Churches and formed the basis of their marriage procedures. Often, a fundamental canonical principle which was found in this *corpus* of canon law was expanded in order to provide for a broader need.

I. *Impediments*: The pastor is required at the beginning of the premarital counseling process to ascertain the freedom of each party to contract matrimony. Impediments which prevent an Orthodox Christian from entering into a valid marriage are absolute; relative impediments do not affect validity. The impediments which follow are contained in the *corpus* of canon law and other ecclesiastical legislation.

Roman Catholic Canonical Procedures

I. *Impediments*: The pastor is required at the beginning of the premarital counseling process to ascertain the freedom of each party to contract matrimony (Canon 1066: Before marriage is celebrated, it must be evident that nothing stands in the way of its valid and licit celebration). In the Code of 1983 only diriment impediments exist (Canon 1073: A diriment impediment renders a person incapable of contracting marriage validly). There are other cases where *permission* is needed; if the *permission* is *not* obtained, then the

A. *Disparity of Worship*: IV:14 and VI:72 prohibit an Orthodox Christian from entering into matrimony with a heretic, Jew or pagan and imposes a penance for violation thereof. The only distinction that is made between disparity of worship (marriage with a non-baptized person) and mixed religion (marriage with a baptized person of another confession) is in the case of an unbaptized person who declares his/her intention to receive baptism after the marriage. (See: *Note* on the mitigation of the rigor of this norm.) Each jurisdiction has its own procedure for obtaining the necessary dispensations. Priests must follow the particular law of their respective provinces,

Note on Trullan Canon 72: It is significant for the purposes of the current dialogue that, over the past few decades, a number of Roman dicasteries have had recourse to Trullan Canon 72 in adjudicating particular cases. The Apostolic Signature, on July 1, 1972, declared that the invalidating clause in the canon had long been mitigated by legitimate custom, imparting to it a simply prohibitive force. The change was legislated for Eastern Catholics by Pope Pius XII in his *motu proprio* of February 22, 1949, *Crebrae Allatae Sunt*, which promulgated the Eastern Catholic marriage law (see C.I.D., vol. 8, p. 5).

The Orthodox Church accepts a mitigation of the ancient rigor as well, but not because of the introduction of custom. According to Dr. N. Milasch, the Church bases this mitigation on the possibilities inherent in the Pauline privilege (see: N. Milasch, *The Canons of the Orthodox Church with Commentaries*, St. Petersburg, 1911, vol. 1, pp.561-4).

marriage is illegal, illicit, contrary to the church law but still valid and binding.

A. *Disparity of Worship* prohibits a Catholic from marrying a non-baptized person. (Canon 1086, 1: Marriage between the two persons, one of whom is baptized in the Catholic Church or has been received into it and has not left it by means of a formal act, and the other of whom is non-baptized, is invalid.) While mixed religion is no longer an impediment in the code, there is still required permission for a Catholic to marry another baptized person who is not a Catholic. Therefore, in the case of Orthodox-Roman Catholic marriages this permission would be needed in accord with canons 1124-1129.

It is therefore possible for both Churches to have recourse to the Trullan Canon 72 in adjudicating marriage cases of mixed religion: Catholic tribunals may refer to it in determining the validity of previously contracted Orthodox-Protestant marriages, and this, because it still has the force of law for the Orthodox: "Consequently, the Council [Vatican II] considered the ancient discipline of the dissident Orientals as still in force and, as a result, not abrogated by the law of Pius XII" (C.I.D., vol. 8, p. 26).

Orthodox tribunals will refer to this canon as their fundamental law in cases both of disparity of cult and mixed religion. Dispensations for disparity of cult are never given by Orthodox ecclesiastical authorities.

B. *Holy Orders*:

1. A canonical marriage constitutes no impediment to ordination to the lectorate, subdiaconate, diaconate or presbyterate (VI:6).

2. Marriage constitutes an absolute impediment to ordination to the episcopate: if a married man is elected a bishop, he must separate from his wife by mutual agreement if he is to be ordained (VI:12).

3. Ordination to the subdiaconate (in some provinces), the diaconate and the presbyterate constitutes an absolute impediment to marriage (VI:3,6).

C. *Monastic Profession* constitutes an absolute impediment to marriage (VI:16). Violation of this canon carries with it severest penalties (Basil: Can. 18).

D. *Successive Marriages*: The Church permits an individual who is widowed or whose first marriage has been legitimately dissolved to enter into a second and even a third marriage. The rites for these marriages are successively more penitential in

B. *Holy Orders*: Ordination to the diaconate, presbyterate, and episcopate constitute an absolute impediment to marriage (Canon 1087: Persons who are in holy orders invalidly attempt marriage).

C. *Perpetual Consecrated Vows* apply to consecrated men and women. (Canon 1088: Persons who are bound by a public perpetual vow of chastity in a religious institute invalidly attempt marriage.)

D. *Successive Marriages*: No one who is considered legitimately married may marry another person. (Canon 1085, 1: A person who is held to the bond of a prior marriage, even if it has not been consummated, invalidly attempts marriage.) This character (Basil: Can. 4,50). A fourth marriage is by immemorial custom absolutely prohibited. Each jurisdiction has its own procedures for canonically dissolving the marital bond. In the event that the ecclesiastical divorce has already been obtained, the priest is required to apply for a dispensation for the couple to enter into a successive marriage, according to the norms of the jurisdiction in which he is acting,

E. *Betrothal* to another party constitutes an impediment which must be dispensed; a dissolution, similar to that required for the marital bond, must be obtained from the competent ecclesiastical authority (VI.98).

F. *Degrees of Consanguinity, Affinity and Spiritual Relationship*

1. *Consanguinity* is a blood relationship existing between persons descended from one another or from the same stock. There is both a canonical and legal importance as to how consanguinity is determined: two lines of consanguinity are determined from the same stock: authority must be consulted in every case of consanguineous collateral relationship.

a. direct line: a descending line from the progenitor (father: son, daughter, grandchild, *etc.*; mother: son, daughter, grandchild, *etc.*)

b. collateral line: the existence of a blood relationship which does not constitute a direct decendance from the progenitor: a brother and a sister are collaterally related to each other but directly related to their progenitor: cousins, aunts, uncles, *etc.*

The degree of relationship is the measure of distance between any two persons descended directly or collaterally from the same stock. Various civil codes take into

rule is so strict that "even if the prior marriage is invalid or dissolved for any reason whatsoever, it is not on that account permitted to contract another before the nullity or the dissolution of the prior marriage has been legitimately and certainly established" (Canon 1085, 3).

E. *Betrothal* is not an impediment to any marriage. (Canon 1062, 2: A promise to marry does not give rise to an action to seek the celebration of marriage; an action for reparation of damages, however, does arise if it is warranted.)

F. *Degrees of Consanguinity, Affinity and Spiritual Relationship*

1. *Consanguinity* in the direct line is always an absolute impediment forbidding marriage between parents and children, grandparents and grandchildren, and so on. In the collateral line, it forbids marriage to the fourth degree of relationship, that is, first cousins. Also it forbids brother-sister unions, uncle-niece, and aunt-nephew unions. Dispensations are available except for brother-sister unions.

Note on *Adoption*: Canon 1094 says "they cannot contract marriage between themselves who are related in the direct line or in the second degree of the collateral line through a legal relationship arising from adoption." Parents may not marry adopted children, nor can adopted children marry each other or natural brothers or sisters.

account sociological customs. For example it is not uncommon for first cousins to marry in some cultures of the Mediterranean world. Local ecclesial jurisdictions often take into account such customs and dispensations can be obtained for certain collateral relationships. Dispensations can never be obtained in the case of direct descendants because such unions violate natural law. The proper ecclesiastical authority must be consulted in every case of consanguineous collateral relationship.

2. *Affinity* is the relationship not by blood that exists between the respective families of two spouses (in-laws). Thus the blood relations of a given spouse become relations by affinity of the opposite spouse in the same degree: the same distinctions between direct and collateral relationships exist. A dispensation may never be given in the direct line; a dispensation may be obtained for certain degrees of collateral relationship by affinity between two persons who desire to marry. The competent ecclesiastical authority is to be petitioned. The legal relationship by adoption falls into this category as well. According to the provisions of VI:54, the following marriages are prohibited: half-brothers and half-sisters; a father and son with a mother and daughter; a father and a son with two sisters; a mother and daughter with two brothers; and two brothers with two sisters. A dispensation may be obtained for certain degrees of collateral relationship by affinity.

3. *Spiritual relationships* are those that exist between a godparent and his/her godchild, according to the provisions of VI:53; the following unions are prohibited: the sponsor with his/her godchild; the sponsor with a widowed natural parent of the godchild; other spiritual rela-

2. *Affinity* forbids marriage in the direct line only (Canon 1092); a man may not marry his mother-in-law or daughter-in-law from a previous marriage and a woman, her father-in-law or son-in-law.

3. *Spiritual relationship* is no longer an impediment.

tionships defined by local custom and particular law.

G. The following impediments derive from the grounds for ecclesiastical divorce established by the Ecumenical Patriarchate since they vitiate the inherent quality of the marital bond from the beginning.

1. *Impotence:* incapacity to have marital relations due to some pathological dysfunction.

2. *Murder* of one's spouse or conspiracy or attempt to do so in order to be free to marry another party.

H. *Public Propriety:* Fornication does not give a couple the right to marriage; this impediment may be dispensed for the greater good (Basil: Can. 22, 25, 26).

G. The following two impediments, though not connected specifically, are listed together here in keeping with the format of this appendix.

1. *Impotence:* Physical or psychic impotence which is certain invalidates marriage. (Canon 1084, 1: Antecedent and perpetual impotence to have intercourse, whether on the part of the man or of the woman, which is either absolute or relative, of its nature invalidates marriage.) Any doubtful impotence does not hinder the marriage from taking place (Canon 1084,2). Sterility is not an impediment as such but may constitute fraud (Canon 1084,3).

2. *Murder:* One who murders one's spouse or conspires to do so may not marry another person (Canon 1090, 1: A person who for the purpose of entering marriage with a certain person has brought about the death of that person's spouse, or one's own spouse, invalidly attempts such a marriage). It should be noted that in ordinary circumstances this impediment may not be dispensed from except by the supreme authority in the Catholic Church. (Canon 1090, 2: They also invalidly attempt marriage between themselves who have brought about the death of the spouse of one of them through mutual physical or moral cooperation.)

H. *Public Propriety* refers to an invalid marriage or from concubinage forbidding marriage with direct relatives of the other party (that is, parents or children). (Canon 1093: The impediment of public propriety arises from an invalid marriage after

227

common life has been established or from notorious and public concubinage; it invalidates marriage in the first degree of the direct line between the man and blood relatives of the woman and vice-versa.)

I. *Age:* Roman law permitted marriage to males having attained the age of 14 years, and to females, the age of 12 years. Current ecclesiastical discipline conforms with the law of the land.

I. *Age:* Males must be 16; females must be 14 (Canon 1083).

J. *Time:* Marriages are prohibited during Lent (Laod. 52) and, by extension of the ratio legis, during other times of fast and feast according to particular law and/or custom.

J. *Time:* Liturgical guidelines discourage marriage during penitential times and All Soul's Day.

II. *Canonical Form and Sacred Minister*

A. The current practice of the Orthodox Church of having a priest bless a marriage can be traced back only about a thousand years. No canon prescribes an ecclesiastical blessing; that marriage was, nevertheless, considered a holy estate from earliest times is substantiated by Holy Scripture and the many canons which legislate concerning the validity and sacred character of the marital bond. Ecclesiastical ratification in the form of a blessing was legislated by Emperor Leo VI in Novella 89.

II. *Canonical Form and Sacred Minister*

A. Strict canonical form was introduced with the Council of Trent (1560) and became universal in the Catholic Church only in 1908. While there are a few exceptions, a Catholic must be married in the presence of the local ordinary, the pastor, or a delegated priest or deacon (Canon 1108).

B. In the case of Orthodox-Roman Catholic marriages the blessing of the Orthodox priest is (absolutely) required in most ecclesial provinces.

B. An explicit exception is made in the law for all Orthodox-Roman Catholic marriages—Canon 1127, 1: If a Catholic party contracts marriage with a non-Catholic of an oriental rite, the canonical form of celebration is to be observed only for liceity. But, the same canon still requires a sacred minister to be present at such a marriage: "for validity, however, the presence of a sacred minister is required along with the observance of the other requirements of law."

C. For couples wishing their marriages to be witnessed in a Roman Catholic church or who want a double ceremony, the conflict arises.

D. Orthodox priests performing an Orthodox-Roman Catholic marriage must inform the pastor of the Roman Catholic party that the marriage has taken place in the Orthodox Church.

E. The official sponsor at an Orthodox wedding must be of the Orthodox faith in good standing.

F. A Roman Catholic priest may bestow a solemn blessing at the conclusion of the marriage rite and may address words of exhortation and congratulations to the couple.

III. *Consent:* In the Orthodox Church, the legal requirements for consent derive from imperial jurisprudence. The individual autocephalous churches have adapted these norms in their particular legislation. Appropriating the principle of Roman law, *matrimonium consensus facit,* the *Basilica* II: 3, 30 states, "Marriage does not mean to sleep together but mutual agreement." That the Orthodox Church requires consent as an integral and constitutive element of the marital contract is indisputable (see: N. Milasch, *Das Kirchenrecht der Morgenländischen Kirche,* Mostar, 1905, pp. 583-4). The local churches, however, have not always seen the need to express this consent verbally. The explicit exchange of consent was made part of the Russian rite of marriage by Patriarch Joachim of Moscow in the late 17th century, under the influence of the Orthodox Metropolitan of Kiev, Archbishop Peter Moghila. Churches coming under the canonical jurisdiction or the theological influence of the Russian Church also introduced an explicit exchange of consent: the Antiochian, Bulgar-

III. *Consent:* Consent is essential to Catholic matrimonial law—Marriage is brought about through the consent of the parties legitimately manifested between persons who are capable according to law of giving consent; no human power can replace this consent (Canon 1057, 1).

ian, Carpatho-Russian, Czech, Polish, Serbian and Ukrainian Churches.

The current Greek practice requires that an ecclesiastical marriage license be obtained 60 days prior to the wedding. The couple signs an affidavit attesting to the fact that there is no legal or canonical impediment to the marriage.

Internal consent is always presumed by the fact that the couple is present at the betrothal rite. This consent must be freely given and without duress. The following factors vitiate the freedom of consent and derive from the grounds for ecclesiastical divorce established by the Ecumenical Patriarch:

A. *Mental Incompetence and Insanity:*
1. violent personality disorders,
2. schizophrenia,
3. paranoia

B. *Force, Abduction and Fear* (Ap. Can. 67; VI:92) deprive one of the parties of his/her freedom of choice: a marriage attempted under such conditions is invalid.

C. *Fraud:* Any deception by fraud renders a marriage invalid.

A. *Mental Incompetence and Insanity:* Those who lack sufficient use of reason are incapable of contracting marriage (Canon 1095, 1).

B. *Force, Abduction and Fear:* "A marriage is invalid if it is entered into due to force or grave fear inflicted from outside the person, even when inflicted unintentionally, which is of such a type that the person is compelled to choose matrimony in order to be freed from it" (Canon 1103). Abduction is treated as a strict impediment. No marriage can exist between a man and a woman abducted or at least detained for the purpose of contracting marriage with her (Canon 1089) unless the woman of her own accord chooses marriage after she has been separated from her abductor and established in a place where she is safe and free. Fear is included in the statement given above.

C. *Fraud:* The 1983 Code explicitly recognizes fraud as an indication of seriously defective consent in Canon 1098: A person contracts invalidly who enters marriage deceived by fraud, perpetrated to obtain consent, concerning some quality of the other party which of its very nature can seriously disturb the partnership of conjugal life. The jurisprudence on this matter must develop, but at least sterility is seen as a probable aspect of fraud in some cases.

D. *Error* concerning the freedom of a party to contract a marriage vitiates consent (VI:93).

D. *Error:* If the error involves the actual person to be married, there is no question that the marriage is invalid (Canon 1091, 1). If the error involves a quality of the person which was directly and principally intended, then the marriage is also invalid (Canon 1092,2). If the error involves dogmatic questions about marriage and concerns the unity, indissolubility or sacramental dignity of marriage, and this was a determinant of the person's will at the time of marriage, the marriage is again invalid (Canon 1099).

E. *Ignorance:* It is necessary that the contracting parties at least know that marriage is a permanent consortium between a man and a woman which is ordered toward the procreation of offspring by means of some sexual cooperation (Canon 1096, 1), but such ignorance must be demonstrated to invalidate the marriage (Canon 1096, 2).

F. *Simulation:* If any party should exclude marriage itself, or some essential element or an essential property (that is, unity or indissolubility) by means of a positive act of the will, then the marriage is contracted invalidly (Canon 1101, 2).

G. *Conditional Marriage:* In the current law, the only permitted condition is one that concerns the past or the present, and the permission of the local ordinary is required to place such a condition (Canon 1102, 2-3). No condition regarding any future situation is permitted any longer, and such a condition would render the marriage invalid (Canon 1102, 1).

H. *Actual Presence:* In order for marriage to be contracted validly, it is necessary that the contracting parties be present

231

together, and this may be done either in person or by proxy (Canon 1104, 1). The rules for proxy marriages are stipulated very carefully in Canon 1105.

I. *Consensual Expression:* Those to be married are to express their matrimonial consent in words; however, if they cannot speak, they are to express it by equivalent signs (Canon 1104, 2). Marriage can be contracted through an interpreter; however, the pastor is not to assist at such a marriage unless he is convinced of the interpreter's trustworthiness (Canon 1106).

IV. *Convalidation:* When the marriage of an Orthodox Christian and Roman Catholic has already taken place in a Catholic church, the marriage can be convalidated by the competent ecclesiastical authority if the following conditions are met: 1) that no absolute impediment to the marriage exists; 2) that any relative impediment that may exist be dispensed; 3) that an appropriate rite be used to bless the union.

IV. *Convalidation:* Convalidation may be needed of a marriage in question due to the fact that an impediment was present at the time of the original marriage, or due to the fact that the proper formalities were not observed, or due to the fact that there was a defect in the consent originally given.

A. In cases involving impediments, they must either have ceased (for example, age, disparity of worship) or be dispensed (for example, consanguinity) and consent must be expressed again (Canon 1156, 1-2).

B. In cases involving improper formalities, it is required that the canonical form be observed, that is, the parties must give consent in the presence of a priest or deacon and two witnesses (Canon 1160).

C. In cases involving defective consent originally given, consent must be given again, and usually according to the required canonical form for marriage (Canon 1159).

D. Another canonical institute known as a "radical sanation" of marriage is possible when the original consent given still exists and the marriage was invalid because of lack of formalities or the existence of certain impediments. In these cases, the original consent is as it were "healed" and the marriage with all it effects is recognized as of the date of the *original* consent (Canon 1161-65).

V. *Dissolution and Annulment*

A. The Orthodox Church teaches that the marriage bond is indissoluble, and this from divine positive law: Mt. 19:3-9; Mk. 10:2-12; Lk. 16:18. Grounded, however, in the recognition of the factors of frailty and error which too often characterize human life, and proceeding from that same divine positive law which admits exceptions to the norm (Dt. 24:1-4; Mt. 19:9; Mk 10:5), the Church, in fact, permits the dissolution of the marital bond on the following grounds:

1. adultery (Basil 9:21) and
2. prolonged absence (VI:93).

B. In addition to the grounds stated above, VI·87 stipulates that a separation/divorce "without reason" is illegal; therefore, we are to conclude that other grounds may exist for the dissolution of the marital bond. Milasch (see: commentary on VI:87 in Vol.I of his Commentaries, p. 578) states that the proper grounds for the dissolution of the marital bond is

V. *Dissolution and Annulment*

A. Dissolution is the recognition that an existing true and valid marriage is no longer. The Catholic Church permits dissolution in certain rare cases. One involves the non-consummation of a marriage between two baptized people (Canon 1142). Another involves the marriages of two non-baptized people (for example, Jews, Muslims, pagans) when one of them wishes to be baptized (the Pauline privilege situation, Canons 1143-49). A third involves a practice of the Holy See to dissolve marriages where only one baptized person is involved provided there is some question of marriage with a baptized person. (These latter situations are the privilege of the faith cases which are not explicitly treated in the 1983 Code except in the general principle: In a doubtful matter the privilege of the faith enjoys the favor of the law [Canon 1150]). In all other cases involving two baptized persons, the only possible path to follow is to challenge the validity of the marriage. This can be done in view of any of the diriment impediments mentioned above or because of the defect of required formalities or because of defective consent. In practice it is rare to discover a marriage of two baptized persons to be invalid on account of an impediment. A few cases do occur involving prior bond, when this has been concealed by one of the parties.

B. Many cases, however, do occur of invalid marriages which were celebrated civilly since this is clearly against the law of the Catholic Church for Catholics. But, if the original marriage was celebrated in a Catholic Church, it is relatively rare to accuse the marriage of nullity on this ground since it would have usually taken place in the presence of a priest and two anything that destroys the moral or religious foundations of the marriage. The grounds for divorce are codified in imperial legislation: Code of Theodosios, III; Code of Justinian, V; Justinian's Novellae 2; 22; 17: 134. The grounds for ecclesiastical divorce are the following:

1. adultery,
2. abandonment,
3. apostasy,
4. monastic profession (by mutual consent).

C. The question of nullity requires further inquiry by Orthodox canonists who read an embryonic theory of nullity in VI:3 which requires that an attempted second marriage of clerics be dissolved, such cohabitation being considered defective from the beginning; also in VI:72 which stipulates that if an Orthodox Christian marries a heretic, "the marriage shall be considered invalid and this illicit cohabitation shall be dissolved."

D. The Ecumenical Patriarchate has established a number of crimes and other causes constituting grounds for ecclesiastical divorce. These causes of action are digested below from directives issued by Archbishop Iakovos to the clergy of the Greek Orthodox Archdiocese of North and South America: Prot. No. 116, June 16, 1966; Prot. No. 106A, Nov, 21, 1973.

1. Force, fear, blackmail;
2. Adultery;
3. Mental Incompetence and Insanity:
   a. Violent personality disorders,
   b. Schizophrenia,
   c. Paranoia;

other witnesses. Most of the nullity cases treated by the Catholic church, therefore, come under the grounds of defective consent. This is due to several causes. First and foremost, it is here that one or both parties can act improperly and without consent or give what is thought to be matrimonial consent which is really very deficient. Secondly, it is in this area that many people claim they wish to marry but are affected by personality defects which make it impossible for them to assume the consortium of common life required by church teaching. If people cannot give of themselves, they are not able to live with another person in a communion of life and love.

4. Concealment prior to marriage of a communicable disease;

5. Conspiracy or attempt to murder one's spouse;

6. Degradation of one's spouse;

7. Lawful imprisonment of a spouse for 7 or more years;

8. Abandonment for a period of 3 or more years, except when such absence is caused by psycho-neurotic disturbance or illness;

9. Coercion of a wife by her husband to prostitute herself;

10. Impotence: incapacity to have marital relations due to some pathological disorder;

11. Addictive alcoholism;

12. Addictive gambling.

A PASTORAL STATEMENT ON ORTHODOX-ROMAN CATHOLIC MARRIAGES

Joint Committee of Orthodox and Catholic Bishops, 1990

Introduction

A growing trust and a spirit of cooperation have developed between the Orthodox Church and the Roman Catholic Church during the last twenty-five years, not only in the United States but also in other parts of the world. Under the inspiration of the Holy Spirit, our churches have been led to recognize more profoundly the need to manifest our unity in Christ and to pray for healing the wounds of centuries-old estrangement.

As bishops of these two churches, we hail this progress in mutual commitment to church unity. We recognize that the Orthodox Church has expressed its seriousness in working for unity in the Church of Christ in this century through encyclicals and gestures of reconciliation. The Pan-Orthodox conferences held at Rhodes and preparations underway for convening a Great and Holy Synod are tangible signs of hope. We also recognize that the Roman Catholic Church, especially at the Second Vatican Council (1962-1965), committed itself to the cause of Christian unity and recognized its close ties with the Orthodox Church. The creation of the Vatican Secretariat (now Pontifical Council) for Promoting Christian Unity is one sign of its dedication to restoring visible unity. Both our churches welcomed the establishment in 1975 of the official Joint International Commission for Theological Dialogue. Notwithstanding the difficulties this commission has encountered and no doubt will continue to encounter, we rejoice in the work which it has already accomplished.

In the United States, under the sponsorship of the Standing Conference of Canonical Orthodox Bishops in America (SCOBA) and the National Conference of Catholic Bishops (NCCB), a fruitful series of theological consultations has been continuing since 1965. Twice each year members of the U.S. Orthodox-Roman Catholic Consultation meet to discuss common doctrinal and pastoral concerns of our two churches. Already this Consultation has met forty times and has published thirteen agreed statements on important religious concerns. It has also shared its work with the Joint International Commission for Theological Dialogue.

A Joint Committee of Orthodox and Roman Catholic Bishops was formed in the United States in 1981 at the suggestion of His Eminence Archbishop Iakovos, Primate of the Greek Orthodox Archdiocese of North and South America, especially to address common pastoral concerns. Foremost among these concerns was the marriage between members of the Roman Catholic and Orthodox Churches.

In this present statement, we, as members of this joint committee, wish to share a number of conclusions from our recent discussions and to propose recommendations that could be implemented in our churches in this country without delay.

To prepare for this statement we have reflected on earlier texts regarding Christian marriage produced by the U.S. Orthodox-Roman Catholic Consultation: three agreed statements on (1) Mixed Marriages (November 4, 1971); (2) the Sanctity of Marriage (December 8, 1978); (3) the Spiritual Formation of Children of Marriages between Orthodox and Roman Catholics (October 11, 1980); and (4) a reaction to an agreement concluded in Boston between Cardinal Medeiros and Bishop Anthimos (April 8, 1981) on ways of regularizing non-canonical marriages between an Orthodox and Roman Catholic spouse (May 29, 1982). Also submitted to us for comment was a document of the Metropolitan New York/New Jersey Orthodox-Roman Catholic Dialogue, an "Agreed Statement on Orthodox-Roman Catholic Marriages" (January 6, 1986). Our own Joint Committee provided a response to its practical suggestions on March 23, 1989. At our previous meetings in 1988 and 1989, we also consulted scholars of Sacred Scripture regarding New Testament perspectives on the indissolubility of marriage.

Meeting now from October 3 to 5, 1990, in Johnstown, Pennsylvania, we wish to make this joint statement about Christian marriage and to offer recommendations which, if implemented, could assist Roman Catholic and Orthodox couples to fulfill more responsibly the requirements of their churches regarding the marriage ceremony, married life in Christ, and the spiritual formation of children.

The Sacredness of Marriage

At a time when the sacredness of married life is seriously threatened by contrary views and "lifestyles," we wish to reaffirm our common faith in the profound reality of married life in Christ. We regard Christian marriage as a vocation from God in which the liberating effect of divine love, a gift of Holy Spirit, is experienced through human love. This human love expresses itself in permanent commitment to mutual fidelity and support in all aspects of life, spiritual as well as physical. It also expresses itself in the generation of new life, that is, in the procreation and nurturing of children on both the spiritual and physical levels. A primary responsibility of parents is the spiritual formation of their children, a task not limited to assuring church membership and providing for formal religious education but extending to all aspects of Christian living.

We regard Christian marriage as having a social dimension which extends beyond the partners and their relatives. Through marriage, husband and wife assume new roles in the church community. Consequently, just as marriage partners have a responsibility for the building up of the Church, so too the church community has a responsibility to help each Christian family foster its life of faith. In particular the church community shares in the parents' responsibility for the spiritual formation of children.

The Sacramentality of Marriage

We share a common faith and conviction that, for Christians in both the Orthodox and Roman Catholic Churches, marriage is a sacrament of Jesus Christ. We profess the presence of Christ in the Holy Spirit through the prayers and actions of our wedding liturgies. We express our belief that it is Christ who unites the spouses in a life of mutual love. Hence, in this holy union, both are seen as being called by Christ not only to live and work together, but also to share their Christian lives so that each spouse, under grace and with the aid of the other, may grow in holiness and Christian perfection. According to our shared belief, this relationship between husband and wife has been established and sanctified by the Lord. Marriage, as a sacred vocation, mirrors the union of Christ with the Church (Eph. 5:23).

The Gospels record that Jesus affirmed the profound significance of marriage. Christian tradition, building upon the teaching of Jesus, con-

238

tinues to proclaim the sanctity of marriage. It is a fundamental relationship in which man and woman, by total sharing with each other, seek their own growth in holiness and that of their children, and show forth the presence of God's kingdom. Having God's love poured in their hearts by the Holy Spirit, husband and wife exemplify and reflect in their lives together the mystery of love which unites the three persons of the Holy Trinity. Thus, marriage becomes a dynamic relationship which challenges the spouses to live according to the high standards of divine love.

In the teaching of our churches, a sacramental marriage requires both the mutual consent of the believing Christian partners and God's blessing imparted through the official ministry of the Church. At the present time, there are differences in the ways by which this ministry is exercised in order to fulfill the theological and canonical norms for marriage in our churches. The Orthodox Church, as a rule, accepts as sacramental only those marriages of Christians baptized in the name of the Holy Trinity which are sanctified in the Church's liturgy through the blessing of an Orthodox bishop or priest. The Catholic Church accepts as sacramental those marriages of Christians baptized in the name of the Holy Trinity which are witnessed by a Catholic bishop or priest (or, in more recent discipline, a deacon), but it also envisages some exceptional cases in which, whether by law or by dispensation, Catholics may enter into a sacramental marriage in the absence of a bishop, priest or deacon. There are also differences in our theological explanations of this diversity. As older presentations of sacramental theology indicate, Orthodox theologians often have insisted that the priest is the proper "minister of the sacrament," whereas Roman Catholic theologians more often have spoken of the couple as "ministering the sacrament to each other."

We do not wish to underestimate the seriousness of these differences in practice and theological explanation. We consider their further study to be desirable. At the same time, we wish to emphasize our fundamental agreement. Both our churches have always agreed that ecclesial context is constitutive of the Christian sacrament of marriage. Within this fundamental agreement, history has shown various possibilities of realization so that no one particular form of expressing this ecclesial context may be considered absolutely normative in all circumstances for both churches. In our judgment, our present differences of practice and theology concerning the required ecclesial context for marriage pertain to the level of secondary theological reflection rather than to the level of dogma.

The Enduring Nature of Marriage

The common teaching of our churches follows Sacred Scripture in affirming the enduring nature of marriage. Already the Old Testament used marriage to describe the covenantal relationship between God and God's people (Hosea). The Epistle to the Ephesians saw marriage as the type of the relationship which exists between Christ and the Church (Eph. 5:31-33). Jesus spoke of marriage as established "from the beginning of creation." He also taught: "And the two shall become one. So they are no longer two but one. What therefore God has joined together, let no man put asunder." (Mk. 10:6,8-9; Mt. 19:4-6)

A number of scholars of Sacred Scripture in our churches consider it likely that Jesus' teaching about the indissolubility of marriage may have already been interpreted and adjusted by New Testament writers, moved by the Holy Spirit, to respond to new circumstances and pastoral problems (cf. Mt. 5:32 and 1 Cor. 7:15). Hence they ask, if Matthew, under the inspiration of the Holy Spirit, could have been moved to add an exceptive phrase to Jesus' saying about divorce, or if Paul, similarly inspired, could have introduced an exception on his own authority, then would it be possible for those exercising authoritative pastoral decision-making in today's Church to explore the examination of exceptions?

Our churches have expressed their conviction concerning the enduring nature of Christian marriage in diverse ways. In the canonical discipline of the Orthodox Church, for example, perpetual monogamy is upheld as the norm of marriage, so that those entering upon a second or subsequent marriage are subject to penance even in the case of widows and widowers. In the Roman Catholic Church the enduring nature of marriage has been emphasized especially in the absolute prohibition of divorce.

Our churches have also responded in diverse ways to the tragedies which can beset marriage in our fallen world. The Orthodox Church, following Mt. 19:9 ("whoever divorces his wife *except for unchastity*, and marries another, commits adultery"), permits divorce under certain circumstances, not only in the case of adultery but also of other serious

240

assaults on the moral and spiritual foundation of marriage (secret abortion, endangering the life of the spouse, forcing the spouse to prostitution and similar abusive situations). Out of pastoral consideration and in order better to serve the spiritual needs of the faithful, the Orthodox Church tolerates remarriage of divorced persons under certain specific circumstances as it permits the remarriage of widows and widowers under certain specific circumstances. The Roman Catholic Church has responded in other ways to such difficult situations. In order to resolve the personal and pastoral issues of failed consummated marriages, it undertakes inquiries to establish whether there may have existed some initial defect in the marriage covenant which provides grounds for the Church to make a declaration of nullity, that is, a decision attesting that the marriage lacked validity. It also recognizes the possibility of dissolving sacramental non-consummated marriages through papal dispensation. While it is true that the Roman Catholic Church does not grant dissolution of the bond of a consummated sacramental marriage, it remains a question among theologians whether this is founded on a prudential judgment or on the Church's perception that it lacks the power to dissolve such a bond.

Study of the history of our various traditions has led us to conclude that some at times may raise a particular theological explanation of relatively recent origin to the level of unchangeable doctrine. The Second Vatican Council's "Pastoral Constitution on the Church in the Modern World" stated that there was need for a renewal of the Roman Catholic Church's understanding and approach to its teaching on marriage. That council implicitly recognized that teaching on marriage had frequently proceeded from a biological and juridical point of view rather than from an interpersonal and existential one.

Spiritual Formation of Children

We also share a common conviction that in marriages in which one spouse is Catholic and the other is Orthodox both should take an active role in every aspect of their children's spiritual formation. Our priests are expected to counsel parents and children against indifference in religious matters. But since unity in Christ through the Holy Spirit is the ultimate goal of family life, all family members should be willing in a spirit of love, trust and freedom, to learn more about their Christian faith. They are

241

expected to pray, study, discuss and seek unity in Christ and to express their commitment to this unity in all aspects of their lives.

In marriages in which our two churches are involved, decisions, including the initial one of the children's church membership, rest with both husband and wife. The decisions should take into account the good of the children, the strength of the religious convictions of the parents and other relatives, the demands of parents' consciences, the unity and stability of the family, and other specific contexts. In some cases, when it appears highly probable that only one of the partners will fulfill his or her responsibility, it seems desirable that children should be raised in that partner's church. In other cases, the children's spiritual formation may include a fuller participation in the life and traditions of both churches, respecting always each church's canonical order. In these cases, the decision regarding the children's church membership is more difficult to make. Yet we are convinced that it is possible to make this decision in good conscience because of the proximity of our churches' doctrine and practice which enables each, to a high degree, to see the other precisely as Church, as the locus for the communion of the faithful with God and with each other through Jesus Christ in the Holy Spirit.

Recommendations

In the light of our discussion together, we submit to our churches the following recommendations which we judge will greatly contribute to promoting Christian charity and honesty in our two sister churches in regard to marriages between our faithful.

(1) We urge that SCOBA and the NCCB establish and sponsor a joint committee to prepare for publication our common teaching regarding Christian marriage, family life, and the spiritual formation of children. Such an ecumenical publication would be produced in common for the guidance of our clergy and the use of all involved in marriages between Orthodox and Roman Catholics. Such material would reflect the profound spirit of love and commitment to Christian unity that has marked our churches in recent times. Such a publication would indicate that our common faith leads to the recognition of the sacramentality of marriage in each other's church.

We recommend that, in this jointly prepared material, pastors and couples be offered up-to-date information about the recent and persistent efforts to foster a closer relationship between our two churches. It would encourage Orthodox-Catholic families to draw deeply from the spiritual wealth of both churches. It would urge them to safeguard the richness and integrity of each tradition by cautioning against attempts to absorb one partner into the other's church.

We also recommend that this material include sensitive and accurate presentation of the present canonical discipline of our churches with regard to marriage in order to aid pastors in counseling couples in a responsible manner, especially if there has been a previous marriage.

(2) We recommend that when an Orthodox and Catholic marry there be only one liturgical ceremony in which either one or both priests are present, with the rite being that of the officiating priest. The guest priest, normally dressed in cassock, would be invited to greet the bride and groom and to offer a prayer toward the end of the ceremony. We recommend that such marriages be recorded in the registries of both churches.

We recommend that in the case of marriages celebrated in the past, if it should be decided that some supplementary liturgical action is needed for a member to be readmitted to full eucharistic communion in one's church, care should be taken that this liturgical celebration avoid the impression of being another marriage ceremony, thereby implying that what had already taken place was not a marriage.

We earnestly submit these recommendations to the NCCB and SCOBA for adoption and rapid implementation by our churches.

While recognizing the integrity of the canonical and pastoral practices and procedures in both our churches which seek to provide for the faithful whose marriages have failed, we also note the major differences which exist between our practices and procedures. We therefore would also encourage further serious and specific study by canonists and others in a common effort to understand and, in so far as possible, resolve these differences of practice and procedure to move toward a commonly accepted declaration of freedom to marry. Our own Joint Committee, with the assistance of the U.S. Orthodox-Roman Catholic Consultation, and

243

of specialists in canon law, church history, and sacramental theology, hopes to pursue this ongoing task.

We realize that this undertaking, as well as the many others that lie before us, is of such magnitude that it cannot be accomplished easily or quickly. Yet, relying on the Holy Spirit, we are confident that it can be achieved, given the spirit of trust and cooperation which exists in our churches and which we have experienced in our own deliberations.

October 5, 1990
Johnstown, PA
Ninth Meeting

Chronology of Orthodox-Catholic Consultation in the United States, 1965-1995

1. September 9, 1965. St. Spyridon Orthodox Church, Parish Center, Worcester, MA.

2. September 29, 1966. Greek Orthodox Archdiocese, New York, NY.

3. May 5-6, 1967. Fr. John Power [RC] Center, Worcester, MA.

4. December 6-7, 1968. Maryknoll Seminary, Maryknoll, NY.

5. December 12-13, 1969. St. Spyridon Orthodox Church, Parish Center, Worcester, MA. **First Agreed Statement, on the Holy Eucharist.**

6. May 19-20, 1970. Mary Reparatrix Retreat House, New York, NY. **Second Agreed Statement, on Mixed Marriages.** [cf. revision at eighth meeting]

7. December 4-5, 1970. Holy Cross Greek Orthodox School of Theology, Brookline, MA.

8. November 3-4, 1971. Barlin Acres, Worcester, MA. **New Text on Mixed Marriages.** [revision of text from 6th meeting]

9. December 6, 1973. Greek Orthodox Archdiocese, New York, NY.

10. May 23-24, 1974. Washington Retreat House, Washington, DC. **Third Agreed Statement, on Respect for Life.**

11. December 9-10, 1974. Greek Orthodox Archdiocese, New York, NY. **Fourth Agreed Statement, on the Church.**

12. May 19-20, 1975. National 4-H Center, Washington, DC.

13. January 23-24, 1976. St. Basil's Academy, Garrison, NY.

14. May 18-19, 1976. Carmelite Fathers Center, Washington, DC. **Fifth and Sixth Agreed Statements, on the Pastoral Office and on the Principle of "Economy."**

15. January 13-14, 1977. Holy Cross Greek Orthodox School of Theology, Brookline, MA.

16. September 28-29, 1977, Washington Retreat House, Washington, DC. **Seventh Agreed Statement: Reaction to the Agenda of the Great and Holy Council of the Orthodox Church.**

17. January 24-25, 1978. Greek Orthodox Archdiocese, New York, NY.

18. May 17-18, 1978. Washington Retreat House, Washington, DC.

19. December 7-8, 1978. Greek Orthodox Archdiocese, New York, NY **Eighth Agreed Statement, on the Sanctity of Marriage.**

20. March 15-16, 1979. Center for Applied Research in the Apostolate (CARA), Washington, DC.

21. November 2-3, 1979. Cenacle Retreat House, Pittsburgh, PA.

22. October 10-11, 1980. Seamen's Institute of New York and New Jersey, New York, NY. **Ninth Agreed Statement, on Spiritual Formation of Children of Marriages between Orthodox and Roman Catholics.**

23. October 1-3, 1981. St. Basil's Academy, Garrison, NY.

24. May 27-29, 1982. St. Francis Seminary, Milwaukee, WI.

25. November 18-20, 1982. Cenacle Retreat House, Pittsburgh, PA.

26. May 23-25, 1983. Bishop Malloy Retreat House, Jamaica, Long Island, NY. **Tenth Agreed Statement, Response to the Munich Statement.**

27. October 27-29, 1983. St. Francis Seminary, Milwaukee, WI.

28. June 4-6, 1984. St. Vladimir's Orthodox Theological Seminary, Crestwood, NY.

29. October 25-27, 1984. Cathedral College, Douglaston, NY. **Eleventh Agreed Statement, Reaction to the BEM Document.**

30. June 3-5, 1985. Holy Cross Greek Orthodox School of Theology, Brookline, MA.

31. October 31-November 2, 1985. Cathedral College, Douglaston, NY.

32. June 2-4, 1986. St. Vladimir's Orthodox Theological Seminary, Crestwood, NY.

33. October 30-November 1, 1986. St. John's Seminary, Brighton, MA. **Twelfth Agreed Statement, on Apostolicity.**

34. June 2-4, 1987. Holy Cross Greek Orthodox School of Theology, Brookline, MA.

35. October 29-31, 1987. St. John's Seminary, Brighton, MA.

36. May 31-June 2, 1988. St. Vladimir's Orthodox Theological Seminary, Crestwood, NY. **Thirteenth Agreed Statement, Response to the Bari Statement.**

37. October 27-29, 1988. St. John's Seminary, Brighton, MA.

38. May 30-June 1, 1989. Cenacle Retreat House, Pittsburgh, PA.

39. October 26-28, 1989. St. John's Seminary, Brighton, MA. **Fourteenth and Fifteenth Agreed Statements, Response to the Valamo Statement on Conciliarity and Primacy in the Church.**

40. May 29-31, 1990. St. Vladimir's Orthodox Theological Seminary, Crestwood, NY.

41. October 18-20, 1990. St. John's Seminary, Brighton, MA. **Sixteenth Agreed Statement, Joint Communiqué on Current Tensions in Eastern Europe.**

42. May 28-30, 1991. Holy Cross Greek Orthodox School of Theology, Brookline, MA.

43. May 26-28, 1992. Holy Cross Greek Orthodox School of Theology, Brookline, MA. **Seventeenth Agreed Statement on Tensions in Eastern Europe Related to "Uniatism."**

44. October 29-31, 1992. Immaculate Conception Center, Douglaston, NY.

45. June 1-3, 1993. St. Vladimir's Orthodox Theological Seminary, Crestwood, NY.

46. October 28-30, 1993. St. John's Seminary, Brighton, MA.

47. May 31-June 2, 1994. Holy Cross Greek Orthodox School of Theology, Brookline, MA.

48. October 13-15, 1994. St. John's Seminary, Brighton, MA. **Eighteenth Agreed Statement: Response to the Balamand Statement.**

49. May 30-31, 1995. St. Vladimir's Orthodox Theological Seminary, Crestwood, NY.

50. October 26-28, 1995. Astor Hotel, Milwaukee, WI.

Bibliography of Documentation:
Statements of Orthodox-Roman Catholic Dialogues
Arranged by Commissions and in Chronological Order

Joint International Commission for Theological Dialogue between the Roman Catholic Church and the Orthodox Church

Note: Official texts are in French; translations in English and Greek are issued by Rome and Constantinople respectively.

"Plan to Set Underway the Theological Dialogue between the Roman Catholic Church and the Orthodox Church" (Patmos/Rhodes, 1980).

"The Mystery of the Church and of the Eucharist in the Light of the Mystery of the Holy Trinity" (Munich, 1982). Published in *Origins*, CNS Documentary Service, 12, 10 (August 12, 1982): 157-60. See also: Pontifical Council for Promoting Christian Unity, *Information Service* [hereafter cited as *IS*] 49 (1982, ii/iii): 107-112. Also published in *One in 2000? Towards Catholic-Orthodox Unity*, ed. by Paul McPartlan (United Kingdom: St. Pauls, 1993), pp. 37-52.

"Faith, Sacraments and the Unity of the Church" (Bari, 1987). Published in *Origins* 17, 44 (April 14, 1988): 743-9. See also: *IS* 64 (1987, ii): 82-7; *One in 2000?*, pp. 53-69.

"The Sacrament of Order in the Sacramental Structure of the Church, with Particular Reference to the Importance of Apostolic Succession for the Sanctification and Unity of the People of God" (Valamo, 1988). Published in *IS* 68 (1988, iii/iv): 173-8. See also: *One in 2000?*, pp. 71-86; *Origins* (incomplete) 18, 18 (October 13, 1988): 297-300.

Note: After the Valamo text was published in Origins, *it was discovered that the English version of the final agreement was lacking two sentences at the end of paragraph 5, and these were included in the text published in* IS *and subsequently but slightly modified in* One in 2000?. *The sentences in* IS *missing from the text published in* Origins *follow: "There is no Church without ministries created by the Spirit; there is no ministry without the Church, that is to say, outside and above the community. Ministries find their meaning and grounds for existence (raison d'être) only in it."*

"Uniatism, Method of Union of the Past, and the Present Search for Full Communion" (Balamand, 1993). Published, with corrections to the English text in italics, in *Ecumenical Trends* [hereafter cited as *ET*] (December 1993) 22, 11: 6-10. These others are incomplete: *IS* 83 (1993, ii): 95-99; *Origins* 23, 10 (August 12, 1993): 166-9; *ET* (September 1993) 22, 8: 1-7.

Note: This text and the plenary meeting of the Joint International Commission which produced it were preceded by a series of meetings with various communiqués and drafts. One meeting was a plenary of the Commission, held in Freising (June 6-15,

247

1990). A text was approved by those present at the end of the Freising meeting and is worthy of note since it resulted from a plenary. The Freising text appears in IS 73 (1990, ii): 52-53, where it is described as "a first step of the Commission in the study of a complex problem of which all aspects must be considered." See also: One is Christ 26 (1990): 362-5. After the English translation of the Balamand text appeared in IS, Origins and ET (September 1993), a notice was received from the Holy See that the English text was defective in three places. Paragraph 13 should conclude with this sentence: "In this context, it is clear that any rebaptism must be avoided." The first sentence of paragraph 26 should conclude with the phrase "at the local level." The third sentence of paragraph 27 should include "moral" among the forms of violence listed and should thus read: "...and to teach them to avoid not only violence, be that physical, verbal or moral, but also all that..." Subsequently ET reissued the Balamand text with corrections, inserted in italics, in the December 1993 issue.

U. S. Joint Committee of Orthodox and Catholic Bishops

Joint statement on "Ordination" (October 1, 1988). Published in *Growing Consensus* [hereafter cited as *GC*], Ecumenical Documents V, ed. Joseph A. Burgess and Jeffrey Gros, F.S.C. (New York, Paulist Press, 1995), pp. 495-6.

"A Pastoral Statement on Orthodox-Roman Catholic Marriages" (October 5, 1990). Published in *Origins* 20, 25 (November 29, 1990): 410-12. See also: *GC*, pp. 497-504.

"Statement" of support for historical Christianity in Eastern Europe and the former Soviet Union (September 19, 1991).

"Communiqué," Tenafly, New Jersey (October 2, 1992). Published in "On File," *Origins* 22, 18 (October 15, 1992): 306.

U. S. Orthodox-Catholic Theological Consultation: Joint Statements

"An Agreed Statement on the Holy Eucharist" (December 13, 1969). The first nine statements from 1969-1978 were published in *Toward Reunion: The Orthodox and Roman Catholic Churches* (hereafter cited as *TR*), ed. by Edward Kilmartin, S.J. (New York: Paulist Press, 1979), pp. 73-91. See also: *GC*, pp. 485-6.

"An Agreed Statement on Mixed Marriage" (November 4, 1971). Published in *Building Unity* [hereafter cited as *BU*], Ecumenical Documents IV, ed. by Joseph A. Burgess and Br. Jeffrey Gros, F.S.C. (New York: Paulist Press, 1989), pp. 326-7. See also: *TR*.

Note: An initial version of this statement was developed at the sixth meeting of the Consultation (New York, May 19-20, 1970), but the final version, printed here and elsewhere, was approved only at the eighth meeting (Barlin Acres, MA, November 3-4, 1971).

"An Agreed Statement on Respect for Life" (May 24, 1974). Published in *BU*, pp. 328-9. See also: *TR*; *Origins* 4, 12 (June 4, 1974): 29.

248

"An Agreed Statement on the Church" (December 10, 1974). Published in *BU*, pp. 330-1. See also: *TR*; *ET* 4, 2 (February 1975): 25-6.

"The Pastoral Office: A Joint Statement" (May 19, 1976). Published in *Origins* 6, 9 (August 12, 1976): 142-3. See also: *TR*; *GC*, pp. 487-90.

"The Principle of Economy: A Joint Statement" (May 19, 1976). Published in *BU*, pp. 332-4. See also: *TR*; *Origins* 6, 9 (August 12, 1976): 143-4.

"Reaction of the Orthodox-Roman Catholic Dialogue to the Agenda of the Great and Holy Council of the Orthodox Church" (September 29, 1977). Published in *TR*.

"An Agreed Statement on the Sanctity of Marriage" (December 8, 1978). Published in *BU*, pp. 335-8. See also: *TR*.

"Joint Recommendations on the Spiritual Formation of Children of Marriages Between Orthodox and Roman Catholics" (October 11, 1980). Published in *BU*, pp. 339-41. See also: *Origins* 10, 22 (November 13, 1980): 347-8.

"A Response to the Joint International Commission for Theological Dialogue Between the Orthodox Church and the Roman Catholic Church Regarding the Munich Document: 'The Mystery of the Church and of the Eucharist in the Light of the Mystery of the Holy Trinity'" (May 25, 1983). Published in *Origins* 13, 10 (August 4, 1983): 167.

"An Agreed Statement on the Lima Document *Baptism, Eucharist and Ministry* by the Eastern Orthodox-Roman Catholic Consultation, U.S.A." (October 27, 1984).

"Apostolicity as God's Gift in the Life of the Church" (November 1, 1986). Published in *BU*, pp. 354-58. See also: *ET* (December 1987) 16, 11: 197-200.

"A Response to the Joint International Commission for Theological Dialogue between the Orthodox Church and the Roman Catholic Church Regarding the Bari Document: 'Faith, Sacraments, and the Unity of the Church'" (June 2, 1988).

"A Joint Reaction by the Orthodox-Roman Catholic Consultation in the U.S.A. to the International Orthodox-Roman Catholic Commission's Text: 'The Sacrament of Order in the Sacramental Structure of the Church with Particular Reference to the Importance of Apostolic Succession for the Sanctification and Unity of the People of God'" (October 28, 1989).

"An Agreed Statement on Conciliarity and Primacy in the Church" (October 28, 1989). Published in *Origins* 19, 29 (December 21, 1989): 469, 471-2. See also: *GC*, pp. 441-4.

"A Joint Communiqué of the Orthodox-Roman Catholic Consultation in the United States on Current Tensions between our Churches in Eastern Europe" (October 20, 1990).

"Joint Statement of the United States Orthodox-Roman Catholic Consultation on Tensions in Eastern Europe Related to 'Uniatism'" (May 28, 1992). Published in *Origins* 22, 5 (June 11, 1992): 79-80.

"A Response of the Orthodox-Roman Catholic Consultation in the United States to the Joint International Commission for Theological Dialogue between the Orthodox

Church and the Roman Catholic Church Regarding the Balamand Document (dated June 23, 1993): 'Uniatism, Method of Union of the Past, and the Present Search for Full Communion'" (October 15, 1994). Published in *Origins* 24, 34 (February 9, 1995): 570-2.

U. S. Orthodox-Catholic Theological Consultation: Special Statements

"A Statement by the Orthodox and Roman Catholic Bilateral Consultation on Persecution of the Greek Orthodox Community in Turkey" (January 25, 1978). Published in *TR*.

"Reaction to the Anthimos/Medeiros Agreement" (May 29, 1982).

A Statement of the Catholic Members of the U.S. Orthodox-Roman Catholic Consultation to Catholics on the vision of unity and the current situation in Eastern Europe (October 31, 1992).

Metropolitan New York/New Jersey Orthodox-Roman Catholic Dialogue

"Agreed Statement on Orthodox-Roman Catholic Marriages" (January 6, 1986). Published in *BU*, pp. 342-53.

Suggestions for Further Reading

Barringer, Robert, C.S.B., ed. *Rome and Constantinople: Essays in the Dialogue of Love.* Holy Cross Orthodox Press, Brookline, MA: 1984. Includes contributions by two members of the U.S. Theological Consultation.

Meyendorff, John. *Rome, Constantinople, Moscow: Historical and Theological Studies.* Crestwood, NY: St. Vladimir's Seminary Press, 1996. Essays by the eminent late Orthodox ecumenist.

Nichols, Aidan, O.P. *Rome and the Eastern Churches: A Study in Schism.* Collegeville, MN: The Liturgical Press, 1992. Useful historical overview of major theological issues, though marred at points by inaccuracies and a polemical tone.

Roberson, Ronald G., C.S.P. *The Eastern Churches: A Brief Survey.* Revised 5th ed. Rome: Pontificio Istituto Orientale, 1995. Available through the United States Catholic Conference, Office of Publishing and Promotion Services, 3211 4th Street N.E., Washington, DC 20017. Complete and up-to-date information on the current state of the Eastern Churches, both Catholic, Orthodox and others.

Storman, E.J., S.J., trans. and ed. *Towards the Healing of Schism: The Sees of Rome and Constantinople* (=Ecumenical Documents III). New York and Mahwah, NJ: Paulist Press, 1987. Public statements and correspondence 1958-1984.

Ware, Timothy (Kallistos). *The Orthodox Church.* Revised 4th ed. London and New York: Penguin Books, 1993. Classic presentation of the history and teachings of the Orthodox Church.

Zizioulas, John. *Being as Communion: Studies in Personhood and the Church.* Crestwood, NY: St. Vladimir's Seminary Press, 1985. Leading contemporary Orthodox theologian and member of the International Joint Commission explores aspects of modern "eucharistic ecclesiology."

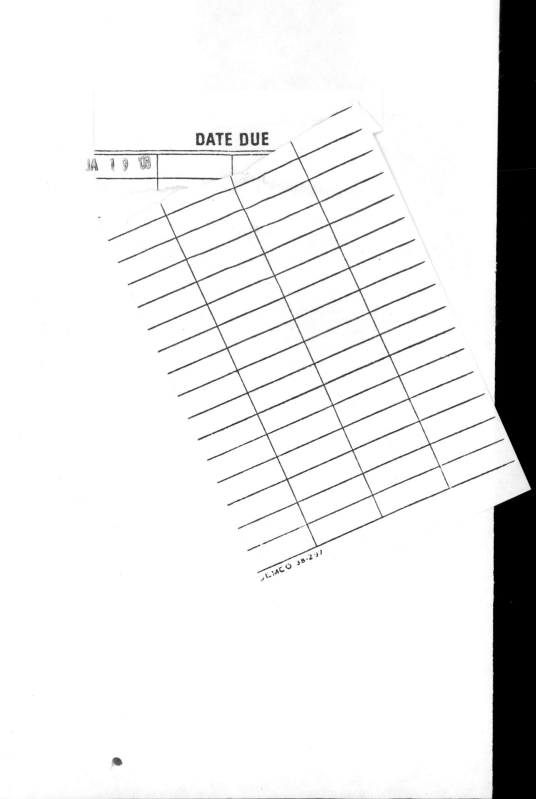